WEALTH, LAND AND SLAVEHOLDING IN MISSISSIPPI

A Planter Family's Life of Privilege

1818-1913

Ray R. Albin

HERITAGE BOOKS
2013

HERITAGE BOOKS

AN IMPRINT OF HERITAGE BOOKS, INC.

Books, CDs, and more—Worldwide

For our listing of thousands of titles see our website
at
www.HeritageBooks.com

Published 2013 by
HERITAGE BOOKS, INC.
Publishing Division
5810 Ruatan Street
Berwyn Heights, Md. 20740

International Standard Book Numbers
Paperbound: 978-0-7884-5484-4
Clothbound: 978-0-7884-6859-9

For Geraldine Elizabeth Albin (1917-1971) who gave so generously

---

For Catherine, Lauren, and Ryan Albin

CONTENTS

LIST OF ILLUSTRATIONS AND MAPS

Maps

x

PROLOGUE

Named after several nearby ancient Indian mounds, the William P. Perkins Mound Plantation was ideally suited for the planting, harvesting, and transporting of cotton. Situated in Bolivar County, Mississippi, on the Mississippi River bank at Choctaw Bend, it also faced on Williams Bayou, which flowed from the river southeast into the county's wild and unsettled interior.[1] The hot, humid, and often rainy Mississippi Delta climate combined with the region's renowned fertile soil yielded frequent bumper crops for the Perkins family and other planters on the few, scattered plantations located mainly along the river. A natural river landing adjacent to his plantation - known locally as Mound Landing - allowed easy downriver transport of Perkins' cotton to the market in New Orleans and then ultimately to the Northeast and Europe. But climate, soil, and geography were only part of the formula for success in this Southern plantation economy. William Perkins, the patriarch, also owned more than 160 slaves.

The traceable roots of William Perkins' rich and influential Southern family dated to sixteenth century Elizabethan England. Beginning in England the Perkins family story moves across the Atlantic to colonial Virginia, then traverses the Appalachian and Allegheny Mountains into frontier Tennessee, and finally reaches the western fringes of an infant United States, early nineteenth century Mississippi. Over generations, the Perkins clan continually ventured west, part of an ongoing national thrust later prominently noted by de Tocqueville and eventually embodied in the concept of *Manifest Destiny*.[2] This westward family movement eventually ended on the shores of the Pacific, with the 1849 journey of William Perkins' oldest son to gold rush California.

---

[1] No author, *Biographical and Historical Memoirs of Mississippi*, (Chicago: original publisher The Goodspeed Publishing Company, 1891), 2: Part 2, 586.

[2] Alexis de Tocqueville, *Democracy in America*, (New York: New American Library, 1954, first published in 1835), 130. Of this westward drive de Tocqueville (1805-1859) wrote, "Millions of men are marching at once towards the same horizon: their language, their religion, their manners differ; their object is the same. Fortune has been promised to them somewhere in the West, and to the West they go to find it. . . . "

In the larger perspective, the Perkins' family story is a microcosm of stages in the development of not only Southern colonial America, but also the developed United States. With its colonial genesis rooted in indentured servitude, first as servants, then later as masters, the Perkins family rose to heights unattainable to them in a rigidly structured seventeenth and eighteenth century English society. As entrepreneurs and landed Southern colonial planters, they first acquired white servants, then Negro slaves, and eventually the affluence and privilege which rewarded their energy and determination. Separation from the social constraints of the mother country had thus allowed these later generations of Perkins men in America to progress and achieve. In America the family's success and wealth, both self-made and inherited, had increased through the decades with each generation laying the foundation on which successive generations flourished in Virginia, and later in Tennessee and Mississippi.

Tracing this generational story provides not just a historical glimpse into an evolving American world of entrepreneurship, affluence, and privilege, but also into the particular nature of the eighteenth and nineteenth century slaveholding American South. Indeed, the Perkins family exemplifies the caste of slaveholding Southern planter-aristocrats - heralded in the South yet often maligned in the North - whose limited numbers belied their significant contributions to the development of the agricultural South and to the texture of a maturing America. Their successes, limitations, faults, and failures became a part of the many personal and generational threads woven into the great American experience that they all shared.

ACKNOWLEDGMENTS

The author wishes to thank Ron Brouillette for his careful editing in the early stages of the manuscript.

The insightful and extremely valuable comments, suggestions, and editing of Gerard S. Grosso were very much appreciated.

PERKINS LINEAGE - England to America

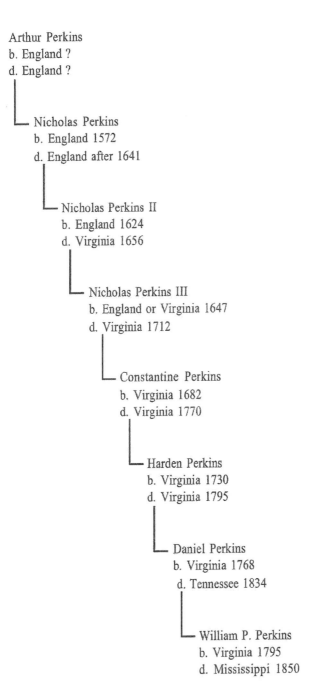

Arthur Perkins
b. England ?
d. England ?

    Nicholas Perkins
    b. England 1572
    d. England after 1641

        Nicholas Perkins II
        b. England 1624
        d. Virginia 1656

            Nicholas Perkins III
            b. England or Virginia 1647
            d. Virginia 1712

                Constantine Perkins
                b. Virginia 1682
                d. Virginia 1770

                    Harden Perkins
                    b. Virginia 1730
                    d. Virginia 1795

                        Daniel Perkins
                        b. Virginia 1768
                        d. Tennessee 1834

                            William P. Perkins
                            b. Virginia 1795
                            d. Mississippi 1850

THE WILLIAM P. PERKINS FAMILY

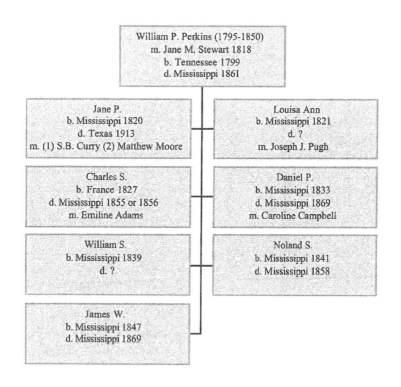

William P. Perkins (1795-1850)
m. Jane M. Stewart 1818
b. Tennessee 1799
d. Mississippi 1861

Jane P.
b. Mississippi 1820
d. Texas 1913
m. (1) S.B. Curry (2) Matthew Moore

Louisa Ann
b. Mississippi 1821
d. ?
m. Joseph J. Pugh

Charles S.
b. France 1827
d. Mississippi 1855 or 1856
m. Emiline Adams

Daniel P.
b. Mississippi 1833
d. Mississippi 1869
m. Caroline Campbell

William S.
b. Mississippi 1839
d. ?

Noland S.
b. Mississippi 1841
d. Mississippi 1858

James W.
b. Mississippi 1847
d. Mississippi 1869

I

Virginia and Tennessee

*"Life is a smoke! -- If this be true, Tobacco will thy Life renew;
Then fear not Death, nor killing care. Whilst we have best Virginia
here."*

Sign on a London tobacco shop in
the 1640s extolling the virtues of
Virginia tobacco

William Price Perkins was born in Washington County,
Virginia, in 1795 the son of Daniel and Bethenia Perkins. This line
of the Perkins clan dated back before 1572 to Arthur Perkins in
Bedfordshire, England, approximately sixty miles north of London. Beginning with Arthur, successive generations of Perkins
males show a son, grandson, and a great grandson all named
Nicholas, then Constantine and Harden, and finally William's father Daniel Perkins. In the seventeenth and eighteenth centuries,
descendants of these Perkins men populated several of Virginia's
early counties (Henrico, Goochland, Pittsylvania, and Buckingham), developed a complicated family tree, and filled land and
probate records with an array of Perkins family members.

By 1641 those awful early years of privation in the Virginia colony, particularly at the Jamestown settlement with its inadequate shelter and food supplies, fatal diseases, and the self-defeating behaviors of some of its colonists were practically over.
Virginia had become self-supporting, and the onset of the tobacco
economy was making some planters rich. Many plantations were
privately owned with settlements developing along the colony's
principal rivers. Virginia's population had grown to more than
10,000 people by 1641, while local representative government, the
House of Burgesses, had been meeting in Jamestown since July
1619. "Given these circumstances, it is not surprising that many
Englishmen sought a new home and a new life in Virginia."[1]

Consequently, the first Perkins in this family line documented in America was William's third great grandfather Nicholas

---

[1] William K. Hall, *Descendants of Nicholas Perkins of Virginia*, (Ann Arbor, Michigan: Edwards Brothers, 1957), 1.

Perkins II who arrived in approximately 1641. According to a land grant dated October 10 of that year, he arrived as an immigrant - indentured servant, transported from England to Virginia, along with a certain Gringall Delahaye; both passages paid for by a Bryant Smith.[2] In exchange Smith received 100 acres of Virginia land in Henrico County under the terms of the headright system.[3]

A little more than a decade after English colonists first settled in Jamestown, Virginia, in 1607, this headright system arose as a means of solving the chronic labor shortage brought about by the colony's developing tobacco economy. The basis for the arrangement was the London Company's "Greate Charter" of 1618, which stated:

> That for all persons . . . which during the next seven years [later extended beyond seven years] after Midsummer Day 1618 shall go into Virginia with the intent there to inhabite [sic], if they continue there three years or dye [sic] after they are shipped there shall be a grant made of fifty acres for every person . . . which grants shall be made respectively to such persons and their heirs at whose charges the said persons going to inhabite in Virginia shall be transported. . . ."

---

[2]Hall in his *Descendants of Nicholas Perkins of Virginia* states that records indicate Nicholas Perkins possessed property in Virginia *and also in England*, suggesting that he *may* have been a man of some means prior to his arrival in America. He explains that some who arrived in America with these prepaid passages were not in fact under-privileged. However, the fact that Nicholas Perkins' *first* recorded deed of land ownership (see below) occurred in 1650, *nine years* after he left England, seems to cast some doubt on the notion he was a "man of means" upon his arrival.

[3]Images and Indexes - "Northern Neck Grants and Surveys/Virginia Land Office Patents and Grants," *Online Catalog The Library of Virginia*, s. v. "Bryant Smith," 783-784, accessed March 17, 2010,
http://lva1.hosted.exlibrisgroup.com:80/F/XY74TIH7DYI3224CKQTYK4RC24J
XSJ5XP615IJSIP2HR5X45CT-39719?func=full-set-
set&set_number=004775&set_entry=000003&format=999. Nicholas Perkins' name appears at the end of the document. The site provides original, printable land deeds in most of early colonial Virginia's counties. Names and grants may be located using the Library's search engine under "Northern Neck Grants and Surveys/Virginia Land Office Patents and Grants." A person whose passage to Virginia was paid for by another was referred to as a 'headright.'

The advent of Virginia's tobacco trade had begun just four years earlier when John Rolfe's first shipment, a meager four barrels, arrived in London in 1614. By 1640, just one year prior to Nicholas Perkins II's arrival in the colony, London was importing nearly a million and a half pounds of tobacco annually from Virginia. But, tobacco production proved to be quite labor-intensive, requiring numerous workers and large tracts of land. As the Charter explained, those able to pay for an indentured servant's passage to Virginia were given fifty acres of land for both themselves (when they arrived) and another fifty for the person transported. In return for their passage, indentured servants like Nicholas II pledged to labor five to seven years for their masters. Likewise, colonists and planters already residing in Virginia who could afford to also availed themselves of the headright system with its twin paybacks of land and labor by importing servants from England. This burgeoning tobacco-based economy initiated by Rolfe, and advanced by the indentured servant labor pool, emerged as the colony's major and most lucrative industry, in short its salvation, generating thousands of pounds in revenue for Virginia and her planters while also benefiting England. The system allowed planters to eventually amass large tracts of land and provided the foundation for Virginia's developing planter aristocracy.

Several years later, having completed the terms of his indenture, Nicholas II may have remained in Henrico County, Virginia, up the James River some thirty miles from historic Jamestown and not far from Richmond. (The family biographer, Hall, reports that Nicholas may have resided in nearby Charles City County southeast of Henrico County.) Later, Perkins paid for the transportation of several indentured servants of his own into the colony. In turn, a deed dated August 30, 1650, and signed by Virginia's Governor William Berkeley (witnessed by Nicholas' wife Mary and two others), granted Nicholas Perkins II 170 acres of land lying in Henrico County's Bermuda Hundred. Situated at the confluence of the Appomattox and James Rivers (on the south side of the James), the land was Perkins' compensation for his cost of "the transport of four persons" (one of whom was Perkins' wife) from England to Virginia:[4]

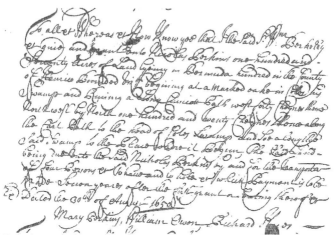

Nicholas Perkins II's 170 acre grant from Virginia Governor Berkeley in Henrico County, August 1650

"To all etc whereas etc Now Know you that I the Said Sr Wm Berkeley etc give and grant unto Nicholas Perkins one hundred and Seventy Acres of Land lying in Bermuda hundred in the County of Henrico Bounded Viz: - beginning at a marked oake in Coles his swamp and Running a Long Cunicott Path west forty Chaynes thence North west by North one hundred and twenty Chaynes thence along the Cart Path to the head of Coles Swamp and Soo along the Said Swamp to the Place where it Begun, the Said Land being due unto the said Nicholas Perkins by and for the transporting of four persons etc to have and to hold etc which payment is to be made Seven years after the first grant or seating thereafter etc dated the 30th of August 1650. [witnessed/signed] Mary Perkins, William Owen, Richard Hues"

---

[4] Ibid.
http://lva1.hosted.exlibrisgroup.com:80/F/XIX3DAD5458HV5HG2RPIVVDKY
D5KFMY95TYX75XPVHBS51RTR9-04370?func=short-jump&jump=000011,
S.v. "Nicholas Perkins." Then see 1650. The fourth person transported remains unidentified. It may have been Nicholas himself.

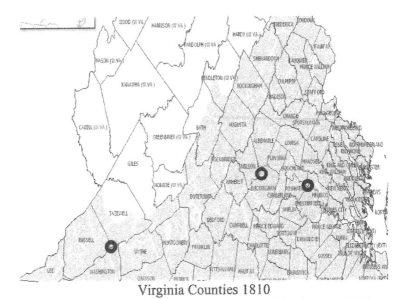

Virginia Counties 1810
The circles show the counties of Henrico, Buckingham, and Washington where early Perkins family members resided.
Map Courtesy of Newberry Library, Chicago.

Governor Berkeley's brief, one paragraph land grant to Nicholas II represents the first record of land ownership for this Perkins family in Virginia, documenting the modest beginning of what eventually developed into a life of prosperity for the former servant. In less than ten years, Nicholas the immigrant had evolved into a Virginia landowner/planter with dreams of additional success replacing the stagnant prospects available to him had he remained in England. (One of Nicholas' descendants later became California's first governor.) As was the case with thousands of Virginia planters, Nicholas II's prosperity, and later that of his son, began with the land they acquired through the headright system and the tobacco produced by their indentured laborers. Later, the land remained, but the indentured laborers were replaced with 'more economic' black slaves imported from Africa.

A record dated September 26, 1674, shows Nicholas' son, twenty-seven year old Nicholas Perkins III, who owned 537 acres in Henrico County north of the James River on Four Mile Creek.[5] Following the death of his father, he had moved there from Charles City County with his mother and stepfather. Born in London (some records indicate Virginia) in 1647, Nicholas III likewise had received a land grant for transporting to Virginia eleven indentured servants whose names appear at the bottom of the document.[6]

According to the grant, one of the eleven was Scipio, a "negro." We have no way of determining if Scipio came as slave, but regardless of his status, it appears that Nicholas may have received a slightly reduced amount of headright acreage for transporting a negro. Perkins, it appears, had been granted five hundred acres for the ten whites he transported, and the other thirty-seven acres may have been the smaller amount allotted for Scipio's passage.

Identifying himself as planter in Henrico County, Nicholas III served on juries and appraised and administered estates, earning the respect of his neighbors in the process. In the span of less than a quarter century, both Nicholas II and III had benefited greatly from a generous system that promised not merely an opportunity to own land, but also the knowledge that they were providing for their futures. Similar stories were being played out all across the Virginia colony.

Though each required a sizeable labor force to work their developing plantations, neither Nicholas III nor his father had augmented their indentured laborers with any documented African slaves. Nor did Nicholas III make mention in his will of any slaves. Times, however, were changing rapidly in Virginia.

By July 1724 Nicholas III's son, Constantine, the first Perkins documented as born in the colonies (1682), continued to expand the family's land holdings and wealth with the acquisition of 847 acres in the area of Henrico County which was later to become Goochland County. Situated on the north and west sides of Beaverdam Creek, in the area where today Goochland, Hanover,

---

[5]Ibid. See the year 1674.
[6]Ibid. See also, Bill Comisford, *History of the Ancestors, Families, and Descendants of Paris Patrick Comisford*, (Westminster, Md.: Heritage Books, 2007), 271.

and Louisa Counties meet (see Virginia Counties map above), the land more than likely produced grains and of course tobacco. Constantine paid "the sum of thirty five Shillings of good and lawful money" for 347 acres of the total of 847 acres he purchased.[7] Constantine earlier had inherited some of his father Nicholas III's land, also in Henrico County, on the north side of the James River. (Nicholas considered Constantine well-provided for and consequently willed him just five shillings cash). Later, in December 1748, at age sixty-six, he purchased 150 acres in Albemarle County in a tract near situated on the south side of the Fluvanna River (James River) that in 1761 became part of Buckingham County.

By the time Constantine's father Nicholas Perkins III died in 1712, Virginia was undergoing a dramatic change in the nature of its labor force. In the latter part of the seventeenth century, slave labor had gradually begun to replace temporary servitude. By the turn of the century, as the slave trade grew and prices dropped, slaves proved to be not just cheaper than indentured servants, but were seen as a more reliable and permanent labor pool. As indentured servants gained their freedom, they had eventually become competitors to their former masters (as Nicholas II had done), owning farms and enterprises, a future unlikely for a black slave. Masters also realized that black slaves, who could be quickly identified, could not easily remain free if they ran off, while escaping white servants simply assimilated unnoticed into the general white population. Lastly, tobacco farming, though labor intensive, did not require any pre-existing skills and language proficiency often possessed by indentured laborers.

In 1712 thirty-year old Constantine Perkins thus found himself exactly in this transition stage - servitude yielding to slavery. And with his inheritance that year and his ongoing land purchases came his need for additional labor. Given these circumstances, Constantine, William Perkins' great grandfather, thus emerged at approximately this time as the first slaveholder in this line of the Perkins family. Constantine Perkins' will of 1761, written nine years before his death, stipulated that his fourteen slaves

---

[7]Virginia Land Office Patents, Constantine Perkins. The price he paid for the remaining acres is unknown.

were to be distributed among his several children.[8] Soon, his heirs,
along with other planter families, would thrive as the evolution of
plantation slavery evolved into the key institutional component of
Southern society.

Meanwhile, in Buckingham County, Harden P. Perkins,
one of the sons of Constantine and his wife, Ann (Pollard) Perkins,
became a successful planter and slaveholder in his own right. Born
in approximately 1730 at Tuckahoe Creek in Henrico County,
Harden was the grandfather of William P. Perkins. He made his
home with his wife Sarah Price Perkins on the James River near
the Albemarle Courthouse at Perkins Falls having inherited some
or all of his father's acreage there.[9] In 1788 he appeared on the
Buckingham County tax list owning twelve slaves and eight
horses.

Copy of the Buckingham County, Virginia, tax list for 1788 showing Harden "Pirkins" (fourth from the top) and the number of his
slaves and horses[10]

---

[8]Hall, *Descendants of Nicholas Perkins*, 11.

[9]No author, *The Compendium of American Genealogy*, (Chicago: Virkus Company, 1930), 4: 277.

[10]"1790 & 1800 Virginia Tax List Censuses," *Binns Genealogy*, accessed December 31, 2010,
http://www.binnsgenealogy.com/VirginiaTaxListCensuses/Buckingham/1788Per
sonalA/11.jpg.

A brief look into the slaveholding world of Harden Perkins provides insight into the changing dynamics of a Virginia planter family now exclusively invested in and reliant on black slaves for labor. With these slaves working his tobacco fields, Harden Perkins saw his profits grow substantially, allowing he and his family to lead an increasingly comfortable life as members of a now well-established Virginia planter aristocracy. But, Perkins, as a slave master, also faced the twin challenges of providing a *lifetime* of 'care' for his human property and the inevitable problem of troublesome slaves and/or 'runaways' experienced by most slaveholders.

In the August 1, 1766, Williamsburg *Virginia Gazette*, for example, Harden Perkins placed a notice seeking to recover his twenty-two year old runaway Negro slave, Guy. Perkins described Guy as "about 5 feet 8 or 9 inches high, full faced, . . . and has a scar on the hind part of each leg; had on when he went away an osnabrug [sic] shirt, a pair of wide trousers, and an old felt hat, and Negro cotton waistcoat."[11] Perkins offered a five-pound reward for the "outlawed slave" to whomever "contrives him to me on [the] James river [sic], near Albemarle old court-house, in Buckingham County, or gives such intelligence so I may get him easily."

Such runaway slave notices were commonplace in the *Gazette* and in later years other Virginia newspapers. Planters' expectations were that black runaways, unlike their white indentured counterparts, could almost always be recovered. Masters thus had every reason to be as forthright as possible in these advertisements, and Harden Perkins was no exception. He further disclosed that Guy had been branded, a practice common in slaveholding annals, but Perkins had placed his brand, the H and P, on each of Guy's *cheeks* instead of on his arms, wrists, or even the neck. Planters and/or their overseers meted out such severe punishment especially for slaves like Guy who were troublesome or repeat runaways. The fact that Perkins willingly published the graphic

---

[11]"*Virginia Gazette*, August 1, 1766, 3, column 2", *Colonial Williamsburg*, accessed April 11, 2010, http://research.history.org/DigitalLibrary/VirginiaGazette/VGImagePopup.cfm?ID=1569&Res=HI. Osnaburg was a coarse type of plain, textile fabric. Slaves wore low quality osnaburg shirts.

description of Guy's disfigurement reveals that he felt no shame in such a penalty. Unexplained, but not surprising, is the mention of Guy's scars on the "hind part of each leg."[12]

Decades later, Frederick Douglass, himself a former slave, summarized a curiosity in the world of slaveholders like Perkins when he wrote: "Give him [the slave] a bad master, and he aspires to a good master; give him a good master, and he wishes to become his own master."

R U N away from the subscriber, a Negro man named G U Y, about 22 years old, about 5 feet 8 or 9 inches high, full faced, branded on the cheeks H?P, and has a scar on the hind part of each leg; had on when he went away an ofnabrug shirt, a pair of wide troufers, an old felt hat, and Negro cotton waiftcoat. Whoever apprehends the faid flave (who is outlawed) and contrives him to me on *James* river, near *Albemarle* old court-houfe, in *Buckingham* county, or gives fuch intelligence fo that I may get him eafily, fhall have 5 l. reward.
HARDIN PERKINS.

Harden (Hardin) Perkins placed this notice in the *Virginia Gazette* in August 1766 in an effort to recover Guy, his runaway. Notice the newspaper's unique icon denoting a runaway slave.

Contrarily, Perkins is found in the records of Tillotson Parish in Buckingham County as a churchwarden.[13] There should be no surprise at such a revelation if we remember that the author of the Declaration of Independence and later the third President, Thomas Jefferson, and America's first President, George Wash-

---

[12]Guy's spirit is enviable, for he had already suffered the indignity of facial disfiguration, in addition to the lashes most likely meted out for previous escape attempts or defiance. Yet despite these punishments, Guy had chosen to run again in another almost hopeless attempt to gain his freedom. In March 1772 Perkins reported another runaway in the *Gazette* whom he later recovered.
[13]Edythe Johns Rucker Whitley, *Genealogical Records of Buckingham County, Virginia*, (Baltimore: Genealogical Publishing Company, 1984), 1.

ington, along with other "Founding Fathers" who demanded 'freedom' from England, all contemporaries of Harden Perkins, held slaves.[14] Less than fifty years later, Harden's college-educated grandson William Perkins, a future member of Mississippi's planter aristocracy, would serve on a jury condemning a slave to death for *burglary*, while at the same time William's slaveholding father-in-law, the presiding judge in the case, was initiating a debating society and a school for young ladies in the town where the slave was hanged.

But slavery, the 'peculiar institution', among other things was always a study in contradictions, and generations of Harden's successors thus became a part of this world. Slave labor in the Perkins family beginning in early eighteenth century Virginia would expand as the family moved into Tennessee and Mississippi, only ceasing in 1865 with the end of the Civil War.

In April 1775 the Revolutionary War broke out pitting the disgruntled thirteen American colonies against their mother country, England. At the outset of the war, the allegiance of those living in the colonies was tested. Little is known, however, of Harden Perkins' wartime activities. It appears that he renounced his King and served the colonial cause by providing the Continental Army with food supplies grown on his Virginia plantation. William Hall writes that Hardin Perkins provided a gun, bacon, beef "cattel," and three bushels of meal for the Revolutionary militia in 1780.[15] Perkins' more than 1,000 acres would have been large enough to allow him to raise and sell the cattle, hogs, and grain the army so desperately needed. Being of middle age at the outbreak of the war, he most likely never participated in any of the fighting.

Following the war, Harden Perkins lived out his days on his plantation in Buckingham County, now a part of the *state* of Virginia. Whether British forces during the conflict ever caused any damage to his plantation is unknown. With Harden's death in January 1795, it appears that the majority of his land eventually

---

[14]In 1775, just one year before the Declaration of Independence was signed, English author Dr. Samuel Johnson wrote in reference to American slaveholding colonists, "How is it that we hear the loudest yelps for liberty among the drivers of negroes?"

[15]Hall, *Descendants of Nicholas Perkins*, 27.

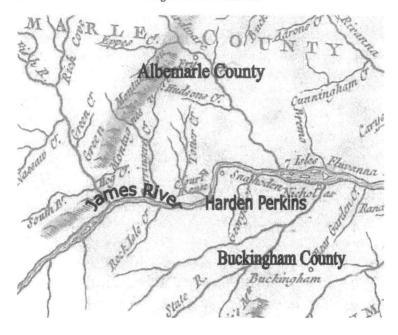

A portion of the 1755 Joshua Fry-Peter Jefferson (Thomas Jefferson's father) map of Virginia. The Albemarle Courthouse Harden
Perkins referred to in his fugitive slave advertisement is distinc-
tively located on the James River. The site of Harden Perkins' land
is based also on his ad in the *Gazette*, ("on James River, near Albemarle old court-house in Buckingham county"). By 1799 expanded Perkins family holdings appear on *both* sides of the James
River. Harden's heir, his son Price Perkins, inherited the land,
eventually totaling 1,101 acres.[16]

---

[16]Virginia Land Office Patents, s. v. "Price Perkins 1799 and 1801" for deed
copies. In Hall, *Descendants of Nicholas Perkins*, 87, the author writes that
Harden Perkins Jr. acquired 300 acres of land on the James River *north of the
courthouse* in 1815, in the same area as his father's land. One of Harden Sr.'s
neighbors on an adjacent tract was Captain Randolph Jefferson, the younger
brother of Thomas Jefferson of Albemarle County and the other son of mapmaker
Peter Jefferson.

passed (after his wife's death) to his oldest son Price Perkins.[17] Harden Perkins Jr., the family's *youngest* male, received a monetary inheritance and 100 acres of land. However, Daniel P. Perkins, the second oldest of Harden's sons, appears to have been disinherited.

Born in October 1768 in Buckingham County, Daniel Perkins left the family home on or before his nineteenth birthday, maybe after a disagreement with his parents. His departure may explain why his inheritance consisted of neither land nor money. Instead he 'inherited' one slave, Abraham, to be provided to Daniel after the death of his mother, which occurred twenty-six years later in 1821!

Too young to have served in the Continental Army, Daniel Perkins, separated from his family by May 1787, appears in the extreme western portion of Virginia (far from Buckingham County) on a Washington County Tax List owning seven slaves, eight horses or mules, and seven cattle. In March 1790 Washington County's land records also mention landowner Daniel Perkins.[18] On March 24, 1795, just two months after his father's death, Daniel paid Andrew Kincannon 1,000 pounds for 311 acres of land.[19] Located on both sides of the Little Holston (spelled Holstein in some documents) River, a branch of the middle fork of the Holston, the acreage lay near the town of Abingdon, Virginia.

While the county was named in honor of George Washington, the city of Abingdon took the name of his wife Martha's ancestral home in England. Located in an area crisscrossed by In-

---

[17]Price Perkins, following his father's death, probably managed the family plantation even though it still belonged to his mother. It was customary for oldest sons to inherit the majority of the family's land and assets. The *Richmond Whig* of June 30, 1843, page 1, column 7, reported Price Perkins' death in his seventy-eighth year, making his birth year 1765.

[18]Rhonda Robertson, "Washington County, VA Survey records abstracts 1781-1797, Part 4 of 5, 384," *USGenWeb archives*, accessed January 11, 2011, http://files.usgwarchives.org/va/washington/deeds/surv1004.txt.

[19]David Trimble, *Southwest Virginia Families,* (San Antonio: 1974), 211-212. Two years later Perkins purchased another twenty-four acres adjoining his original purchase: Twenty-four acre land grant to Daniel Perkins in Washington County, Virginia, 1797, Library of Virginia Online Catalog, 416, s.v. Daniel Perkins (assignee of Andrew Kincannon). See Andrew Kincannon for his original deed for the entire 361 acres he purchased on July 5, 1785, 179.

dian trails early on, Abingdon had emerged by 1795, only twenty-five years after its first settlement, as a gateway to the West through the Cumberland Gap into Kentucky and Tennessee. It soon became the first incorporated town west of the Allegheny Mountains. Though several overland trails linked Abingdon with distant east coast cities, it remained somewhat isolated.[20] In this western Virginia setting nestled in the foothills of the Appalachian Mountains, Daniel Perkins raised a large family, and it was here that his son William P. was born in 1795.

As a planter of some means, Daniel must have been well respected by his neighbors and the citizens of Washington County for in 1795, when Daniel was twenty-seven years old, and again in 1796, they elected him to the House of Delegates in the Virginia General Assembly, the successor to the House of Burgesses. His election meant that Perkins was compelled occasionally to make the more than 600 mile roundtrip horseback ride to the new state capital at Richmond, a journey made all the more difficult by the state's near absence of roads. However, soon after completing his second term in the House of Delegates, Daniel chose to leave Virginia for the lure of the middle Tennessee countryside. Perhaps his recent land purchases in Washington County had left him yearning for additional, *cheaper* acreage in Tennessee.

In 1798 Daniel, with his wife of thirteen years, Bethenia, who was also his cousin (she was the daughter of Nicholas and Leah Perkins), and their six children settled in Williamson County, Tennessee, near Nashville, some five miles from Franklin.[21] It seems likely that prior to leaving Virginia Daniel would have sold his plantation, but no record of any such sale appeared in the sources consulted. Other members of the extended Perkins clan accompanied Daniel, with some also settling in Franklin. This move marked the second time in eleven years dating back to his boyhood home in Buckingham County that Daniel had ventured westward. Though his young son William Perkins had spent the

[20]Aaron D. Purcell, "A Damned Piece of Rascality, The Business of Slave Trading in Southern Appalachia," *Journal of East Tennessee History*, 78, (2006), 4.
[21]Hall, *Descendants*, 86-87, and Thomas McCormick, *Carson McCormick Family Memorials*, (Madison, Wisconsin: 1953), 40. Daniel's brother, William, also married a cousin, the sister of Daniel's wife Bethenia.

first three years of his life in Abingdon, it was in Tennessee that he (and his siblings) would grow into adulthood.

In Franklin Daniel and his family lived near its few white settlers who resided in log cabins dotting the landscape of the small village. Situated on the edge of Indian country, Williamson County was far from a wilderness haven. Barely one year earlier in 1797, Indians had killed a white man at the head of the Harpeth River close to Franklin.[22]

Soon, Daniel Perkins sought public service positions in Franklin as he had done in Virginia. In October 1799 Daniel gained appointment with several others as a commissioner tasked with choosing a site for a Williamson County courthouse, prison, and stocks and to see to their construction.[23] Perkins became one of the county's first justices of the peace in 1800, and in 1806 he assumed the position of a trustee at the local Harpeth Academy.

On March 24, 1800, five months after he had taken up his building commissioner duties, Daniel purchased 640 acres of land from Thomas Edmondson for $3,200, or five dollars per acre.[24] On this property standing just across the bridge on the north side of the Harpeth River on the Del Rio Pike, he apparently built the first Perkins home in the Franklin area. An imposing brick structure, the house contained several rooms with high ceilings and an elegant, curved stairway. Across the road from this, the "original" Perkins home, a Perkins family graveyard was established. On the opposite side of the river toward Franklin stood two other large brick Perkins clan homes, also constructed during this early period.

As it turned out, the timing of Daniel's move to Tennessee had been impeccable, though probably fortuitous. In the early

---

[22] John Davis, "Indian Murders Around Nashville," *South-Western Monthly*, January 1, 1852., accessed July 31, 2011, http://books.google.com/books?id=1LcRAAAAYAAJ&pg=PA214&dq=%22will iam-son+county+south+western+monthly%22&hl=en&ei=wh9DTunvO4LiiALTxuz CAQ&sa=X&oi=book_result&ct=result&resnum=1&ved=0CDIQ6AEwAA#v=o nepage&q&f=false.
[23]"County Formation in Acts of Tennessee 1799, Chapter 3," *Tennessee State Library*, accessed September 10, 2011, http://tennessee.gov/tsla/history/county/actwilliamson.htm.
[24]McCormick, *Family Memorials*, 41.

1800s just two years after Perkins' arrival, the settlement of the
Cherokee Indians' claims opened the doors to white colonization
in Middle Tennessee. Cheap land tempted these newcomers, but
Daniel's early arrival had allowed him to choose among the most
desirable locations and to buy at a more favorable price.

For thirty-six years, Daniel Perkins would remain in Williamson County, living among his relatives and supporting his
large family. He managed his cotton/tobacco plantation and his
dozens of slaves, acquired more wealth, served his community,
and raced thoroughbred horses at Franklin racecourses.[25]

It was from this family of immigrants, and indentured servants, then later planters, plantations, privilege, power, wealth, and
slaveholding that William P. Perkins grew into manhood. William
spent his early years in Franklin and Williamson County on the
family plantation no doubt learning the methods of farm management from his father and absorbing the manner of the planter lifestyle as well. He is described as an intelligent young man of strong
character and excellent judgment, of medium height, with blue
eyes and a dark and ruddy complexion.[26]

---

[25]James Douglas Anderson, *Making the American Thoroughbred, Especially in
Tennessee, 1800-1845*, (Norwood, Massachussetts: Plimpton Press, 1916), 130,
133.
[26]*Biographical and Historical Memoirs of Mississippi*, 586. William's daughter,
Jane Perkins Curry Moore, provided this description.

II

Wilkinson County, Mississippi

Mr. P[erkins] has respectable and extensive family connections here [Mississippi] as well as in the State of Tennessee. No doubt should he be pleased with your country and future prospects there, he will ultimately move there and be the means of many valuable citizens moving there both from this State and from Tennessee. . . .

William Johnson to Stephen Austin,
referring to William P. Perkins
March 1, 1825

Every master of slaves is born a petty tyrant.

George Mason, 1787,
Virginia slaveholder, delegate to the
Constitutional Convention, and co-
father of the Bill of Rights

By the time the War of 1812 against Great Britain had broken out, William Perkins was a restless youth of seventeen. He, along with thousands of other Tennesseans, immediately responded to a call for volunteers issued by a local man from Davidson County, near Nashville, the future seventh President of the United States, Major General Andrew Jackson. Their courage and character in responding to America's need for soldiers in 1812 would become the basis for Tennessee's nickname, the Volunteer State. Each man was to supply his own rifle, ammunition, camp equipment, and blankets, with the government providing an allowance later to cover the costs. On December 10, 1812, the 2,070 volunteers, "comprised of the choicest of our citizens" according to Jackson, assembled in Franklin, Tennessee, not far from the Perkins plantation.

William was awarded the rank of fourth sergeant in Captain McEwen's Company of the Second Regiment of Tennessee Volunteers under the command of a prominent Franklin jurist and later U.S. Senator, Colonel Thomas Hart Benton.[1] Young Perkins'

---

[1]"MS Wilkin Archives," *Roots Web*, November 24, 2006, accessed May 27, 2010, http://archiver.rootsweb.ancestry.com/th/read/MSWILKIN/2006-

sudden advancement in rank appears to be related to not only his intelligence and martial skills but maybe also due to his father's acquaintance with Colonel Benton.

Daniel Perkins, as a Franklin justice of the peace, and Benton, who had been admitted to the Franklin bar in 1806, both appeared over the years in the local courts and across Williamson County and had undoubtedly met each other on any number of occasions. It may have been during those first weeks in the military that young William learned a life lesson, how suitable connections could prove beneficial.

Weeks later on January 7, 1813, with Jackson's preparations as complete as possible, his force embarked. The two 700-man regiments of infantry, in a flotilla of flat-bottom boats, journeyed first down the Cumberland River, then navigated the ice-clogged Ohio, and the Mississippi to Natchez, Mississippi.[2] Jackson's cavalry corps would ride overland and eventually rendezvous with the infantry in Natchez. The volunteers' primary, long-term mission, to support the seizure of Mobile, Pensacola, and St. Augustine by the Army's regular troops, was expected to be a difficult task for an inexperienced militia. Thirty-nine freezing days later on February 15, 1813, Jackson and his men arrived some 1,000 miles downriver near Natchez, Mississippi Territory. There, the entire contingent encamped on the outskirts of the city, established Fort Jackson, and waited.

Jackson's expedition never moved past Natchez. The general unexpectedly received notice that the federal government had provided neither provisions nor quarters for the next leg of his expedition to New Orleans. After remaining in Natchez until late March 1813, Jackson's discouraged troops began the agonizing

---

11/1164386438. In 1852 Jane Stewart Perkins attested to William Perkins' service in the War of 1812. On November 17, 1852, at Jane's request, her cousin James Alexander Ventress of Wilkinson County and another cousin, Frances M. Currier, both provided sworn statements supporting Jane's declaration regarding William's service under Colonel Benton. Benton in 1813 fought a duel with Jackson, but later both men reconciled. Benton was a staunch advocate of westward expansion.

[2]During part of his journey down the Mississippi River, Sgt. William Perkins may have viewed the untamed and unsettled landscape of what would later become the fabulously productive cotton-producing region known as the Mississippi Delta.

return trek to Nashville, this time via a 500-mile overland route through the wilderness. Though they arrived half starved weeks later, most men had survived the arduous return march. For William and his fellow soldiers the return march would be remembered as an exercise in determination, stamina, and courage. In Nashville William and other volunteers were promptly dismissed from military service by a Presidential order dated February 6, 1813, nine days before they had even arrived in Natchez!! However, many men in Benton's regiment reenlisted in September 1813 and served under Colonel William Pillow, retaining their same unit designation, the Second Regiment, West Tennessee Volunteer Infantry.

William may have been one of those who reenlisted. His name appears in the service records for the War of 1812, first as a sergeant in Benton's regiment, then in Pillow's unit as a second lieutenant, later promoted and discharged as a first lieutenant (see War of 1812 enlistment cards below). However, because his wife omitted any reference regarding his time with Pillow's unit on a document she later completed attesting to William's wartime service, there is some doubt as to William's reenlistment. If this Lt. Perkins is in fact our William, according to the unit history for Pillow's regiment, he would have taken part in General Jackson's first Creek campaign, serving in the same regiment as his older brother Harden Perkins and participating in the fighting at the Battle of Talladega (Alabama) on November 9, 1813.[3]

Significantly, William's presence with Jackson's military expedition to and from Mississippi, along with his time spent at Natchez, greatly impacted his future. In the coming decades, Perkins would purchase large tracts of land and establish highly prof-

---

[3]"War of 1812 Service Records," William P. Perkins, *Ancestry.com* accessed May 27, 2011. For the service cards see, United States War of 1812, Index to Service Records," images 2695 and 2696. For Hardin Perkins see number 2381, accessed September 25, 2011, *Family Search,* https://familysearch.org/pal:/MM9.3.1/TH-1942-21916-9617-78?cc=1916219&wc=11893876. Interrupting his law practice in Nashville, Harden Perkins had likewise enlisted, as a private in Pillow's Second Regiment West Tennessee Volunteers. He ended up fighting under Jackson's command against the Creek Indians and later, upon returning to Tennessee, attained the rank of Major.

itable plantations in several of the areas he had become acquainted with during his army days in Mississippi.

War of 1812 Service cards for Sgt. William P. Perkins in Benton's Regiment and for a Lt. William P. Perkins in Pillow's Regiment
Family Search.org

Following his military service in the War of 1812, William, apparently unscathed, returned home to Franklin and enrolled in nearby Cumberland College, later the University of Nashville. Earlier, his older brothers Harden, a lawyer, and Nicholas, a doctor, had likewise attended and then graduated from Cumberland. With William's graduation the Daniel Perkins family could claim three college-educated sons under one roof, evidence of the Perkins family's social status and a rare achievement in an early nineteenth century America where illiteracy was often the norm.[4]

---

[4]William Russell Smith, *Reminiscences of a Long Life; historical, political, personal and literary*, (Washington, D.C.: W.R. Smith Sr., 1889), 294, accessed December 11, 2010,

Mississippi counties[5]

http://books.google.com/books?id=6aUEAAAAYAAJ&pg=PA294&dq=perkins+at+cumberland+college+1817&lr=&cd=5#v=onepage&q=perkins%20at%20cumberland%20college%201817&f=false. This source provides a brief look at the successful life of William's older brother Harden Perkins in Alabama.

[5] U. S. Census Bureau, accessed January 10, 2012, http://quickfacts.census.gov/qfd/maps/mississippi_map.html

Upon graduation, circa 1817-1818, an ambitious twenty-two year old William left the relative economic security of the family plantation in Tennessee to seek his fortune in Mississippi, an agriculturally promising region on the very fringe of civilization that had only recently attained statehood. William's arrival there coincided with the postwar period's second phase of the ongoing great migration to Mississippi/the Southwest.[6] Opportunity had drawn Perkins and thousands of others to this dynamic region. Many of these early pioneers undoubtedly hoped to profit by growing primarily cotton along with sugar cane. Some, like William, were young sons eager for a chance to prove themselves.

William's decision to migrate in 1818 also reflected a generational tendency in his own family beginning with Nicholas Perkins II in the 1650s. Searching for new land and opportunities, subsequent Perkins generations (Nicholas III, Constantine, Harden, and Daniel) undertook a gradual, nearly always-westward progression. From Henrico County, Virginia, to Goochland, Buckingham, and Washington Counties, Perkins folks moved, eventually spilling into Williamson County, Tennessee, and culminating with William's venture, even further west, into Southwestern Mississippi.

In the broader scope, other push-pull factors also influenced this westward migration. Tobacco over the decades simply had exhausted the soil in many areas of the original easternmost colonies driving farmers to search for virgin, fertile, and affordable acreage. With seemingly endless tracts of such unspoiled land available "over the next hill", it became commonplace for Southern planter families to move west.[7] Furthermore, following the War of 1812, tobacco prices had steadily declined from fifteen (in 1816) to five cents (in 1824) per pound. To make matters worse, tobacco exports fluctuated, exceeding prewar totals just twice

---

[6]Westward migration became a recurring theme in American history well into the nineteenth century. Over the decades thousands of Americans, both northerners and southerners, joined the westward movement as America eventually expanded its boundaries to the Pacific Ocean.

[7]Later, Mississippi's location in the deeper South away from the threat of abolitionist influences that had begun to affect the Border States also contributed to its population increase.

from 1815-1821.[8] As a result, many planters immigrated to Mississippi anticipating improved revenues and profits from its vast agricultural potential. (Evidence of the extent of this westward trend is found in the election of the seventh President, Andrew Jackson, in 1829, the first President representing a state, Tennessee, *west* of the Appalachian Mountains).

Perkins' choice of rural Wilkinson County in the extreme southwest corner of Mississippi, south of Natchez, near the city of Woodville was probably no haphazard decision. He most likely had become familiar with the Woodville area during the six weeks Jackson's army had encamped near there in the aborted Natchez expedition. William's uncle from Franklin, Nicholas Perkins, the Mississippi Territory's first attorney general, may also have influenced his decision as he related stories back in Tennessee of the opportunities to be found in southwestern Mississippi.[9]

Once Perkins and other planters arrived in Wilkinson County to begin the tasks of settlement and choice of money crop, they quickly learned that while sugarcane grew well, cotton would be more profitable. Mississippi's climate and soil often yielded bumper crops of cotton, and its high demand in Europe and suitability to inexpensive slave labor made growing this "white gold" a highly lucrative undertaking.

The area prospered despite the fact that unlike most plantation settlements in southwestern Mississippi only Woodville lacked a creek to float its cotton to the Mississippi River. Early on, resourceful, local planters had compensated and transported their bales overland, by wagon, to the landing at Bayou Sara, Louisiana, where they would then be shipped downriver to New Orleans for eventual export overseas or to domestic markets.

In October 1816, near the time of William's arrival, a territorial census for Wilkinson County counted 7,277 inhabitants, consisting of 3,218 whites, 4,057 slaves, and two persons of

---

[8]No author, *American Almanac and Repository of Useful Knowledge for the Year 1838*, (Boston: Charles Bowen, 1838), 122-123.
[9]Nicholas Perkins was the brother of William's mother Bethenia. He is credited with the capture of the fugitive Aaron Burr in 1807.

color.[10] Just four years later, its white population had increased to
3,582 while the black total jumped to more than 5,000, testimony
to a continuing influx of both planters and their slaves.[11] Woodville, the county's most thriving city despite its remote location,
soon boasted a public square, a bank, stores, and a courthouse
where slave auctions were held. A Female Academy and a debating and literary society would soon be established. Mississippi's
oldest newspaper, the *Woodville Republican*, began printing in
1823. That same year the County Court in its January term even
established rates for taverns and innkeepers:

Breakfast	$.37^{1/2}$(cents)
Dinner	half dollar
Supper	$.37^{1/2}$
Lodging	.25 per night
Feed horse	.45 all night
French brandy	$.25^{1/2}$ pt
Whiskey	$.12^{1/2}$ pt
Madeira wine	2.00 btl
Claret wine	1.00 btl
Whiskey	.25 (toddy) [12]

---

[10]Mississippi, State Archives, Various Records, 1820-1951, Wilkinson County,
1816 Territory Census Returns, Image 18, accessed October 21, 2011, *Family
Search*,
https://www.familysearch.org/search/image/index#uri=https%3A//api.familysear
ch.org/records/collection/1919687/waypoints. These voluminous, unindexed
records cover an amazing array of primary source documents, ink drops and
smudges included, for each county in Mississippi beginning in 1810. Caution,
however, must be used in relying on Mississippi's county census records. County
enumerators sometimes included all citizens in their population totals. On other
occasions, they only tallied white male voters. Moreover, when counting slaves,
sometimes they included just those less than sixty years of age.
[11]Ibid., Box 4939, image 26. Wilkinson's slave population numbers for 1820 vary
depending on the source consulted. All indicate a population exceeding 5,000
slaves.
[12]"County Court January Term 1823," *Wilkinson County Chancery Court Records, Suits 1822-1871*, Mormon Family History Library (FHL), Salt Lake City,
microfilm roll 877088, 27.

With planting and slaveholding his primary interests, William had arrived in Woodville with a substantial amount of money, either his own or the family's. He soon married Jane Mell Stewart in a ceremony conducted by Jane's uncle, Justice of the Peace James Carraway, on April 28, 1818. As a result of his marriage, Perkins became part of an elite, local family at least as affluent as his own in Tennessee, with the added benefit that the intermarriage of a Perkins and a Stewart served to reinforce the social standing of both the bride and the groom.

Jane, born in Montgomery County, Tennessee, in approximately 1799, was the daughter of Charles Stewart of the famous Scottish Stewarts. Her grandfather was descended from King James I of Scotland. Earlier, Jane's father had left North Carolina and settled in Montgomery County on a tract known as Peacher's Mill. For twelve years Jane resided there on the family's estate situated on a large expanse of valuable land. The Stewarts soon emerged as one of the richest and most influential families in Tennessee, and Jane could claim that Stewart County was named after her Uncle Duncan.

In approximately 1811 Jane's father Charles Stewart (born May 1773), a former member of the Tennessee House of Representatives from 1801-1803, left Tennessee.[13] With his family he settled in Wilkinson County joining his older brother Duncan Stewart who had arrived earlier. Charles, "being full of enterprise and fond of making money," believed that cotton planting in this rugged, virgin land would prove more profitable than any business opportunity in Tennessee. He appeared on the Wilkinson County tax rolls as a landowner on Thompson's Creek southeast of Woodville.[14] There, he claimed fifty slaves and 320 acres. Later, at a

---

[13]United States Bureau of Land Management Tract Books, 1820-1908, Mississippi, Volume 1, Additional, Image 155, accessed December 28, 2012, *Family Search*,
https://familysearch.org/pal:/MM9.3.1/TH-1942-32488-12403-28?cc=2074276&wc=M9MF-GXY:1183216191. This record shows that Charles Stewart purchased 162 acres of land on March 25, 1811, in Wilkinson County.
[14]Mississippi, State Archives, Various Records, 1820-1951, Wilkinson County, County Tax Rolls 1812, Box 141, image 12, accessed October 21, 2011, *Family Search*,
https://www.familysearch.org/search/image/index#uri=https%3A//api.familysearch.org/records/collection/1919687/waypoints.

different site some three miles east of Woodville near Buffalo Creek, he constructed a "hospitable mansion" destined to be his primary plantation and permanent residence.[15] By 1819, in the short span of eight years, Stewart had become one of the county's wealthiest planters claiming nearly 2,000 acres, and by 1820 he owned 130 slaves.[16] He also claimed slaves and land on two other plantations on each side of the courthouse in Pointe Coupee Parish, Louisiana.[17]

Stewart's older brother, fifty-six-year old (in 1819) Duncan, eventually established his own plantation near Woodville and southwest of Centreville. Claiming nearly 1,000 acres (by 1820) and sixty-eight slaves (1819) on Comite Creek, Duncan Stewart constructed his grand plantation house, Holly Grove:

> a massive Colonial building with large brick pillars, [nine fireplaces] and galleries on both upper and lower floors. Its many rooms were filled with choice pieces of mahogany and rosewood furniture, (today considered antiques fit for a museum), family portraits, old silver and rare books, which enhanced its beauty -- certainly a home of real charm. From the marks on one of the bricks, authorities state the house was erected one

---

[15]James Ross, *Life and Times of Elder Reuben Ross,* (Philadelphia: Grant, Faires & Rodgers, 1882), 271. See also, Oleavia Neil Wilson Wiese, *Woodville Republican, Mississippi's Oldest Existing Newspaper,* (Bowie, Maryland: Heritage Books, 2009), 1: 160: "Mary Stewart, exec'x [executrix] of the Charles Stewart, Sr. estate [1834] will apply for her dower, 1200 acres three miles east of Woodville. . . ."

[16]Wilkinson County, County Tax Rolls, 1819, Box 3768, image 19, and 1820, image 21, accessed October 21, 2011, *Family Search.*

[17]Charles Stewart seeking compensation for a murdered slave. "Charles Stewart, Louisiana, 1821, Petition 20882124," *Digital Library on American Slavery,* accessed December 11, 2010, http://library.uncg.edu/slavery/about.aspx. This primary source based website is particularly valuable in searching for slave owners and their slaves across the South. Its information is gleaned from court records, and the search feature makes locating a particular owner very easy. See Charles Stewart's advertisement announcing the sale of his two Louisiana plantations and his slaves in the *Woodville Republican,* August 1, 1827.

hundred and fifty years ago [1821, or perhaps earlier].[18]

The Stewart brothers' wealth, much of it accumulated in North Carolina and Tennessee real estate ventures, clearly had not diminished with their arrival in Mississippi.

Duncan Stewart, a former member of the North Carolina legislature, Tennessee state senator, and trustee of Cumberland College (which William Perkins had attended) from 1806-1808, reentered politics soon after his arrival in Mississippi. In short order voters elected him to the Mississippi House of Representatives. He held positions as Mississippi's surveyor general and president of the state senate, and when Mississippi achieved statehood in 1817, Duncan became the state's first lieutenant governor.

Although the wealth of the younger newlyweds, William and Jane Perkins, at first could not be expected to equal that of the Stewarts, William began acquiring both land and slaves soon after his arrival in Woodville. Slight discrepancies appear in the various county records for the size and location of William's subsequent holdings following his first land purchase of 600 acres in 1819 on Thompson's Creek. However, it is safe to say he acquired an additional 760 acres on Buffalo Creek, approximately five miles east of Woodville by 1822. Combined, his total holdings amounted to between 1,300 and 1,400 acres.[19] The price he paid for the land is unknown, but it must have exceeded the two dollars per acre his father-in-law Charles Stewart had paid several years earlier in 1811.

Plantations of this size in Mississippi of course required sizeable amounts of labor. In 1824 Perkins, having increased his slave numbers during the previous years, reported owning seventy-nine slaves. Perhaps William had used his proximity to Natchez, the renowned slave-trading hub just north of Woodville,

---

[18]Herman de Bachelle Seebold, *Old Louisiana Plantation Homes and Family Trees*, (Gretna, Louisiana: Pelican Publishing Company, 1971), II: 63.

[19]Wilkinson County, County Tax Rolls, 1822, Box 3768, image 20, accessed October 21, 2011, *Family Search*. While the 1822 record shows his land is located only on Thompson's Creek, the 1824 tax rolls show acreage on *both* Thompson's Creek and Buffalo Creek. See Tax Rolls, 1824, Box 3293, image 25.

to help account for this large increase.[20] Or, he may have acquired some at the slave auctions held in the Woodville town square in front of the Court House.

The Counties of Middle Tennessee[21]
Williamson County, the home of the Perkins clan in William's boyhood, appears just southeast of Montgomery County, where William's wife Jane was born. Given this proximity, it is possible that the Perkinses and Stewarts knew each other in Tennessee. Stewart County, named after Jane Stewart's Uncle Duncan, lies just to the west of Montgomery County.

.   Only five years after his college graduation, William had achieved remarkable success in Mississippi attaining a home, land,

---

[20]Perkins claimed thirty-one or thirty-three slaves in 1820 and thirty-four slaves in 1821. He more than doubled that amount by 1824. See 1824 Tax Rolls, Box 3293, image 25. See also, Fourth Census, 1820, Wilkinson County, Mississippi, s.v. "William Perkins, Charles Stewart, and Duncan Stewart" *Heritage Quest*, accessed through the author's library account on November 9, 2010. The 1820 Federal Census was Mississippi's first since it had achieved statehood three years earlier. That year, the Stewart brothers claimed nearly 200 slaves between them. Duncan Stewart is reported in various sources as having died in 1819 or 1820, but according to *The Journal of Wilkinson County History,* 1: March 1990, he actually died on November 27, 1821.
[21]Austin Foster, *Counties of Tennessee* (Greenville, South Carolina: Southern Historical Press, 1923). See maps, "1810-1820."

slaves, and a fine pleasure carriage while enjoying the privileged planter lifestyle he had experienced as a youth in Tennessee. Residing over the next dozen years in this pastoral setting on Buffalo Creek, William and Jane developed their cotton plantation and raised their children in close proximity to Jane's parents who earlier had purchased more than 1,000 acres, also on Buffalo Creek.[22]

In the years both preceding and following Mississippi's statehood, Perkins' Stewart relatives, along with several other prominent citizens, attempted to bring elements of civilization to rural Wilkinson County. In the winter of 1816, Charles Stewart prevailed upon a close friend and preacher from Montgomery County, Tennessee, Reuben Ross, to visit Woodville the following spring. According to Ross's son, Stewart hoped the elder Ross might bring the faith "to a people almost entirely destitute of religious instruction."[23] However, the son described his father's impressions of 1817 Woodville in such a way that suggests Charles' hopes would be in vain:

> the manners and customs of the people seemed so strange to him [his father Reuben Ross], and their thoughts so full of cotton, sugar, and money that he did not think the voice of the preacher was likely to be heard by them to much advantage.[24]

Later, each Stewart brother played a role in chartering a bank for Woodville (1818), opening and becoming trustees of Wilkinson Female Academy (1819), and initiating the Franklin

---

[22]Close to the Perkins family lived Samuel Davis and his wife Jane, owners since 1810 of a cotton plantation. The Davises were the parents of young Jefferson Davis, the future president of the Confederacy, who was attending elementary school in Woodville at the time. Given the proximity of the Perkins plantation to that of the Davises, William and his family had to have known and conversed with Samuel and Jane Davis.

[23]Ross, *Life and Times of Elder Reuben Ross*, 272. In this book James Ross, the son of Reuben Ross, describes among other things his father's life as a preacher in Tennessee, his close friendship with Charles Stewart, and this visit to Woodville.

[24]Ibid., 271. After spending nearly three months in Woodville during the spring of 1817, Ross decided against moving his family there and returned to Tennessee.

1819 Wilkinson County Tax Roll. This copy of the original document shows William P. Perkin[s] (fifth from the bottom) paying $8.10 tax on his 600 acres on T[hompson] Creek. In addition, he paid a tax of $1 per head on each of his twenty-one slaves and $1 for himself as a head of household. William's tax bill for 1819 totaled $30.10 (last column).

Wilkinson County 1820, showing the location of Woodville and the Duncan Stewart plantation (arrow) in the lower right. Just north of Stewart's plantation (and east of Woodville) were the plantations of his brother Charles Stewart and William Perkins on Buffalo Creek.[25]

Debating and Literary Society for the county (1819).[26] But, despite all the financial accomplishments and suggestions of "cultural progress" by the Perkins, Stewarts, and other plantation families, an unsettling anxiety lurked on every plantation near Woodville and across Wilkinson County.

---

[25]"Mississippi Digital Map Library, Mississippi, 1820", *U. S. GenWeb Archives Mississippi*, accessed March 26, 2010,
http://usgwarchives.org/maps/mississippi/statemap/ms1820.jpg.
[26]No author, *Revised Code of the Laws of Mississippi*, (Natchez: Francis Baker, 1824), 469, 587, and 594. Charles Stewart and three others opened a branch of the Bank of Mississippi in Woodville. See also, John Wesley Monette, *History of the Discovery and Settlement of the Valley of the Mississippi*, (New York: Harper & Bros., 1848), fn., 384.

In Wilkinson County, as throughout the South, probably nothing caused more concern among slaveholders like William Perkins than the nagging specter of violence and/or insurrection directed at them or their families by their "labor force." Simply put, being outnumbered by their blacks sent shivers down white spines. And the situation was growing more pronounced with time.

According to Wilkinson County records, its white population had begun a gradual decline following its peak years, 1816 to 1823. By 1825 Wilkinson's whites numbered 2,933, some 285 less than in 1816.[27] On the other hand, and monitored carefully by whites, black numbers during the same period had soared from 4,057 to 6,033, an increase of nearly 2,000 slaves in nine years. By 1825 slaves constituted slightly more than two thirds of Wilkinson County's population. Certainly, these slave numbers were a growth indicator of the plantation "industry", but they did nothing to ease the white owners' sense of anxiety and concern.

Not surprisingly, in slave states the punishment meted out in cases of black violence against whites was uniformly swift and harsh, and in remote areas in the Deep South, like Woodville, white vigilance and discipline rarely relaxed. In 1823 and in 1826 Woodville's citizens' fears were fully realized in several incidents of black violence against white owners.

For example, Charles Stewart, an associate judge in the Wilkinson County court, heard a murder case in 1823 involving three slaves, Lewis, Dick, and Jim. Ultimately the jury convicted the three of murdering their master, William Sojourner, and sentenced them to be hanged on August 22, 1823, at gallows erected

---

[27]Wilkinson's white population in 1816 stood at 3,218, but by January 12, 1825, it had decreased to 2,933. Mississippi, State Archives, Various Records, 1820-1951, Wilkinson County, 1816 Territory Census Returns, Image 18, and 1825 State Census, Wilkinson County, image 21, accessed October 21, 2011, *Family Search,* https://www.familysearch.org/search/image/index#uri=https%3A//api.familysearch.org/records/collection/1919687/waypoints. A possible explanation for the decline in the white population at this time could be that as local planters became increasingly established many, along with their families, relocated to larger cities like Natchez or New Orleans leaving reliable overseers in charge of their Wilkinson County plantations. As time passed this concept of absentee ownership became prevalent among Mississippi's planter elite in many counties.

in the Woodville public square "within thirty feet of Bank Street and opposite the court house."[28]

While the Sojourner case had captured whites' attention in 1823, in 1826 another local incident involving a slave and his master caused further alarm in Woodville. That year, an escaped slave took an axe to his owner, William Cason, William's brother Mason in the Woodville Lodge, and Cason's wife, seriously injuring Cason and killing the woman.[29] Angry whites pursued and killed the slave.

While incidents of such extreme violence were unusual, even non-violent acts directed at whites could produce the most severe punishments. In a simple burglary case heard in Judge Charles Stewart's court involving a slave, Jerry, a jury convicted the defendant, who was hanged some three weeks later.[30] Whether Perkins, a juror in the case, felt any regret about the severity of the punishment is unknown. But as a slaveholder and a product of several generations of slaveholders in Virginia and Tennessee, it is highly unlikely that he ever doubted its legitimacy. Indeed, throughout the South, burglary and many other lesser crimes perpetuated by slaves were also considered capital offenses. In the words of North Carolina Chief Justice Thomas Ruffin in his opinion in *State v. Mann 13 NC 263* (1829): "The power of the master must be absolute, to render the submission of the slave perfect."[31]

---

[28]*Wilkinson County, Court Minutes, July & August, 1823*, FHL, microfilm roll 877088, 54, 57.

[29]Hezekiah Niles (ed.), *Niles Weekly Register*, (Baltimore: Franklin Press, April 12, 1826), 30: 83. The *Register* mistakenly refers to the master as Carson.

[30]*Wilkinson County Mississippi Court Minutes*, August 6, 1823, 59.

[31]Between 1825 and 1830 William Perkins' Masonic Lodge, along with the Columbus, Mississippi, chapter, contributed monetarily to the American Colonization Society. Founded in 1816, the Society helped establish the country of Liberia in 1821-22 as an African home to "repatriate" free African-Americans. While Southern slaveholders opposed abolition, some supported the American Colonization Society. Nationally, the Society eventually managed to relocate thousands of freed blacks to Liberia over the years. Locally, the *Woodville Republican* ran advertisements in twenty issues in 1824 promoting settlements in *Haiti* for freed blacks. In September 1827 the paper printed a letter describing the virtues of Liberian settlement. See Early Fox, "The American Colonization Society 1817-1840," *John Hopkins University Studies in Historical and Political Science*, Series XXXVII, no. 3, (1919), 377.

* * * * *

Meanwhile, during the 1820s, William Perkins continued to expand his land holdings in Wilkinson County. He purchased these additional parcels of land, not from an individual, but instead from the United States government. Under a law titled "An Act for the Further Provision for the Sale of Public Lands" authorized by an "Act of Congress on April 20, 1820", citizens were required to pay cash for all purchases at a minimum rate of $1.25 per acre. The legal document supporting the transaction indicated the name of the purchaser, date of purchase, number of acres, a description of the land's location, and the name of the President at the time. Absent, however, was the total cost of the transaction. The terms of this generous land program over the years would allow thousands of private citizens like Perkins the opportunity to buy undeveloped tracts of land in not only Mississippi but also in other states. From the mid 1820s until close to his death, William would take full advantage of this government program, purchasing tracts first in Wilkinson County only, then later, during the 1840s, in the Mississippi counties of Attala, Neshoba, and Bolivar. This was prime acreage, sold at bargain prices, in one of the finest cotton growing regions in the world. Part of William's great wealth in later years can be linked to these transactions and the amount of cotton he produced thereon.

Today, the Bureau of Land Management's records of the period are replete with transactions in Mississippi alone totaling thousands of acres, many made by individuals whose purchases easily eclipsed William's modest total.[32] The scope and impact of this bountiful land program not only benefited individual planters, but it also impacted Mississippi's economy, allowing the state to develop its agricultural wealth at a faster pace than could otherwise have been expected. But notwithstanding the generosity of this domestic government program, William also looked *outside* the United States for land investment opportunities.

---

[32]Search for each purchase at: "Land Patents," *Bureau of Land Management*, s. v. "Wilkinson County, William Perkins," accessed March 17, 2010, http://www.glorecords.blm.gov/. The documents, surveys, and plat images are located by entering the name of the individual being researched along with the county and state.

On March 1, 1825, seated at his office desk in Woodville,
attorney William Johnson, planter and slaveholder, penned a brief
note of introduction for the man then waiting in front of him, William P. Perkins. Both men had been acquainted for many years
beginning in Franklin, Tennessee. In 1818 Johnson had even appeared as a bondsman at William's marriage in Wilkinson County.[33] Johnson jotted down the following:

Woodville, March 1st 1825.
Dear Sir,
This will be handed you by Mr. William P. Perkins: a respectable
and wealthy planter of this country [United States] – Mr. Perkins
visits your Province [Texas] with the view of acquiring Land and
ultimately establishing a sugar or Cotton farm in your province –
Mr. P. has respectable and extensive family connections here as
well as in the State of Tennessee. No doubt should he be pleased
with your country and future prospects there, he will ultimately
move there and be the means of many valuable citizens moving
there both from this State and from Tennessee – I have been personally and [?] acquainted with him for many years and have no
hesitation in saying [he] would be a valuable acquisition to your
settlement – Mr. P. is now waiting and you will therefore excuse
this crude Note. –
Wm Johnson[34]

Johnson had addressed his note to none other than Stephen
F. Austin. Austin then was in the initial stages of founding a settlement at San Felipe, Texas, on the banks of the Brazos River,
approximately forty-five miles west of today's Houston and about
360 miles from Woodville. Claimed by Mexico, Texas was actu-

---

[33]In a demonstration of trust and generosity Johnson's brother, Joseph, had
agreed with William on seven promissory notes of $5,343 each charging him no
interest if William repaid the sums on time in installments from 1825-1831. Perkins and Johnson signed the agreement on April 30, 1824. This Joseph Johnson
was probably the politically prominent Woodville planter who later became
president of the local railroad. *Wilkinson County Courthouse Land Records Book
D*, FHL, microfilm roll 876533, 264.
[34]Eugene Barker (ed.), *Annual Report of American Historical Association*, "The
Austin Papers", (Washington, D. C.: Government Printing Office, 1924), 2: 1053.

ally a foreign country then, but Mexican authorities had granted
Austin permission to settle Americans there. Credited with being
the founder of present day Texas, Austin, by late 1825, had settled
the first 300 families in his Austin Colony. Of those several came
from Woodville.

Austin could be very selective in his choice of settlers.
Most were literate, industrious men of a higher economic class
than average immigrants. Most brought property with them.
Twenty-five percent brought slaves. William, if he chose to immi-
grate (again westward), would mesh quite nicely with the kind of
men Austin sought to populate his colony. Furthermore, as Johnson remarked, William's prestigious social status and family connections in both Mississippi and Tennessee could prove to be a
valuable asset for Austin in his efforts to entice additional settlers
to Texas. Potential settlers were all lured by the economic potential of the vast Texas landscape and the price Austin charged for
any land purchased, twelve and a half cents per acre.

During the spring or summer of 1825, Perkins actually
made the trip to San Felipe and took title to an unspecified amount
of land in Austin's colony. However, he did not commit to moving
his family there quite yet. From Mississippi in the early fall of
1825, William wrote to Austin:

Woodville, 27th Sept. 1825
Dear Sir,
I have now made my arrangements to send two or three hands
[slaves] to your country some time in the winter, to make a crop
next year, but I find it impracticable for me to move my family
and hands for several years, therefore I write this particularly to
know from you, if I am there myself and make a Crop, will it be
sufficient to hold my land, with the title I already have. I am anxious you would write to me by the first of November on this subject – if you think this will not answer I will probably decline the
undertaking.
        Wm. P. Perkins
Give my respects to Col' Pettis and Mr. William
[Addressed to] Col' Stephen F. Austin, Texas[35]

---

[35]Ibid., 1208.

William's double reference to making a crop revealed his concern for the prevailing rule then in effect in Austin's colony, if titled land were not cultivated within two years of the receipt of the title, the claim would be forfeited. Whether Austin ever responded or if William ever sent his hands or returned personally to plant a crop there is unknown. Later, the impracticality of the undertaking evidently caused William to forgo the Texas move and remain in Mississippi, a decision he probably never regretted.

Though twenty-five years later William would still refer to himself as a planter, this Texas episode reveals that at age thirty, despite his success in Woodville, an entrepreneurial spirit burned inside him, one that would remain for the rest of his life. William's focus, seeking maximum profits in planting, land and slave acquisition, *and as an investor and creditor*, would dominate his business activities in the coming decades and contradict, to a degree, the stereotypical notion that planters were primarily farmers. However, William's 'world' *depended* on slave labor and to pass over this principle is to fail to understand the man. The profits he gained from the labor of his slaves made possible his and his family's way of life, as well as other ancillary enterprises, exemplified by a partnership he formed in the late 1820s with his brother-in-law.

By 1828 slaveholders in the Woodville area could select from a number of sources to outfit their slaves with shoes. In addition to those Woodville merchants who imported slaves' shoes from Boston and New York, some local businesses also manufactured such shoes and sold them at a cheaper price than the imports. Perkins and Duncan Stewart (son of Charles Stewart) in 1828 had seen a need in the Woodville area and acted, forming their own business that year to manufacture shoes locally while also producing tanned leather. Using slave labor, most likely overseen by an experienced shoemaker, Perkins and Stewart began to compete for local business - Wilkinson County counted more than 6,000 slaves in 1825 - in what they hoped would become a lucrative endeavor.[36] Though they ran advertisements in the *Woodville Republican* for their shoe enterprise, the two men most likely had already

---

[36]Franklee Gilbert Whartenby, *Labor and Labor Productivity in United States Cotton Production, 1800-1840*, (New York: Arno Press, 1977), 164.

gained the business of William's father-in-law, Charles Stewart, the owner of more than a hundred slaves.[37] The fact that many slaves went barefoot during the summer calls into question the profitability of the venture, but again it demonstrated how motivated Perkins was to leverage profits from the backs of his slaves.

Near the end of the 1820s, William and Jane Perkins still resided on their comfortable and productive Wilkinson County plantation. The family now totaled five with the births of two daughters, Jane P. born in December 1820, Louisa Ann in 1821, and a son, Charles Stewart, born surprisingly in France in 1827.[38] (The fact that the Perkins family could afford a trip to France further demonstrates the wealth William had accumulated in Mississippi.) Despite experiencing more than a decade of financial success in Wilkinson County, William soon initiated steps resulting in his resettlement to a potentially more lucrative area of an ever-expanding Mississippi.

As a part of this strategy, William began a gradual downsizing of his land and slave holdings in Wilkinson County. By 1830 William claimed just thirty-four slaves.[39] In May 1831 he

---

[37]Charles Sydnor, *Slavery in Mississippi*, (Gloucester, Massachusetts: Peter Smith Publisher, 1965), 25. See also footnote twelve on the same page.

[38]Seventh Census, 1850, Yuba County, California, s. v. "C. L. Perkins," line 18, accessed August 1, 2011, *Family Search*, https://familysearch.org/pal:/MM9.1.2/MWHD-JGJ/p_171689208. The enumerator erred in listing Charles' middle initial as L. William and a pregnant Jane had evidently journeyed to France in 1827, possibly accompanying or visiting one of Jane's cousins (perhaps James Alexander Ventress who may have been attending college there at the time). (William's daughter, Louisa Ann Perkins Pugh of Madison County, Mississippi, appears as a twenty-nine year old in the 1850 census.)

[39]Fifth Census, 1830, Wilkinson County, Mississippi, s. v. "Wm. P. Perkins," 280, accessed November 11, 2010 *Ancestry.com*. Included in his thirty-four slaves were "two certain Negro children . . . a Boy named William about the age of six or seven years & [a] girl named Charlotte about the same age. . . ." He had purchased them on March 19, 1824, for "the sum of three hundred dollars . . ." from Charles Stewart. *Wilkinson County Land Records, Book E*, FHL, microfilm roll 876533, March 19, 1824, 263. Counted also was Louisa, a three-year old slave girl *given* by Grandpa Charles Stewart to his granddaughter Jane P. Perkins as a gift in 1826, *Wilkinson County Land Records, Book E*, FHL, microfilm roll 876533, June 10, 1826, 234? There is minor confusion in the granting of the slave Louisa. In the document the recipient of the gift is written as Jane Mell Perkins

received $7,500 for the sale of 600 acres of "land on which Perkins resides."[40] In July 1831 William sold five slaves to William Richardson for $1,400.[41] These transactions had followed another, a group of twenty slaves offered at his plantation by his cousin D. Hardeman in February 1831. As a result, by mid 1831 William held only seventeen slaves (above five and less than sixty years old) and just his remaining 760 acres on Buffalo Creek, which it may be assumed he also eventually sold. Understandable is William's desire to sell his land before he moved, but unexplained is his motive for selling his slaves who could have been easily transported to his new plantation.

FOR SALE
(ON LIBERAL TERMS)

20 LIKELY YOUNG NEGROES (Men, Women & Boys)

Apply to the subscriber at W. P. Perkins' five miles East of Woodville
D. Hardeman, February 5, 1831

Copy of slave advertisement appearing in the *Woodville Republican* placed by William Perkins' cousin, D. Hardeman

---

who is actually Stewart's daughter and of course William's wife. Stewart's intended beneficiary was his granddaughter Jane P. Perkins.

[40] *Wilkinson County, Land Records Book G*, FHL, microfilm roll 876534, May 17, 1831, 146-147. William Perkins may have received installment payments on the sale from the purchaser, William Reid, totaling $10,500 due each January from 1832 to 1835, 193-194. Or, possibly, the $10,500 represented the proceeds of a separate transaction.

[41] Ibid.,191. The five slaves were forty-year old Johnson, and his four children, Dempsey, Cathy, Randall, and Josephine. Richardson may have sold the five to another slaveholder soon thereafter.

NOTICE.

IN pursuance of a Deed of Trust executed by *William Yerby*, on the 19th day of April, 1824, for the use of *John F. Carmichael*, the undersigned Trustee, therein named will proceed to sell to the highest bidder. for ready money, on the 5th day of December next. at the Court House of the County of Wilkinson, the following

NEGRO SLAVES, to wit.

Anthony, Jack, Jim, Dennis, Ellison, Louisa, Martha, Rose, Jane, Lewis, Criss, Sally, Charlotte and Chelson.

or so many thereof as may be necessary to satisfy the several sums of money mentioned in said Deed, with the costs attendant thereon.

T. H. PROSSER, *Trustee.*

November 4. 1825.   99

Wilkinson County slave sale notice from November 1825. Yerby was a Wilkinson Masonic Lodge brother of William Perkins. William had served on a jury in the court of Judge Thomas H. Prosser.

III

Madison County

*For in a warm climate, no man will labor for himself who can
make another labor for him.*

Thomas Jefferson, "Notes on the
State of Virginia," 1781

In October 1833 William Perkins' name first appears in
the tax records of the central Mississippi county of Madison, north
of Woodville, dubbed the *Land Between Two Rivers*, the Pearl
River to the east and the Big Black in the west. However, the absence of any customary tax data, such as acres claimed, location,
or number of slaves, suggests he hadn't yet settled there. One year
later, according to local records, he and his family had taken up
permanent residence northwest of Livingston, the nearest town to
William's new plantation. Then the most prosperous settlement in
Madison County and also its county seat, Livingston provided a
meeting place for its citizens and a hub for profit-hungry planters
to market their cotton or purchase recently arrived slaves transported from the slave markets and pens in Natchez.[1]

On the other hand, if new citizens arrived in Madison
County expecting to find numerous available community services,
many were disappointed. At first, despite the county's economic
potential, only a few banks and stores existed. The few schools
and academies lacked funding. Often, school money came from
unconventional sources. To support the county's Pearl River Female Academy, a state lottery had to be organized, offering prizes
of twenty-five Negro slaves valued at $1,600 each.[2]

William's decision to leave Wilkinson County in favor of
this untamed country near Livingston and Canton (map below)
undoubtedly involved family considerations. His brother Daniel P.
Perkins Jr. and his wife had recently moved there from Tennessee

---

[1]Dunbar Rowland, *Encyclopedia of Mississippi History*, (Madison, Wisconsin:
S.A. Brant, 1907), 110. Later, nearby Canton became the county seat.
[2]*Canton Herald*, April 21, 1837, 3, column 5.

circa 1830.[3] In addition, William's four cousins, William, "D.," Thomas, and John Locke Hardeman resided several miles away on Burnt Corn Creek near Livingston by at least 1835.[4]

This Perkins-Hardeman family connection ran deep. Frequent marriages between members of each family over the years resulted in the births of many offspring in Tennessee and in Virginia beginning as far back as the 1750s. The proximity of the two families would eventually spill over into gold rush California and continue into the twentieth century. As late as 1940, William's great grandson Jack (John) Morrison and his wife resided in Gainesville, Texas, with their niece, Virginia Hardeman.

Despite this proximity of relatives, William may well have viewed the tremendous economic opportunities available in this promising agricultural region as the paramount attraction – Southern cotton expansion had just begun to reenergize slavery in the South. Intent on reaping a fortune in an area on the verge of a cotton boom, Perkins was joining the already emergent migration into Madison County. His arrival in 1833 no doubt invoked memories of his first journey there decades earlier.

In March 1813 Perkins and other Tennessee volunteers had slogged and sometimes cut their way through the region, following the Natchez Trace, the storied, old Native American pathway. As members of General Jackson's army returning to Tennessee from Natchez, their line of march took them through this isolated and unsurveyed area to within five miles of where Canton would eventually develop. Now, in 1833, William observed a still largely rustic region with relatively few plantations (in comparison to Wilkinson County) dotting its landscape.

At the time of William Perkins' arrival, one of Madison County's most striking features was the huge imbalance - similar

---

[3]Fifth Census, 1830, Madison County, Mississippi, s. v. "Daniel Perkins," 94, accessed January 18, 2011, *Ancestry.com*. Daniel Perkins Jr. reported owning one slave in the 1830 census and four in the 1840 census, but the 1840 census figure may be far less than the actual number he owned at the time of his death in 1841. From 1831-1840 Daniel purchased approximately 670 acres in Madison and nearby Hinds County through the same government program as William. Daniel Perkins apparently lived alternately in both counties but maintained his primary plantation in Hinds County.

[4]By 1838 William Hardeman had become the president of the Citizens Bank of Madison County in Canton. *Canton Herald*, December 19, 1838.

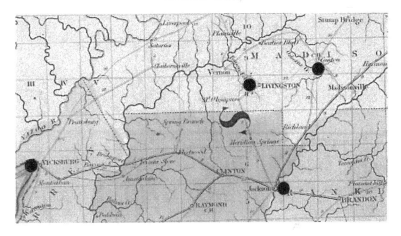

1839 map showing the Madison County cities of Canton and
Livingston. To the west is Vicksburg on the Mississippi River, and
south of Livingston is Jackson, the state capital.[5]

to that found in Wilkinson County - between its slave and white
populations. Two factors contributed to this overwhelming black
majority: Some recently arrived planters brought with them large
gangs of slaves.[6] Secondly, absentee plantation owners continued
to reside in the older, more settled parts of the state - "leaving on a
plantation containing perhaps, several sections of land, no white
person except the overseer. . . ."[7] As a result, Madison County, as
early as 1834, counted 4,904 slaves and substantially fewer
whites.[8] While the county census enumerator's practice of listing

[5]"Mississippi Digital Map Library, Mississippi 1839," *US GenWeb Archives*,
accessed January 18, 2013,
http://www.usgwarchives.net/maps/mississippi/statemap/ms1839.jpg.
[6]David J. Libby, *Slavery and Frontier Mississippi 1720-1835*, (Jackson: University Press of Mississippi, 2008), 104.
[7]Edwin Miles, "Mississippi Slave Insurrection Scare of 1835," *Journal of Negro
History, 42* (January 1957): 48-49.
[8]Mississippi, State Archives, Various Records, 1820-1951, Madison County,
County tax rolls 1834, Box 3718, image 65, accessed October 22, 2011, *Family
Search,*
https://www.familysearch.org/search/image/index#uri=https%3A//api.familysear
ch.org/records/collection/1919687/waypoints. This image provides a recap of the
county's 1834 tax rolls. Along with the slave count (those blacks older than five
but less than sixty years old), the compiler listed only the 658 white polls and two

only white polls in his frequent tallies makes it difficult to determine the exact count of whites for any given year, it can be stated
with some certainty that in 1834 blacks outnumbered whites by a
margin of at least three to one. Yet, despite Madison's County's
large slave population, local planters continued to require more
'hands' for their plantations.

Slaves in a cotton field. Image courtesy of Documenting the
American South, The University of North Carolina at Chapel Hill
Libraries

　　　　With cotton selling high at $76 per bale in 1835 according
to a Livingston slave trader, demand for slaves increased. But,
twin impediments initially hampered planters' attempts to acquire
additional slaves.[9] First, demand for slave labor in Madison's de-

free men of color. (Madison County records showed 659 white polls in 1837).
The white polls are those males, ages 21-50, who qualified to vote. This group,
when combined with the unknown number of remaining males, plus women and
children, would still total a far *smaller* number than the county's slave population.
[9] Joseph Meek letter in Purcell, "A Damned Piece of Rascality," 9. Meek wrote in
June 1835 that cotton sold for eighteen to twenty cents per pound. Using nineteen
cents a pound as a basis, a 400-pound bale would bring $76.

veloping plantation economy had quickly surpassed supply. Furthermore, since 1808 the United States Congress had outlawed African slave imports into America. As a result, the laws of economics demonstrated they also applied to slavery because the ensuing slave labor shortage led to higher domestic slave prices, especially in Madison County. As an example, in January 1835 a Livingston resident and William's neighbor, Josiah Newman, paid almost $1,000 each for the forty slaves he purchased from a local dealer.

As had been the case in Wilkinson County, a constantly expanding force of slaves meant planters could expect to earn progressively greater profits. In October 1835, hoping to benefit from planters' increasing demands for slaves, seven slave traders established offices in Livingston. At about the same time, one such local trader reported to his partners and suppliers in Virginia his urgent need for more slaves, "as many as possible [to sell]," adding, "the house now collected full of people . . . a greate [sic] gathering here to buy [slaves]."[10]

Despite the aforementioned obstacles to slave acquisition, these Madison County slave dealers soon had been able to satisfy their customers' needs by creatively importing domestic slaves from Virginia or Tennessee. Accordingly, by 1836 the county's slave population had reached 8,158, an increase of more than 3,200 slaves since 1834.[11]

Shortly after his arrival, William Perkins seized upon the opportunity to begin making money. He soon claimed fifty slaves (in light of his selling spree before he left Wilkinson County, many were probably purchased from local slave traders) and 1,320 acres (assessed at three dollar per acre). This acreage, part of

---

[10]Joseph Meek, letter to his partner Samuel Logan, September 27, 1835, *Seth Keller, Inc.*, accessed September 14, 2011, http://www.sethkaller.net/catalogs, partially transcribed copy (downloaded) in author's possession. Keller was offering the letter for sale on or about the access date. The author's later attempts to view the letter online were unsuccessful.

[11]Madison County tax rolls, 1830-1854, 1836, Box 3718, images 68-84, accessed October 22, 2011, *Family Search,* https://www.familysearch.org/search/image/index#uri=https%3A//api.familysearch.org/records/collection/1919687/waypoints. Presumably, the census enumerator's tally included only those slaves older than five years and less than sixty years as was customary.

which straddled Persimmon Creek, was situated along a road that ran from Livingston to Canton.[12] Two years later in 1836, Perkins' land expenditures totaled $42,700 for the nearly 3,200 acres he had acquired in Madison County, more than double the amount he had claimed in Wilkinson County.[13]

While cotton formed the foundation of Perkins' wealth, other sources added to his increasing prosperity. During his more than twelve-year residence in Madison County, William invested thousands of dollars in additional land parcels, and then sold portions of that same acreage for profit. Inheritance also contributed to Perkins' assets. With the death of his father, Daniel Perkins, in Tennessee in September 1834 (William's mother, Bethenia, predeceased his father) and the death of Jane's father six months later in 1835, William and Jane may have inherited slaves, money, and/or land from one or both parents (Charles Stewart held approximately 116 slaves in Wilkinson County by 1830 and Daniel Perkins in Tennessee claimed thirty-nine.).[14] In his will dated Feb-

---

[12]Mississippi, State Archives, Various Records, 1820-1951, Madison County, County Tax Rolls 1834, Box 3718, image 58, accessed October 22, 2011, *Family Search*, https://www.familysearch.org/search/image/index#uri=https%3A//api.familysear ch.org/records/collection/1919687/waypoints. The assessment was dated November 1834.

[13]*Madison County, MS, Deeds Book B*, FHL, microfilm roll 886074, 215 and *Book D*, microfilm roll 886075, 64 and140. Part of the land was located in Sections 4, 28, and 33 in Townships 8 and 9 in Range 1 East. Since the total sale price per acre seems high given the times, perhaps Perkins' transactions included more than just land.

[14]Wiese, *Woodville Republican*, 144. Weise cites the March 21, 1835, edition of the *Republican* for the following: "Judge Charles Stewart of this county [Wilkinson] died in Hancock County [Mississippi] on March 15, [1835] in his 62nd year." According to *The Journal of Wilkinson County History*, "Wilkinson County Cemetery Records," (Woodville, Mississippi: March 1990), 1: 239, Charles Stewart is buried at the Stewart 3 Cemetery located outside of Woodville. His brother Duncan rests in Stewart Cemetery 2. For Charles Stewart's slave count, see Fifth Census, 1830, Wilkinson County, Mississippi, s. v. "Charles Stewart," 276, accessed November 11, 2010, *Ancestry.com*. Stewart is listed as Dr. Charles Stewart on the census roll. For Daniel Perkins' slave count, see Fifth Census, 1830, Williamson County, Tennessee, s. v. "Daniel Perkins," image 206, accessed November 11, 2010, *Ancestry.com*. Daniel Perkins Sr. of Tennessee provided that on his death his property should be divided between his children, William P. Perkins and others (Appendix A). Perkins Sr. willed his slaves to his

ruary 24, 1835, Grandpa Stewart left a $5,000 cash bequest (held in trust by William Perkins) to his grandson, Charles Stewart Perkins, further evidence of the wealth available to Perkins family members.[15]

By 1840 not only had William acquired slaves and land, but he also had begun to further diversify his investments. He purchased 400 shares of stock in the Mississippi Union Bank (headed by the former Mississippi governor Hiram Runnels) for an unspecified price and $2,250 worth of "bloodstock" racehorses (for breeding).[16]

William's calculated shift from Wilkinson to Madison County was proving to be one of the wisest and most profitable business decisions of his life. By 1840 his income and assets, based in part on his economic success in Madison, were allowing his family to enjoy a life of increasing privilege and affluence. Only in the closing years of the Civil War, with the demise of the American Southern slave owning society at hand, would the family ever be financially challenged.

While residing in Madison County, William and Jane began sharing some of their growing wealth. They generously provided gifts to their children in the form of land and slaves. On October 1, 1838, William and Jane deeded several tracts of land in Madison County to their daughter Louisa (Ann) Pugh and her hus-

---

children in a manner of speaking. He specified that all his slaves except Lizza be sold among his offspring. Lizza was permitted to choose her owner from among Daniel's children. Perkins then specified which of his Negro families were not to be separated. Daniel is supposedly buried "at the old Scales place at Eagleville, Tenn., near Franklin, the Scales being relatives," McCormick, *Family Memorials*, 40.

[15] *Wilkinson County, Will Book 2*, FHL, microfilm roll 877079, 126-128. See also, *Madison County, MS, Deeds Book G*, FHL, microfilm roll 886078, 614, mentioned in papers filed by William P. Perkins recorded April 20, 1840. In his will Charles Stewart granted three of his more than 100 slaves freedom and generous cash grants provided that the Mississippi legislature confirmed their emancipation which was not a certainty. Stewart also left his slave Phillip, who was not freed and was to remain in the household of Stewart's wife, $100 annually to be paid to him each Christmas morning.

[16] *Madison County, MS, Deeds Book G*, microfilm roll 886078, February 19, 1840, 410 and *Book K*, microfilm roll 886082, 667. Perkins purchased the bank stock in April 1839, and following in his father Daniel's footsteps, he acquired the racehorses in February 1840.

band Dr. Joseph Pugh.[17] Slightly more than a year later on October 15, 1839, the William and Jane transferred ownership to the Pughs of twenty slaves ranging in age from five to forty years, and valued at between $10,000 and $12,000 by William's own estimate.[18]

In February 1840 the Perkins' eldest son, Charles S., received a gift of slaves and also cash from his parents. William and Jane transferred to Charles "twelve Negro slaves for life," and the $5,000 inheritance from Grandpa Stewart.[19] Thirteen-year old Charles now owned Sandy Jones, approximately forty-years old, and his wife, Patience, approximately thirty-seven years old, both described as "of a dark complexion." Their two children, Simon and Wake, Wake's wife Matilda, and their two children, Sandy II, age six (?), and Sophia, six months, were also included in the conveyance as were five teenagers; Green eighteen, John and Aaron both sixteen, and Elizabeth and Samy each fifteen. Of these dozen slaves one in particular bears further mention - the male adult slave, Sandy Jones.

The random mention of the elder slave Sandy Jones provides the first documentation of his connection to his master Charles Perkins. Their relationship would continue for the next twelve years on the plantation and later in the California goldfields. Interestingly, because the names and ages of Sandy's wife, children,

---

[17]Ibid., *Book F*, microfilm roll, 886077, 11.
[18]Ibid., 643. Of these twenty blacks, two groups may have been families based on the sequence in which their names are listed in the transfer document and the ages of the children. William had chosen to keep them intact when he transferred ownership to the Pughs. The deed lists the names, ages, and color of the slaves involved in the transfer:

Family 1	Family 2	
Mack, black, age 40	John, copper, 30	Susan(?), 6
Mary, copper, 35	Lucy, copper, 24	
Jim, yellow, 13	Janey (?), 9	
Elizabeth, yellow, 11	Milly (?), 5	

With the economic Panic of 1837, slave and cotton prices had tumbled. The value of the slaves is based on William's testimony regarding slave prices in December 1839 and is found in W. C. Smedes and T. A. Marshall, *Reports of Cases Argued and Determined in the High Court of Errors and Appeals for the State of Mississippi*, (Boston: Charles C. Little and James Brown, 1849), XI: 514-515.
[19]Ibid., *Book G*, microfilm roll 886078, 614. See *Bolivar County Deed Book C*, microfilm roll 886086, 11, for mention of some of these slaves in another transaction.

and grandchildren appear in these records, a unique opportunity emerges to track an entire slave family well into the post Civil War era, decades later.

* * * * *

Madison County, in the first years of its development, maintained a reputation for aggressiveness and a certain callousness on the part of some of its citizens. As a result, its residents witnessed violent episodes not often seen in Mississippi's more established counties. In 1838 two men fought a duel with Bowie knives inflicting severe wounds on each other. Such duels could occur in the most unlikely of locations. In the town square at Canton, two *lawyers* discharged pistols "without effect" then commenced to beat each over the head with the emptied weapons. Finally, after bystanders had separated the two, one of the men secured another weapon then shot his opponent to death. In yet another dramatic incident, again involving two lawyers, a prosecutor in a Canton *courtroom* attacked a defense attorney as he (the defense attorney) addressed the jury. The victim responded by stabbing his attacker with a sword cane killing him.[20] However, the most striking example of lawlessness had occurred earlier, shortly after William Perkins arrived in Madison County.

By the 1830s Southerners viewed slavery not as an inherited evil from the past but, instead, as a lasting and valued institution of immeasurable good. Any efforts to disrupt this entrenched way of life, even attempts made by white Southerners, would not be tolerated. A disturbing incident occurred in slave-rich Madison County midway through the decade that brought this canon to the forefront.

In 1835 the Madison County that William and his family

---

[20]The episodes were reported in the: *Columbia Democrat*, (Bloomsburg, Pennsylvania), September 15, 1838, 2, column 5, *New Orleans Picayune*, cited in the *Rutland Herald* (Vermont), February 2, 1840, 2, column 3, and *New York Tribune*, June 5, 1843, 2, column 3. Accessed January 21, 2012, "Historic American Newspapers," *Library of Congress*, http://chroniclingamerica.loc.gov/search/pages/results/?state=&date1=1836&date2=1845&proxtext=canton%2C+mississippi&x=14&y=9&dateFilterType=yearRange&rows=20&searchType=basic.

had just recently called home experienced an episode of dramatic violence. An uncharacteristic steady rainfall had descended on the area from mid May to July causing concern among local planters that the cotton crop would be diminished or even ruined. Meanwhile, as a result of the continued downpour, slaves remained idle in their shacks, unable to perform their necessary and customary tasks in the drenched cotton fields. The forbidding weather proved to be a threatening omen.

For the previous four years, Madison County's whites, and in fact whites across the entire South, had lived with the traumatic memory of Nat Turner leading a band of his fellow slaves in 1831 on a countywide rampage, murdering nearly sixty Virginia whites in an extraordinary two day rebellion.[21] In late June 1835, amidst the continuing rainfall, rumors of a slave revolt began circulating around Livingston, increasing anxiety there among the white population. This specter of a local slave insurrection fueled in part by the ongoing anxieties of Madison County's outnumbered whites, combined possibly with their haunting awareness of the Turner revolt, finally erupted in a wave of hostility and retribution.

As the episode unfolded, Livingston's citizens initially remained calm but watchful. Later, as fear of a rebellion began to take hold, women and children sought refuge in their homes, while vigilante groups of local slaveholders, self-described as committees of "safety" and "investigation," formed. They rooted out alleged black revolt perpetrators and through "interrogation" and eventually the whip extracted "confessions", supposedly implicating several whites - "the most wicked and abandoned white men in the country; highway robbers, murderers, and abolitionists," - who allegedly intended to lead a slave rebellion on July 4.[22]

---

[21]Whites quickly mobilized and in putting down the rebellion executed not only the insurrectionists but scores of innocent slaves as well. Turner was captured two months later, brought to trial, and executed.

[22]H.R. Howard, compiler, *The History of Virgil A. Stewart and His Adventure in Capturing the Great Western Land Pirate*, (New York: Harper and Brothers, 1836), 233, Libby, *Slavery and Frontier Mississippi*, 110, 111, and Lee Sandlin, *Wicked River: The Mississippi When It Last Ran Wild*, (New York: Pantheon Books, 2010), 177. The description of the implicated whites is found in the biased *Proceedings of the Citizens of Madison County.*

The so-called Livingston Committee of Safety consisted of thirteen prominent men with broad, extralegal, self-appointed powers to investigate and punish any person, regardless of color, involved in helping or inciting slave revolts. Though William's future son-in-law, Dr. Joseph Pugh, played a role in these events, he held no position on the committee. However, it was Pugh who had suggested its organization. After its formation the committee placed the Doctor in charge of mounted and foot patrols whose job was to secure the towns and the countryside against any revolt-minded slaves or collaborating whites.

Pugh, however, may not have behaved quite as radically as the actual committee members. Through "the wise interference and prudent suggestions of a very spirited and enterprising young gentleman, Dr. _____ Pugh" three whites accused in the insurrection plot were saved from instant massacre by an angry Livingston mob.[23] Their reprieve was short-lived. Two days later on July 4, the committee convicted two of the three, and before a crowd of Livingston's citizens hanged them from a makeshift scaffold.

Contributing as much as anything to this approximately three-week long 'rebellion' episode was the lawlessness of local citizens. Mob hysteria, as a result of the "confessions" coerced from terrified slaves, had formed the basis for the revolt scare. The *Vicksburg Register* on July 16, 1835, supposed five whites and ten to fifteen blacks had been hanged in Livingston. Later, a local observer in a July 27, 1835, Nashville newspaper account titled "Insurrection of Slaves in Mississippi," noted that "about ten negroes and five or six white men have been hung without any forms of law or trial, except an examination before the examining committee. They are still going on trying and hanging."[24] The situation had become so dangerous that Henry Foote, well known in and near Livingston and later a United States Senator and the Mississippi Governor, did not cross-examine witnesses against his white

---

[23]Hezekiah Niles (ed.), *Niles Weekly Register*, (Baltimore: E. Niles, October 17, 1835), 49: 119.

[24]*National Intelligencer*, July 29, 1835, cited in Davidson Burns McKibben, "Negro Slave Insurrections in Mississippi, 1800-1865," *The Journal of Negro History*, Volume 34, no. 1, (Jan. 1949), 77-78, accessed May 2, 2012, http://www.jstor.org/discover/10.2307/2715628?uid=3739560&uid=2129&uid=2&uid=70&uid=4&uid=3739256&sid=21101521078897.

client out of fear of retribution from the Livingston mob. Less than twenty minutes later his client, whose innocence Foote never doubted, was hanged by decision of the committee. Ultimately, the committee may have condemned a total of seven whites and an undetermined number of blacks (the total may have been as high as thirty) to the gallows for their roles in plotting a rebellion that never occurred.

Stories regarding some of the accused whites emerge from the conflicting sources. Some, like Foote's client, were innocent victims. One, William Earle, was tortured and hanged himself, while the mob executed his brother the following morning. Two other whites *may* have been involved in the rebellion plot, even though a so-called gallows confession uttered by one of them is suspect.[25] A fourth white victim, Ruel Blake, a slave owner and planter executed on July 10, lived near William in Livingston. Another alleged white conspirator, Matthew Sharkey, killed a member of the Livingston Committee of Safety who was pursuing him, then turned himself in to the Hinds County committee (similar to the Livingston committee, but less virulent). Its members soon acquitted him of any wrongdoing. In the midst of all the turmoil lived William Perkins and his family.

Perkins resided near the focal point of the rebellion rumors and the scene of the hangings where, according to the vigilance committee's report, slaves in the vicinity of Livingston (and the Perkins plantation) outnumbered whites fifty to one. Given William's proximity to the events and his stature within the community, it would be entirely reasonable to assume that Livingston locals approached him about joining the committee. As a college educated, wealthy, respected slaveholder, a relative of Mississippi's former first lieutenant governor, and the nephew of the territory's first attorney general, William would have lent immense prestige and solid judgment to their group. Yet, his name does not appear in any of the committee's records.

Whether any of Perkins' slaves were involved in the rumored uprising is uncertain. Later, testimony given before the

---

[25]Daniel S. Dupre, *Transforming the Cotton Frontier: Madison County, Alabama, 1800-1840,* (Baton Rouge: Louisiana State University Press, 1997), 225, and Libby, *Slavery and Frontier Mississippi,* 112, 113.

committee in July 1835 regarding an accused plotter, Albe Dean, revealed, "when on his way to Livingston he had asked a witness, among other things, if some of W. P. Perkins's negroes were not engaged in the conspiracy."[26] However, nothing in any subsequent testimony implicated any of William's slaves.

Eventually calm was restored in Madison County. But, two months later another black suspected in the rebellion was caught and executed in Livingston in September 1835.[27] More than two and a half *years* later Canton's whites still remained cautious. The *Canton Herald* reported a new city ordnance making it unlawful for any Negro or Negroes to visit the city on Sunday without a special permit from the owner or overseer, on penalty of twenty lashes.[28]

Across the country Americans had taken notice of the events in Madison County. In January 1838 a young Abraham Lincoln delivered a speech in Illinois titled "The Perpetuation of Our Political Institutions." In it he referenced the Livingston episode. Speaking specifically about the "increasing disregard for law which pervades the country" he declared, "Next, negroes, suspected of conspiring to raise an insurrection, were caught up and hanged in all parts of the State [Mississippi]: then, white men, supposed to be leagued with the negroes [were hanged]." Only later, in the last years of the 1840s, would Madison County's wild-west mentality subside.

In March 1836, not long after the rebellion turmoil in Livingston had ended, a less incendiary incident involving William Perkins occurred there which provides us with an absorbing, unusually detailed human insight into the multi-faceted world of plantation owner culture and practice. Beginning with a business transaction involving a single female slave, the incident would expand to involve other characters and various sub plots, eventually culminating in a Mississippi Supreme Court decision seven years later.

---

[26]H.R. Howard, *The History of Virgil A. Stewart*, 247.
[27]Niles, *Register*, October 31, 1835.
[28]*Canton Herald*, February 21, 1838, 3, column 6. A similar law had been enacted in 1836 in Woodville.

In the mid-1800s numerous, affluent slaveholding planters, especially those managing larger plantations like Perkins,
typically maintained a significant distance between themselves
and their field hands. (The select few household slaves obviously
came into direct daily contact with the master and his family because of their assigned domestic duties within the 'big house'.)
Many masters achieved separation from their field hands through
their frequent absences or by allowing overseers direct and daily
control over the slaves. Still others became absentee owners living
in different counties, sometimes even in a different state. William,
as a resident owner, practiced close control and personal participa-
tion, however, in all the commercial aspects of slave ownership,
including the purchase or exchange of slaves.

In April 1836 William Perkins hired another overseer,
thirty-six year old Tennessee-born James T. Barr, to help manage
the nearly eighty slaves now laboring on his plantation.[29] William
had met Barr just weeks earlier as the result of a business transaction with Barr's previous employer.

In early 1836 William chose to rid himself of one of his
female slaves. Consequently, he sought out a sixty-five year old
itinerant Madison County man, Joseph Meek Jr., probably not a
stranger at all. Meek, had lived in Washington County, Virginia,
near William's early boyhood home in Abingdon, and given this
proximity, almost certainly the Meeks and Perkins families had
been acquainted there. Like William, Meek later also maintained a
Tennessee connection.

By 1836 Meek held claim as an experienced, interstate
slave trader/speculator, one of Nashville's leaders in that profession. From Nashville, an important crossroads of the domestic
slave trade, Meek traveled throughout Virginia, Tennessee, Louisiana, and Mississippi, on occasion ranging as far east as Maryland. On these journeys he would purchase slaves, transport them
in coffles (slaves chained together in a line) to corrals located on
property he owned just north of Canton, and then quickly auction

---

[29]W. C. Smedes and T. A. Marshall, *Cases Argued and Determined in the High
Court of Errors and Appeals*, (Boston: Little and Brown, 1844), 1: 414, (*Munn v
Perkins*, 9 Mississippi 412). In court testimony Barr reveals how he came to work
for Perkins in 1836, leaving the employ of Joseph Meek, an infrequent Madison
County resident. Barr later became the Sunflower County, Mississippi, assessor.

them on behalf of Meek, Haynes, Logan, and Company or another partner Benjamin Little.[30]

On March 19 Perkins and Meek struck their deal in a seemingly uncomplicated exchange of slaves. William would hand over Mary, a mulatto, and in return Meek would allow William to select one of two slaves, Lucinda or Charlotte, from his plantation.

For William or any slaveholder to offer such an exchange usually signified a troublesome slave. Trading a slave to a neighboring plantation owner, a common occurrence among planters, was construed as a sort of punishment, but not as severe as "selling a slave down the river." Both involved matters of proximity. A slave exchanged or sold to a neighboring plantation still maintained an opportunity, albeit rare, to see family and friends. A slave transferred to a new owner a great distance from his/her home plantation likely would never again enjoy that privilege.

Before Perkins had closed the deal, Meek had hastily conducted Mary to Natchez, the slave-trading hub on the Mississippi River. There, he promptly sold (literally down the river) the presumably troublesome Mary, receiving $1,500 for her. In the meantime, back at Meek's plantation, James T. Barr, Meek's overseer at the time, was showing William the two slave girls, explaining that Meek was absent in Natchez on business (selling slaves, including Mary).[31] Perkins "examined them carefully and selected the girl Lucinda" (Meek had recently purchased her in Natchez), noting at the time that she "seemed to be affected with a bad cold, and had great difficulty of breathing."[32] Trusting his own judgment in such matters, William likely thought nothing else of the girl's malady. At this point, William had no reason to distrust Meek, a fellow Virginian.[33]

---

[30]Two of Meek's partners, brothers in law and Abingdon lawyers Samuel Logan and Christopher Haynes, privately acknowledged risking their reputations by entering into slave trading deals with Meek.

[31]Perkins had conveyed the following written order from Meek to James T. Barr who acted in Meek's absence: "Mr. Little [Meek's slave trading partner] or Mr. Barr will deliver to William P. Perkins or order, one of my two girls, giving him [a] choice-either Lucinda or Charlotte. [signed] Joseph Meek, 19th March, 1836." *Munn v Perkins*, 413, 414.

[32]Ibid., 414.

[33]Early in 1835 Meek had expressed the belief that the health of slaves had to be guaranteed or "law soots" would ensue and courts might reverse a slave sale due

One month later, in April 1836, Lucinda was engaged in scraping cotton in Perkins' field, but she still suffered from the cold and breathing difficulty. Consequently, Perkins arranged for Lucinda to perform light duties about the house. When her condition failed to improve, Perkins asked his personal physician, who also administered to his slaves, Dr. Pugh, known for his involvement with the Livingston Committee of Safety of 1835, to examine her. Pugh treated Lucinda for bowel problems for a "considerable length of time," then discovered she was suffering not from a cold but from incurable consumption (tuberculosis). Pugh also found that *Lucinda suffered from the illness at the time Perkins had purchased her from Meek* based on overseer Barr's description of the girl's symptoms.[34]

When Lucinda eventually died of the lingering disease in early 1838, William's relationship with the Meek family soured. Nearly one year later on March 4, 1839, William and his brother Daniel P. Perkins attended a slave sale at the Newman Plantation on Panther Creek seven miles west of Canton where William

---

to a slave's poor health. Purcell, "A Damned Piece of Rascality," 8. Furthermore, William likely remained unaware of the fact that six years earlier one of Meek's customers had won a judgment against the defendant Meek in a court case regarding the sale of another slave. In Louisiana in 1829, Joseph Morris Back had purchased a twenty-eight year old male slave, Andrew, from Meek for $457.50. Meek had warranted the slave "free from all the vices and maladies prescribed by law." Later, Back had learned that Andrew had "long before been addicted to running away." Back alleged that Meek knew about it and "failed to make full disclosure of it." The court agreed with Back and compelled Meek to repay Back for the cost of the slave, in addition to paying damages of $300 plus interest. Meek also was "condemned to take back Andrew." *Digital Library on American Slavery*, s. v. "Joseph Meek Jr., Louisiana," 1829, Petition 20882996.

[34] *Munn v Perkins*, 414-415. Pugh charged Perkins $100 for the medical attention. Further testimony indicated that the sale of a healthy Lucinda, had she been purchased in March 1836, would have brought $1,000. Despite the problem he experienced with Lucinda's health issues, William continued to conduct additional business with Meek (and Little). In May 1837 Perkins sold land to the two for $4,000. With his slaves sales and profits increasing, Meek planned to construct a large brick family residence on the property. *Madison County Deeds, Book E*, FHL, microfilm roll 886076, 3 and Purcell, "A Damned Piece of Rascality," 19.

An 1850s engraving of a slave coffle, under the close supervision of armed, mounted whites. Notice the first two slaves are playing instruments as they march, while other males in the file are restrained. Beginning in the 1830s, such overland slave coffles became a common sight along established trails leading from the Upper Old South to slave markets in the Deep South (like the infamous Natchez, Mississippi, slave market) where slave traders would then offer them for sale.

hoped to purchase several of the thirty plus slaves being offered.[35] There, William unexpectedly met Jesse Meek. Jesse, Joseph's younger brother, had assumed the role of estate administrator upon his brother's death (intestate) in February 1838. Perkins then probably related to the younger Meek the story of Lucinda and how he had, following the onset of Lucinda's illness, first requested that Joseph Meek take her back because she had been of no use to him and an expense. Meek initially refused, but William explained he had finally secured a verbal promise from Joseph Meek that he (Meek) "would pay all expenses and if the girl died she

---

[35]John D. Freeman, Robert H. Bruckner. *Reports of Cases Decided in the Superior Court of Chancery of the State of Mississippi,* (Cincinnati: E. Morgan and Company, 1844), *"Newman and Beck v Jesse Meek et al,"* 445, 449, 453. William and his brother Daniel had testified as witnesses in this, a separate case, involving the Meeks.

would be his [Meek's] loss."[36] Perkins indicated that Jesse Meek, as the estate's administrator, should compensate him (Perkins) for his monetary loss in the death of Lucinda per his previous agreement with Joseph Meek. Jesse Meek apparently refused Perkins' demand.[37]

Three months later on June 3, 1839, Perkins sued Meek. In all, over the next three years, Perkins won three separate suits against Jesse Meek for $1,380, $1,700, and $1,686.66.[38] Two judgments were overturned on appeal, but the court refused to overturn the third and final judgment.

With that the new administrator of the estate, John Munn, Joseph Meeks's son-in-law, brought the case to the Mississippi Supreme Court in 1843. A staunch opponent of abolitionism despite his New England upbringing, Munn had only recently settled in Canton.[39] Based largely on the strength of overseer Barr's key testimony as a witness to Joseph Meek's verbal promise/guarantee to Perkins mentioned above and the fact that Munn was attempting to gain another trial to which he "is not entitled under the law," the court upheld the judgment in favor of Perkins.[40] Presumably, the $1,686 judgment covered both William's personal property loss (Lucinda) and the labor he was "denied" as a result of the girl's death.

William's determination in using the courts – over a lengthy period of time (four years) – to gain a remedy in a dispute

---

[36]*Munn v Perkins*, 414, 418. Overseer Barr had overheard this crucial conversation between Joseph Meek and Perkins. William's courtroom experiences date back to Wilkinson County. There, William became involved in a court proceeding, winning a small judgment against Robert Bowden for $120.47 on December 4, 1830, and February 26, 1831. Wiese, *Woodville Republican*, 1: 69, 74.

[37]In an effort to settle claims against his brother's estate, Jesse Meek had begun selling off Joseph Meek's slaves as early as May 2, 1838, ten months before he encountered Perkins. A notice in the *Canton Herald*, May 2, 1838, 4, column 2, announced the sale of some thirty slaves.

[38]In testimony Jesse Meek stated the slave girl, Mary, whom Perkins had traded to Joseph Meek was "not very saleable, because she was too white." Yet, Joseph Meek had managed to resell her for $1,500, *Munn v Perkins*, 414, 415.

[39]University of Notre Dame Rare Books and Special Collections, John Munn Letters, 1836-1837," *Manuscripts of Early National and Antebellum America*, accessed July 8, 2010,
http://www.rarebooks.nd.edu/digital/early_american/letters/index.shtml.

[40]*Munn v Perkins*, 422.

regarding a female slave reveals that he viewed his slaves (and all slaves) in term of economic and property matters, and not as human subjects. His statements to Meek that the gravely ill Lucinda had been an economic burden, and he desired Meek to reclaim her further underscore Perkins' calculating, practical business approach regarding slave matters.

The Lucinda episode also demonstrates the reality of how deeply slavery was embedded into the structure of American culture and particularly the law. An already embattled institution and the subject of hot debate fanned by a Northern abolitionist press, slavery increasingly occupied the workings of all three branches of government at both the state (more so in Southern states) and federal levels with its central theme of property law. Nine years later, following his father's precedent, Charles Perkins, William's oldest son, sought a legal remedy in the California courts to recover his slave property.

Lastly, and not to be overlooked is Perkins' slave, Mary, the enigmatic catalyst of the Lucinda affair. Unfortunately, more questions arise concerning her role than there are answers. The very scant references to Mary in the *Munn v Perkins* proceeding remain the lone source of information regarding her and serve to tantalize more than inform. The basic question that arises is what had she done that would cause William, at some effort and inconvenience on his part, to exchange her with the slave trader Meek? William's actions over the years indicate that he was not an ignorant man, but in such apparent haste to be rid of Mary (the only slave he felt obliged to part with that day), William had accepted an obviously sick slave in return. Furthermore, was Meek, in acting with equal swiftness when he sold her downriver, doing so at William's instigation or by mere coincidence? From court testimony, we learn that the mulatto Mary was "too white", and that when he sold her, Meek received $1,500, an apparently excessive price for a female slave at the time. (Lucinda, in the same month as Mary's sale, would have sold for $1,000 according to court testimony.)[41] For Mary to warrant such a price, she must have been young and either skilled or very beautiful.

---

[41]In 1835 William's neighbor, Josiah Newman (mentioned above) paid roughly *$1,000* apiece for slaves he purchased. In June 1836 in Natchez, just three months

Given what we know, could William have had a secret
relationship with Mary and then because of "circumstances" been
forced to sell her with all possible haste, removing her in the process as far away as possible, while accepting a less than healthy
slave in return to expedite the agreement? Or, had William discovered she had played some role in the county rebellion scare of
1835? While the answers to these questions may never be known,
William's decisive actions regarding Mary on March 19, 1836,
indicate something was amiss.

        Meanwhile, in 1837, despite recent years of growth in cot-
ton production and profits for Madison County planters, a financial catastrophe struck not only Madison County and Mississippi,
but also the entire country. Caused in part by rampant land speculation and excessive borrowing, the *Panic of 1837* wreaked havoc
on America.
        The Panic was actually a depression, the results of which
hit Mississippi particularly hard. Statewide, it demolished the
economy. Banks across the state failed as planters, businessmen,
and other workers struggled to stay solvent. Money was scarce and
bankruptcies abounded. Cotton prices dropped from seventy-six
dollars per bale in 1836 to thirty-six dollars a bale by 1840.[42]
Planters who could not pay their taxes and other debts experienced
foreclosures.
        Locally, Madison County citizens faced the same difficul-
ties. During 1838, beginning with only a few at first, the *Canton
Herald* printed daily notices of sheriff's sales and foreclosures, but
as the depression worsened, the number increased dramatically,
eventually filling multiple columns in each issue. The Madison
County sheriff, Samuel Flournoy, reportedly could not bring himself to enforce eviction declarations on his defaulted neighbors.
        Evidence of the depression's negative impact on Madison
County's citizens is further revealed in the county censuses for
1837 and 1838. In 1837 659 white polls, the movers and shakers

---

after Meek had sold Mary there, an observer reported that Negroes were worth
$1,200 each. George H. Marble, letter from Natchez, June 12, 1836.
[42]The first figure is based on the statement of Joseph Meek, the Livingston slave
trader, and the second is from testimony William Perkins provided in another
court case mentioned below.

within the county, appeared on the Madison County tax sheets. One year after the depression struck, only 505 names remained, a loss of twenty-three percent. Among those included in the white polls count was a significant number of local planters. During this same one-year period, the county's slave population (slaves older than five and less than sixty years) declined by 1,050, or nearly twelve percent. Many planters who faced foreclosure and the loss of their plantations and slaves left the county or the state, often resettling with their slaves in Texas.[43] Moreover, county tax revenues dropped from a high of $9,217 in 1837 (before the depression had taken hold) to $7,811 in 1838, and then bottomed out at $1,234 in 1839.[44] Not all of Madison County's citizens, though, experienced the adverse effects of the economic downturn.

William Perkins appears to have withstood the ravages of the debilitating financial meltdown better than most. In 1838, the first full year after the onset of the depression, William's number of slaves actually increased, from ninety to 100.[45] In a statement he made several years later, William believed that in December 1839 (the closest year to 1838 for which figures are available) choice field hands would have sold for $500 apiece and were "intrinsically worth $600 apiece on an [average?] in gold and silver."[46] (Compare to the $1,500 sale price William's slave Mary

---

[43]Madison County tax rolls 1837, Box 3717, image 24 and 1838, box 3717, image 22, accessed October 20, 2011, *Family Search*.

[44]Ibid., and 1839, Box 3717, image 32.

[45]Madison County Tax Rolls, 1838, Combined Assessment-State Tax, Box 3717, image 15, accessed October 20, 2011. In 1839 Perkins reported fewer slaves than the 100 he declared in 1838 due to his gift of twenty slaves to his daughter and her husband in October 1839.

[46]Smedes, *Reports of Cases Argued*, XI, 514-515, *Farmers Bank et al v Douglass*. In November 1848 Perkins was called to testify in *The Farmers Bank et al vs Douglass* fraud case. Heard in Mississippi's High Court of Errors and Appeals, it involved several of Livingston's citizens and one of William's neighbors. Perkins provided testimony regarding the economics of plantation slavery in 1839-1840. As Perkins was well aware, a slave's value depended on a complex set of factors: sex, age, strength, health, childbearing capability (for females), and possession of a skill, such as a blacksmith. Furthermore, the market price for the cash crop (cotton in Perkins' case) also played a role. Higher market prices usually resulted in increased slave prices due to greater demand.

In an unrelated case in 1839, William and his two cousins, William and D. Hardeman, became defendants in a suit brought by their neighbor Edward Ander-

brought in 1836.) Thus, the value of his 100 slaves in 1838 would have approximated $50,000-$60,000, far below their pre Depression value, but nonetheless a considerable sum.

Combining his slave count with the 2,600 acres he then owned on Persimmon Creek and the 1,115 acres he co-owned with son-in-law Joseph J. Pugh in other counties, Perkins' wealth in land and slaves had elevated him to the planter aristocracy. This elite group, even years later in *1860*, boasted nationwide only "ten thousand families who lived off the labor of gangs of more than fifty slaves."[47] By 1838, in the midst of the depression, Perkins had become the county's fourth largest landowner while ranking third in slave ownership.[48] Furthermore, unlike many of his defaulting fellow citizens, William was able to meet his tax obligations during the crisis. His taxes, an indicator of his overall wealth, even *increased* in 1838 but dipped slightly in 1839 and 1840.

Others factors show that the effects of the depression somehow bypassed William for the most part. His gifts of land and slaves to his daughter Ann Pugh and her husband in 1838 and 1839 had occurred during the height of the crisis. Most certainly, if Perkins' financial solvency had been challenged during this time, he could not have provided these gifts, nor could he have afforded his April 1839 investment in stock shares of the Mississippi Union Bank. Perkins also made a payment of $15,444, presumably for a land purchase in October 1838 at a time when many of his neighbors struggled just to pay their property taxes.[49] Fur-

---

son. Due to several errors made at the local level, Perkins and the Hardemans took their case to the United States Supreme Court. Seven years later in January 1846, the Supreme Court ordered a stay in the judgment against the Hardemans and Perkins on account of the Circuit Court clerk's error. See *Wm. and D. Hardeman and Wm. P. Perkins, Plaintiffs in error v. Edward Anderson*, 4 Howard U. S. 640 (1846).

[47]Kenneth Stampp, *The Peculiar Institution*, (New York: Random House, 1956), 30-31.

[48]Mississippi, State Archives, Various Records, 1820-1951, Madison County, County Tax Rolls, 1838, Combined Assessment-State Tax, Box 3717, images 1-23, accessed October 20, 2011, *Family Search,* https://www.familysearch.org/search/image/index#uri=https%3A//api.familysearch.org/records/collection/1919687/waypoints.

[49]Shipp, acknowledging receipt of a payment from William P. Perkins, *Madison County, MS, Deeds Book F*, FHL, microfilm roll 866077, 1.

thermore, near the end of the crisis in February 1840, William had indulged in his lavish $2,250 purchase of racehorses. At approximately the same time, William faced the reality, however, that his recently purchased stock shares in the struggling Mississippi Union Bank were virtually worthless. Nonetheless, he must have felt extremely fortunate to emerge from those dark economic times in remarkably sound financial shape.

In 1840 with the depression winding down and to the delight of the local tax collector, Madison County tax revenues rebounded and actually exceeded the yearly amounts collected in 1838 or 1839. Cotton, however, did not recover so quickly. William recalled that it sold for $36 a bale in 1840 and $32 in 1841, more than forty dollars less than its pre depression high.[50]

Each of these recent events William experienced, the 1835 rebellion scare, the problems with slaves Mary and then Lucinda, and the ills associated with the Panic of 1837, exemplified the unpredictable nature of the Mississippi cotton culture. On the other hand, planters like Perkins understood full well that the potential profitability of slave-based cotton agriculture outweighed the risks involved. And after all, weren't planters essentially gamblers?

During their time in Madison County, William and Jane Perkins saw both growth and change in their immediate family. The births of sons Daniel P. in 1833 and William S. in 1839 in-

---

[50]Smedes, *Reports of Cases Argued*, XI, 514-515, *Farmers Bank et al v Douglass.* Perkins had augmented his testimony in this case heard in November 1848 most likely with the aid of his own plantation records from the years in question. Much like a company would maintain a business record of all its transactions, large plantation owners maintained meticulous books showing acreage under cultivation, yield per acre, income, slaves' production levels, and expenditures. Events occurring on the plantation often were logged in as well, especially those that related to the master's "bottom line." Perkins, always practical and efficient, retained just such records and others, likely dating back to his first plantation in Wilkinson County. Indeed, over the years he relied on these records to provide, among other things, name and age data for the slaves he regularly used as collateral for the various loans he assumed. The author recalls poring over just such a plantation record found on the shelf of some refurbished slave quarters on a plantation near Natchez, Mississippi, some twenty years ago. Carefully and neatly noted over the years by the master were debits and credits ranging from the cost of nails, and slaves' clothing to the price he received for his cotton to his yearly Christmas expense for his slaves when he provided them with an extra ration of molasses.

creased their number of children to five.[51] Also, the *Canton Herald* reported that the Perkins' youngest daughter Louisa (Ann) Perkins, age sixteen, had wed the family physician, thirty-year old Dr. Joseph J. Pugh of Livingston on December 18, 1837: "Married on Tues evening last by Rev. Mr. Monroe Dr. Joseph J. Pugh to Miss Ann, daughter of William Perkins Esq. of this county."[52] Louisa's marriage left her seventeen-year old sister Jane as the only remaining daughter in the household.

The newlywed, Dr. Joseph James Pugh, a man of considerable means, belonged to a large and prominent North Carolina family. Two of his brothers were also physicians as were many other Pugh relatives. In approximately 1809 Pugh's family had relocated to Tennessee, settling near Franklin on Murphy's Fork in Williamson County close to the Perkins clan. By 1835 Pugh resided in Livingston, maybe on the Perkins plantation. Later, he established a practice in Canton (fifteen miles away). In time he became an active member of the local Whig Party, a surgeon holding the rank of captain in the 25th regiment Mississippi militia, and in 1841 the president of the county Board of Police (Board of Supervisors).[53] A small-scale planter, Pugh shared ownership of

---

[51]Seventh Census, 1850, Bolivar County, Mississippi, s. v. "William P. Bekins," line 13, accessed August 1, 2011, *Family Search.* The *Family Search* search mode incorrectly lists Perkins as 'Bekins' due to the census enumerator's poor handwriting. The 1850 census was the first to list names of all family members whereas previously just the heads of household had been shown. The census of 1850 shows William's son Daniel Perkins' age at what appears to be fourteen, Appendix B. In a later document, completed by Daniel himself after the Civil War, he states that his age in 1865 was thirty-two, thus making his actual birth year 1833, not 1836.

[52]Betty C. Wiltshire, (compiler), *Marriages and Deaths from Mississippi Newspapers*, (Bowie, Maryland: Heritage Books, 1990), 1: 35, from the *Canton Herald*, December 22, 1837, 2, column 5. The "Esquire" following William's name in the *Herald's* notice indicates that he was a highly respected member of the community. Early in 1840 Louisa Pugh gave birth to the couple's first son, William Perkins Pugh, named after his grandfather, but on March 10, 1840, the infant died unexpectedly (*Madison Whig Advocate* of Canton, Mississippi, March 14, 1840, in Wiltshire, *Marriages and Deaths*, 125). A year later William and his wife Jane became grandparents again with the birth of Florence Pugh, Ann and Joseph's first daughter. In the ensuing years, the Pughs would add five more children to their family.

[53]The doctor was also a visionary. In 1841 he joined with many other prominent men of Canton and Jackson to establish the first railroad between their cities.

some of his Mississippi property with William Perkins, while he also owned land, later known as the Bonnie Doon plantation, on the banks of Joe's Bayou in Madison Parish, Louisiana.[54] In 1840 Pugh claimed thirty slaves. Ten years later, he owned just five slaves in Madison County but thirty-five in Madison Parish.[55] As described by William's cousin Ann Hardeman, Pugh "was greatly beloved and [a] kind and affectionate husband . . . conscientious in the discharge of his domestic and professional duties."[56]

In the early 1850s, Dr. Pugh gradually became involved in Mississippi's thriving spa business in Madison County. In August of that year, he penned a brief explanation of the beneficial health effects of Madison County's Artesian Springs, northwest of Canton. Published in a medical journal, Joseph Pugh's note describes the Spring's benefits to sufferers with "debility of the digestive organs, including diarrhea, and dysentery . . . and functional diseases of the kidneys. . . ."[57] He wrote his commentary both as an informative medical piece and also as a description of the benefits

---

Completed many years later, the railroad linked New Orleans (via Canton) to Chicago. Nancy Chambers Underwood, compiler, *Fifty Families, A History*, (Dallas: Nortex Press, 1977), 263-264.

[54]*Bureau of Land Management*, s. v. "William P. Perkins," 1841.

[55]Sixth Census, 1840, Madison County, Mississippi, s. v. "Jos. J. Pugh," 88, image 626, accessed February 15, 2011, *Ancestry.com.* and Seventh Census, 1850, Madison County, Mississippi, s. v. "J. J. Pugh," line 15, accessed May 27, 2011, *Family Search*. Also, Seventh Census, 1850, Slave schedules, Madison County, Mississippi:
https://www.familysearch.org/pal:/MM9.3.1/TH-267-12047-160999-76?cc=1420440&wc=6145360. See 1850, Slave schedules, Madison Parish, Louisiana, s. v. "Joseph J. Pugh" and "Jos. J. Pugh," images 24-25, accessed September 15, 2011, *Family Search*, https://familysearch.org/pal:/MM9.3.1/TH-267-11664-115929-76?cc=1420440&wc=6145409.

[56]Ann Hardeman to Michael O'Brien, *An Evening When Alone*, (Charlottesville: University Press of Virginia, 1997), 264. Ann Hardeman, Perkins' cousin from Tennessee, lived a few miles south of Jackson, Mississippi, in Hinds County not far from Perkins' plantation in Livingston. Her brother was William Hardemnan.

[57]No author, "The Medical Examiner and Record of Medical Science", (Philadelphia: Lindsay and Blakiston, 1851), 466. The grand Artesian Springs Hotel in Madison County, just twenty-two miles from Canton, could accommodate 500 people according to an ad in the *Madisonian*. It remained open and packed with guests year round. For a description see Mary Carol Miller, *Lost Landmarks of Mississippi*, (Jackson: University Press of Mississippi, 2002), 57.

of the Artesian Springs that could only have helped create additional interest in the waters there.

Pugh eventually moved his practice to Cooper's Well, a competing spa likewise renowned statewide for its waters and hotel. Located in neighboring Hinds County seventeen miles southwest of Jackson and some forty miles from Vicksburg, the resort welcomed both rich planters who enjoyed the spa's proximity to their plantations and other affluent citizens.[58] Though his family continued to reside in Madison County, Pugh spent more and more time working at the "watering place" tending to the medical needs of its wealthy patrons. Eventually, in February 1854 Pugh and seven other men formed the Cooper's Well Company, a partnership that owned and managed the spa at Cooper's Well.[59] Because of its picturesque views and elevated location among lofty pines, combined with its accommodations, waters, billiard rooms, pin alleys, bars, and ballrooms, the resort never lacked for customers.

* * * * *

In late 1841 William Perkins contemplated a bold new business venture. Despite enjoying financial success and the proximity of the Daniel Perkins, Hardeman, and Pugh families to his plantation in Madison County, Perkins anticipated yet another move.[60] With visions of larger profits guiding his thoughts (as always), William looked to the virgin soil of the Mississippi Delta in Bolivar County. This move, too, would require William to develop a plantation in an area where civilization was just beginning to arise.

---

[58]O'Brien, *An Evening*, 425, fn 32.

[59](No author), *Laws of the State of Mississippi*, (Natchez: Barksdale and Jones, 1854), 239.

[60]Sixth Census, 1840, Madison County, Mississippi, s. v. "W. P. Perkins," 94, accessed February 12, 2011, *Ancestry.com* and Mississippi, State Archives, Various Records, 1820-1951, State Census Return Madison County, 1841, image 12, accessed October 30, 2011, *Family Search*, https://familysearch.org/pal:/MM9.3.1/TH-1951-20904-20777-69?cc=1919687&wc=13645947.

IV

Bolivar County

Whereas the said William P. Perkins is justly indebted and owes to the said William B. Cook one hundred and ninety-four thousand three hundred and thirty-three pounds of ginned cotton.

> Part of a payment agreement
> signed by William Perkins for his
> first land purchase in Bolivar
> County, January 15, 1842

    The Native Americans who resided in Mississippi for centuries saw their lands gradually fall into the hands of whites beginning with European exploration in the sixteenth century. In 1541 the Spanish explorer Hernando de Soto became the first known white to cross the Mississippi River. Later, in 1682 the Frenchman Robert de La Salle boldly claimed the entire Mississippi River basin for France resulting in an increasingly larger white presence in the region during the next century and a half. By 1842 the Choctaw, Chickasaw, and other tribes for the most part had abandoned their Mississippi homeland. They had ceded parts to the United States government by treaty, while encroaching throngs of eager American pioneers and planters, desirous of claiming each available acre of tillable land they encountered, had provided a further impetus for these Native Americans to resettle westward.

    An agrarian frontier society throughout its formative years, Mississippi, with cotton producing counties similar to Wilkinson and Madison arising statewide, eventually became the most dynamic and productive cotton producing state in pre Civil War America. By 1850 its most vital component - along with its fertile soil – was a huge slave labor force numbering nearly 310,000, easily eclipsing the state's white population of 296,648.

    Soon to be at the forefront of Mississippi's cotton monoculture (more than 1,200,000 bales produced statewide by 1860) were the counties of its fabulously fertile Delta region.[1]

---

[1]This Delta is not to be confused with the Mississippi River Delta 300 miles south at the mouth of the Mississippi River.

This distinctive area of northwest Mississippi included ten counties on or near the Mississippi River, one of which was Bolivar.
Bolivar and the several other counties had been formed by the
Treaty of Dancing Rabbit Creek from part of the Choctaw Indian
Cession of 1830. It was in Bolivar County that William Perkins
planned to invest in and develop his third plantation that ultimately would sustain his heirs and descendants for the next half
century.

Prior to William's resettlement in Bolivar County, his
brother, Daniel P. Perkins, passed away in Hinds County, Mississippi, in approximately March 1841.[2] Daniel's death allowed
William to further expand his cash reserves and slave-holdings.
Daniel had died childless and intestate, leaving only a wife who
soon remarried and moved to Texas. After his brother's death,
William purchased 1,240 acres, part of Daniel's land on his Canebreak Place Plantation, at a sheriff's sale in February 1841.[3] William then promptly sold the acreage for cash to John Yerger, a
member of the prominent Yerger family of Hinds County. The
sale and profit eventually helped fund part of Perkins' upcoming
land acquisitions in Bolivar County. Later, to solve his growing
need for labor, William purchased thirty slaves (in 1844), probably the thirty known to have belonged to his deceased brother's
estate.

---

[2] An October 26, 1842, estate notice showed that Daniel Perkins Marr and the
widowed wife, M. B. (Mary) Perkins, administered the estate in Hinds County.
Mary Hendrix (compiler), *Mississippi Court Records 1799-1859*, (Greenville,
South Carolina: Southern Historical Press, 1999), 123.
[3] Mississippi Probate Records 1781-1930, Hinds County, Estates (series 1) 1844-
1855, no. 665-707, images 114, 118-124,
https://familysearch.org/pal:/MM9.3.1/TH-1961-30881-22528-
37?cc=2036959&wc=MMY2-7HS:409918074. Other Hinds County records for
1841-1842 show William claiming only 640 acres of land and paying taxes on
seventeen slaves. Almost immediately following his brother's death, William
Perkins and his nephew, Daniel Perkins Marr, became involved in a prolonged
lawsuit regarding Daniel Perkins' estate brought by William's widowed sister-in-
law Mary Perkins (remarried name Lea). The litigation continued for nearly sixteen years, eventually involving William's children, their spouses, and another
relative, attorney W. Hardeman. It appears no settlement was ever reached, and
apparently the only ones receiving any money from the suit and countersuits were
the lawyers involved.

Some ten months after his brother's death, William reached an agreement in January 1842 that would eventually culminate in his move from Madison County northwest to wild and rural Bolivar County. He purchased seven prime riverfront lots totaling 582 acres in the southern part of the county from fellow Virginian William B. Cook. One of the county's early pioneers and in 1836 one of its organizing commissioners, Cook had sold a marvelous piece of undeveloped land which may have first attracted William's attention some twenty-nine years earlier.[4]

In 1813 from the deck of one of General Andrew Jackson's riverboats floating down the Mississippi to Natchez, a young Sgt. Perkins may have observed on the port side (eastern) the overgrown landscape of what eventually would become Bolivar County. He may have made a mental note of this site and any potential river landing. Two features made the location even more memorable: the distinctive Indian mounds a little more than a mile inland and possibly visible from the river and a convenient river-fed bayou. In 1842 this location, along with several of Perkins' later Bolivar County land acquisitions, would become the defining purchases of his lifetime.

This first transaction called for Perkins to pay Cook $18,000 for the property. However, the two men worked out a deal where Perkins would finance the purchase by paying Cook in kind, 194,333 pounds of ginned cotton (approximately 485 bales) in three yearly installments of 64,777 pounds each, beginning in 1842. (A bale weighs roughly 400-500 pounds.) If that amount could not be raised in any given year then, according to the promissory note, William became obligated to deliver the balance to Cook or his agent at Yazoo City, about thirty miles from William's Madison County plantation near Livingston.[5] Using the $32 per bale price for 1841 (which Perkins later quoted in his 1848 court testimony in *Farmers Bank et al v Douglass* referenced above), the value of his cotton indenture to Cook equaled more than $15,500, with the remaining $2,500 presumably being

---

[4]Located in Township 20, Range 9 West, lots 3-8 in section 3 and lot one in section 4, the acreage fronted the Mississippi River.

[5]William B. Cook to William P. Perkins, *Bolivar County, Mississippi, Deed Book B*, FHL, microfilm roll 886085, January 13, 1842, 257-259, copy in author's possession.

the interest that would accrue during the three-year life of the debt.[6]

CARVER'S IMPROVED COTTON GINS.

G. BURKE & CO.,

Cotton Factors and General Commission Merchants, Chief Agents for the sale of

E. CARVER & CO.'S IMPROVED COTTON GINS.

☞ They have on hand a large assortment of the usual sizes. ☜

No. 145 Canal street, State House Square,

NEW ORLEANS.

1851 magazine advertisement for a cotton gin

Beneficial geographic features were undoubtedly a primary factor in William's astute decision to acquire this property. Located on the Choctaw Bend of the Mississippi River approximately two miles west of today's small town of Scott, this acreage proved well suited for a cotton plantation. A unique feature, Williams Bayou, the clear running stream fed by the Mississippi first observed by Perkins in 1813, and now presumably named after the land's first owner in 1831, William Cook, passed somewhat diagonally through Perkins' property. Bordered by cypress swamps in certain areas, the bayou ran eastward, then southeastward from the Mississippi (Map 1). The waterway divided the

---

[6]Ibid. It is possible that this transaction with Cook involved other attendant costs, because the price per acre William paid, thirty dollars, was exceedingly high for the times.

lots William owned in sections three and four and those he would eventually purchase in sections ten and seventeen while serving as an inlet to the more remote parts of his plantation and to the county's interior. (Generally, a complete section would include approximately 640 acres.) More importantly, Perkins' purchase also included a river access point at Mound Landing where his slaves could load ginned cotton bales onto a waiting steamboat for prompt transport downriver to markets in New Orleans, the capital port of King Cotton. Not only was the landing convenient, but it also played a vital role in Perkins' bottom line.

Because of this direct river access, Perkins and other planters who resided in Bolivar, Washington, Coahoma, and Issaquena counties along the Mississippi River, benefited from cheaper transportation costs when shipping their cotton to New Orleans or Memphis. Unlike some inland county planters, they no longer had to bear the *additional* costs of *first* moving their cotton overland to the Mississippi (as William had been compelled to do in Wilkinson, then Madison County), with the accompanying un-certainties of narrow, muddy, or obstructed roads that could fur-ther delay getting their crops to market.

Following his agreement with Cook, William, in a series of transactions post 1842, closed deals for additional Bolivar County acreage. He acquired the remaining two lots in section three adjoining the six others in that section he had previously purchased from Cook (Map 1). Later, in March 1844 Perkins added large parts of sections seventeen and ten, also located on Williams Bayou, parts of section twenty-one, all of twenty-two, and a triangular portion of section twenty-three. (Map 1).[7] Also, Perkins and land speculator and former member of President's

---

[7]Ibid., 533, 544. By 1854 the Perkins family owned all of section seventeen, to-taling 585 acres. William's impressive and logical land acquisitions in Bolivar County later included two final purchases through the government land program. Though they were dated in 1848 and 1852, these transactions had been finalized much earlier. Both tracts, located approximately three miles from the river in section twenty-nine, totaled 480 acres. William Perkins also owned 640 acres of untaxed and unimproved land designated for schools in Section 16, shown on Map 1, that I have not included in his total of holdings.

Polk's cabinet, Robert J. Walker, shared ownership and taxes on 417 additional riverfront acres in section one.[8]

These purchases, many assessed at five dollars per acre, when combined with others William made later in the decade, meant that his Mound Plantation, as it came to be called, consisted of approximately 3,200 acres, making him one of the county's leading landowners. Perkins' acreage, much of it located on preferred Mississippi riverfront property, would yield substantial yearly food crops, enough to sustain his family and slaves. At the same time, other sections produced enough cotton to provide the Perkins clan over the years with remarkable wealth representative of the South's elite planter aristocracy.

William's strategy for launching his new plantation in Bolivar County involved a division of his labor force. Madison County tax records show that in 1841 Perkins claimed eighty-one slaves, but in the year following he recorded only thirty on his Persimmon Creek plantation. While retaining in Madison County mainly his house slaves, the cooks, maids, laundresses, gardeners, and carriage driver, he had not sold the 'missing' fifty-one hands, but instead by 1842 he had put them hard to work in Bolivar County.

William thus delayed his permanent move for approximately five years. During that interval these slaves and others, in a staggering effort, cleared the dense growths of towering cane, evergreen, and bamboo from large swaths of Bolivar County's virgin land, sowed the same with cotton, built the plantation house, slave cabins, and a mule barn, added a cotton gin, a mill house, and erected both a stable for Perkins' recently acquired thoroughbred breeding horses and other structures. Throughout this phase between his purchase and settlement, Perkins shuttled back and forth from Madison County to Bolivar County super-

---

[8]Mississippi, State Archives, Various Records, 1820-1951, Bolivar County Tax Rolls 1846-1858, Box 9845, 1850, (Bolivar County Land Roll), images 30-31, accessed October 31, 2011, *Family Search,* https://www.familysearch.org/search/image/index#uri=https%3A//api.familysearch.org/records/collection/1919687/waypoints. Each paid taxes on 208.6 acres of the total. Robert J. Walker (1801-1869), a passionate defender of slavery, a former United States Senator from Mississippi and the Treasury Secretary in the Polk administration, owned dozens of tracts of land across Mississippi.

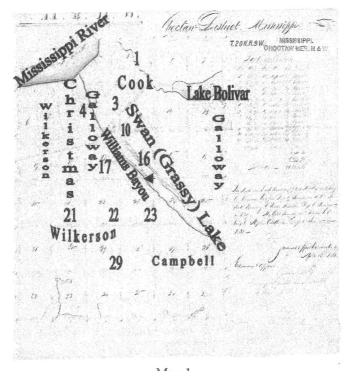

Map 1
William Perkins' Bolivar County land purchases and neighbors (looking west)[9]

Section 1 - 209 acres - Lots 4-8 - Perkins' portion of land shared with Walker
Section 3 - 668 acres – all, straddles Williams Bayou - extends to the river
Section 4 - 78 acres - Lot 1
Section 10 - 46 acres
Section 16 - 640 acres - Perkins' unimproved and untaxed (school) land
Section 17 - 585 acres - part, later all
Section 21 - 240 acres - part
Section 22 - 640 acres - all
Section 23 - 319 acres - part
Section 29 - 480 acres - part- Later sold to C. S. Perkins

---

[9]*Bureau of Land Management*, s. v. "Plat Image, T. 20N, R. 9W," accessed April 11, 2010. Original April 1831 survey map with William's purchases and owners of adjacent land superimposed. Today, Williams Bayou no longer extends to the river, and Highway 1 passes through sections 37, 26, 25, 14, and 13 near the former Perkins property. The small town of Scott now stands near the land later owned by Charles Scott in sections 12-15.

View of a young Bolivar County cotton field looking west in the
direction of the Mississippi River. Located just over the tree line
in the distance lies a portion of the land owned by William P.
Perkins in 1850. Photo taken by author in July 2010.

vising his slaves and the bustle of activity on his developing plantation.[10] Making things easier for William during this hectic

---

[10]A notice dated August 25, 1843, mentions the death of Sarah Henry (widow of
the former Madison County deputy sheriff) in the residence of Colonel William
P. Perkins of Madison County, (not Bolivar County) Mississippi. See (abstracted
by) Jonathan Kennon Thompson Smith, "Death Notices from the Western
Weekly Review, Franklin, Tennessee 1841-1851," 2004, accessed July 28, 2010,
http://www.tngenweb.org/records/williamson/obits/wwr/wwr2-15.htm.
Another source also indicates that the Perkins family continued to reside in Madison County past 1843. William's son, Charles Stewart Perkins, attended the College of New Jersey at Princeton (later Princeton University) from 1844 to1848. In
the college's catalog for his sophomore and junior years, 1846-1847, Charles
declared Canton, Mississippi, in Madison County, near Livingston, as his place
of residence. See, No author, *Catalog of the Officers and Students of the College
of New Jersey*, (Princeton, New Jersey: John T. Robinson, printer 1845-1848), s.
v. "Charles Perkins," 36, 59, 82, 103, for years 1845-1848, accessed July 4, 2010,
http://books.google.com/books?id=SS1LAAAAYAAJ&pg=PA82&dq=charles+s
+perkins+the+college+of+new+jersey&lr=&cd=2#v=onepage&q=perkins&f=fal
se. Curiously, as a freshman in 1844, Charles listed his residence as St. Louis,

period was his reunion with an old acquaintance.

Though the exact date is uncertain, during the developmental stage of his new plantation, Perkins hired a new overseer, North Carolina-born, fifty-one year old William Fisher Paquinette. In approximately 1823 Paquinette had moved to Wilkinson County and settled east of Woodville on Buffalo Creek. He and Perkins soon became acquainted, perhaps because by then the two lived within miles of each other or because a Paquinette family member had introduced them.[11] Joined by his twenty-one year old son, Remson, Paquinette now reunited with William in Bolivar County (Appendix B).[12]

At fifty-one (in 1850), Paquinette was considerably older than Bolivar County's twenty-four other overseers/agents, who ranged in age from twenty to thirty-seven years in the 1850 census. Their average age of just under twenty-nine years was not unusual, as most overseers tended to be younger, unattached men, in their twenties or early thirties often lacking skill in the difficult task of slave management. Although Paquinette had claimed no slaves since 1840, he brought a measure of experience and forcefulness to the job, as he had previously held and sold slaves in Wilkinson County on his plantation. In assuming the role of Perkins' agent, Paquinette thus defied the stereotypical notion of an 1850's overseer.

Tasked with the major dual responsibilities of overseeing the development of the expanding plantation (while William spent time in Madison County) and the daily supervision of its slaves, Paquinette answered only to Perkins. Assisting Paquinette in a secondary supervisory role may have been his son and also one of Perkins' black drivers.

No one was of greater importance in the managerial hierarchy of the Southern plantation system than the overseer. Yet,

---

Missouri, while in his senior year in the fall of 1847, he claimed Belmont in Tishomingo County, Mississippi, as his home.

[11]Paquinette served on a Wilkinson County jury as early as April 1823. See *Wilkinson County Court Minutes*, FHL, microfilm roll 877088, 37. Perkins had acted as a real estate appraiser with John Paquinette (a brother to William Paquinette?) in August 1828.

[12]Paquinette's name and that of his son Remson appear just above that of William Perkins in the 1850 census, Appendix B.

competent, trustworthy plantation overseers were rare commodities in the South. A lack of social prestige and monetary rewards
meant the profession did not attract the most capable men. As the
chief custodian of the plantation's slaves, the overseer planned
(often in conjunction with the master) work schedules designed to
extract the maximum amount of labor from each slave, maintained a constant, vigilant supervision of all field slaves, and
meted out punishment to the 'hands' for rule infractions, slacking,
or disrespect.[13] As a result, slaves generally despised their overseers. Over and above these responsibilities, the overseer was also
expected to care for the livestock and the plantation's agricultural
equipment (plows, hoes, etc.).

Overseers had to contend with not only a rigorous work
routine and often-unrealistic job requirements, but also with demanding masters who frequently considered and treated them as
social inferiors. Due to such negative factors and the thankless
nature of the job, the most ambitious overseers often aspired to
jobs as independent farmers or modest slaveholders. In turn, this
resulted in a restricted number of available, high quality, professional overseers. Because of the rapid turnover of these men,
owners coveted those overseers who were especially competent.

Part of the definition of "competency", though, depended
on the quantity of cotton the overseer's slave gangs produced for
market. The overseer received credit for a large crop and blame
for a small one, and his reputation to a great degree depended

---

[13]Thomas Affleck, *The Cotton Plantation Record and Account Book, No. 3,* cited
in, Thomas Knox, *Camp-fire and Cotton-field,* (New York: Blelock and Company, 1865), 363. Affleck devoted a portion of his book to the "Duties of an
Overseer." Typical of the book's suggestions for overseers is the following:
"Never be induced by a course of good behavior on the part of the negroes, to
relax the strictness of your discipline; but, when you have by judicious management, brought them to that state, keep them so by the same means. By taking
frequent strolls about the premises, including of course the [slave] quarters and
the stockyards, during the evening and at least twice a week during the night, you
will put a more effectual stop to any irregularities than by the most severe punishments. The only way to keep a negro honest is not to trust him. This seems to
be a harsh assertion; but it is, unfortunately, too true."

upon the number of bales he was able to harvest.[14] William's expectations for Paquinette would most likely have been exceedingly high given the size of the Mound Plantation and its large number of slaves.

Though we have no way of knowing the extent of Paquinette's reliability and efficiency, William Perkins at least had found a man with whom he was familiar. (The best overseers tended to secure employment with the largest and most affluent planters.) He relied on his overseer's slave management skills and judgment to the extent that by 1850 William had placed him in charge of one half of the Mound Plantation's land and slaves. On one occasion, after the plantation's completion William, while absent with his family from Bolivar County for several days, left Paquinette in charge of the entire plantation.[15]

Either before or during the time William was developing his Bolivar County plantation, he acquired *another* plantation, perhaps in a trustee capacity, in a remote and sparsely populated section of eastern Washington County. Located some fifty miles southeast of the Mound Plantation and approximately sixty miles northwest of Perkins' Madison County property, this new plantation was described as "situated opposite midway the lake," (Cold Lake, a body of water about twenty miles in length, 100 yards wide and from fifteen to twenty feet deep).[16] While Perkins remained an absentee owner, records from July 1844 indicate that on this new plantation he counted sixty slaves and probably at

---

[14]Frederick Law Olmsted, *The Cotton Kingdom: A Traveller's Observations on Cotton and Slavery in the American Slave States*, (New York: Mason Brothers, 1861), II, 189.

[15]O'Brien, *An Evening,* 223. In August 1850 while making a solo journey to visit his Hardeman relatives near Jackson, Mississippi, (the rest of the Perkins family was visiting in Tennessee), William had left the operation of the plantation to Paquinette.

[16]*New York Tribune* on August 23, 1842. The *Tribune* reprinted from the *New Orleans Bulletin* a curious fish story involving some of Perkins' slaves on his Washington County plantation. One morning the slaves observed a "great commotion among the fish" in Cole [Cold] Lake. Exhibiting bizarre behaviors as if they were mad, some of the fish were seen beaching themselves while others surfaced then dived suddenly to the lake's bottom. The following morning the lake and the adjacent banks were covered with dead fish for a mile in each direction.

least one overseer.[17] The fact that sixteen of these sixty were
children under five years old meant that slave families, rather
than just male slave work gangs, resided on the plantation. (The
county tax assessor categorized the other forty-four slaves as "5
and upwards" meaning that some in that group were possibly also
children.) Though county records do not disclose the overall acreage of this plantation (it was described as "a large amount of
valuable land & about 60 slaves"), the fact that he controlled a
second Delta plantation reveals William's intention of aggres-
sively expanding his holdings and increasing his wealth in the
Delta region.[18]

In contrast to his recently acquired Bolivar County acreage, this inland plantation in Washington County had no immediate access to the Mississippi River. Therefore, transporting any
cotton grown in the Cold Lake area to market could not have been
accomplished with the same relative ease as cotton grown on his
Mound Plantation. (In the absence of any tax and land records
showing his Washington County holdings post 1844, Perkins may
have sold the property sometime after that date.)

Uncertainty shrouds the exact date the *entire* Perkins family settled permanently in Bolivar County. Based on available
documents, the move occurred between 1846-1847. William Perkins' name first appears in Bolivar County on the September 1,
1846, tax rolls. He claimed slaves and eighty head of cattle, but
significantly he did not itemize any of the family's personal effects, the piano, watches, clock, pistols, carriage, or his racehorses, indicating that his family and possessions still remained in
Madison County.[19]

---

[17]Mississippi, State Archives, Various Records, 1820-1951, Washington County
Tax Rolls, 1844, Box 3783, image 9, accessed October 31, 2011, *Family Search,*
https://www.familysearch.org/search/image/index#uri=https%3A//api.familysear
ch.org/records/collection/1919687/waypoints.
[18]Mississippi Probate Records 1781-1930, Hinds County, Estates (series 1) 1844-
1855, no. 665-707, image 118,
https://familysearch.org/pal:/MM9.3.1/TH-1961-30881-22528-
37?cc=2036959&wc=MMY2-7HS:409918074.
[19]Mississippi, State Archives, Various Records, 1820-1951, Bolivar County
1846, Tax Rolls 1846-1858, Box 9845, images 13, 14, accessed October 31,
2011, *Family Search,*

Despite his apparent non-resident status in Bolivar County, Perkins still paid taxes there, a general tax $35.50, a special tax of $17.75, a poor tax of $7.10, and a state tax of $71.00, levied for his 117 slaves at the rate of sixty cents per slave ($70.20) and a penny each for his eighty cattle. (*Cattle and slaves* were lumped together under Mississippi's state tax.)[20] William was also assessed a property tax of $91.43 on his 3,200 acres.

Of particular significance on William's tax bill are the thirty-six additional slaves he reported compared to four years earlier. Since his first land purchase in Bolivar County in 1842, Perkins' slave holdings had increased from eighty-one to 117 slaves, evidence of his increasing number of acres under cultivation. In the coming years, his slave count would grow even more dramatically to accommodate the further development of his plantation.

While these 1846 records do not conclusively show the complete Perkins family's residency in Bolivar County then, a county historian confirmed that William resided there (presumably with his entire family) by at least November 1847. That year, William Perkins served as an elected member of the county's Seventh Board of Police (Board of Supervisors), his only known venture into the world of public service.[21]

Though Perkins had avoided public office until his stint with the Board of Police, he most likely claimed a political affiliation. At the time he resided in Livingston, Madison County was traditionally a Whig stronghold. Moreover, in Mississippi's other large slaveholding counties, planters traditionally supported

---

https://www.familysearch.org/search/image/index#uri=https%3A//api.familysear ch.org/records/collection/1919687/waypoints.

[20]Ibid. Perkins paid no school tax, as there were no county schools at that time. Historically, Perkins generally paid a tax of seventy-five cents per slave from 1820-1824 in Wilkinson County and fifty cents per slave in 1827, 1828, and 1831. See FHL, Wilkinson County: Box **3768**, 1820 - image 19, 1821 - image 21, 1822 - image 20. In box **3293**, 1824 - image 25, 1827 - image 87, 1828 - image 120, and 1831 - image 153. In Madison County Perkins paid approximately seventy-five cents per slave in 1834 and between fifty and seventy-five cents in 1841. See Madison County: Box **3718**, 1834 - image 58 and 1841 - image 110.
[21]Florence W. Sillers (compiler), *History of Bolivar County, Mississippi*, (Jackson, Mississippi: Hederman Brothers, 1948), 17. While residing in Livingston, William had served briefly as an election judge in October 1837.

the Whig Party, whose main interests - anti-Jacksonism and strong states' rights policies - aligned with their own.[22] We do know that William's brother, Daniel P. Perkins, and son-in-law, Dr. Pugh, claimed Whig affiliations.[23] Later, in a predominantly slaveholding Bolivar County, many of Perkins' neighbors and acquaintances also aligned with the Whigs: Peter Starke, Lewis Galloway, Charles Clark, John Lobdell, and the jurist William Yerger. Given these details, it is probable that if Perkins became politically affiliated, he too supported the Whig Party.

In the mid 1840s, at approximately the same time William was preparing to occupy his new plantation, two northern archaeologists, Ephraim Squier and Edwin Davis, set out to scientifically document the numerous ancient Indian Mounds so prevalent in the Mississippi Valley. By the winter of 1846, the two had excavated nearly 150 such sites. The subsequent report of their findings published by the Smithsonian Institution in 1848 remains a landmark in scientific research and a classic study of North American Indian mounds.[24] During the course of their investigations, Squier and Davis personally visited the sites of all the mounds in their report except two. These two they left to an associate, James Hough. Hough of Hamilton, Butler County, Ohio, was probably related to Joseph Hough, also of Butler County, and a prominent Mississippi landowner with whom William had transacted several Bolivar County land purchases.

In 1846 James Hough called at the Perkins plantation in Bolivar County, intent on surveying and documenting the four mounds there. Built by Native Americans who inhabited the land during the Mississippian Period (1000-1500 AD), the four mounds and their circular enclosure occupied a little less than ten acres of William's property. Located approximately *one and a half miles east* of the Mississippi River on Williams Bayou (this

---

[22]The Whig party ultimately became a victim of the slavery issue, unable to find a compromise between its pro and antislavery factions. Four members of the party held office as President, William Henry Harrison (1841), John Tyler (1841-1845), Zachary Taylor (1849-1850), and Millard Fillmore (1850-1853).

[23]*Canton Herald*, "List of Whig Delegates", September 1, 1837.

[24]The report, *Ancient Monuments of the Mississippi Valley*, was the first publication ever issued by the Smithsonian Institution on any subject.

Squier and Davis description seems to place the mounds in either William's section three or its bordering section seventeen shown on Map 1), the mounds somewhat resembled others that checkerboarded this region but with one exception. Two of the mounds displayed a unique platform appearance and were enclosed by an immense circular embankment (Figures A and B below).[25] Rising as stately monuments of an earlier era, these two mounds towered above the otherwise flat expanse of Perkins' recently cleared cotton fields lending to his plantation its name while also providing a conspicuous appearance to any passersby.

    Describing the mounds' appearance, Squier and Davis wrote:

> They [the structures] consist of two truncated pyramidal mounds, accompanied by two small conical mounds, the whole surrounded by a circular embankment of earth 2,300 feet in circumference [732 feet in diameter] and 4 feet high, there being no ditch [moat]. A gateway opens into the enclosure from the east. Mound A is 150 feet square at the base, 75 feet square on top, and 20 feet high, with a graded ascent [ramp] from the east. Mound B is 135 feet square at the base, 50 feet at the top, and 15 feet high, with ascent [ramp] from the north. The two small conical mounds are about 30 feet in diameter and 5 feet high. The sides of the pyramidal structures do not vary two degrees from the cardinal points of the compass [in other words the pyramids were not canted], probably as near as they could be located without instruments.[26]

----

[25]The author consulted the Research Libraries of Archaeology at the University of North Carolina, Chapel Hill, in a further effort to locate the exact site of the mounds on William's property. In their undated report (copy in author's possession) they refer to a 1940 effort in which a shanty boatman described the *location* as having gone into the river in *1939*. His description approximated the point described earlier by Squier and Davis (and Hough). This portion of the submerged Perkins land can be identified as most of the land in section three. Today, his section seventeen remains intact. See Chapter XI for a further explanation and a valid contradiction as to the date.

[26]Ephraim Squier and Edwin Davis, *Ancient Monuments of the Mississippi Valley*, (Washington, D. C.: Smithsonian Institution Press, reprint 1998, original 1848), 116-117, and Calvin Brown, *Archaeology of Mississippi*, (Jackson: Uni-

The shapes of the pair of truncated pyramidal mounds revealed that their Native American builders - Mississippians of the
Mississippian culture - might have constructed residences or tem-
ples on their platforms while both the pyramidal and/or the coni-
cal mounds may also have been used as burial sites. In their report Squier and Davis included Hough's findings. Their precise
sketch of the Perkins mounds remains the only surviving drawing
of these ancient earthworks (Figure A). In later decades the
mounds would take on a life of their own, becoming the subject
of books and archaeological journal articles. Undocumented,
however, was the obvious fact that the four structures, along with
their accompanying embankment and untillable soil, limited Perkins' cultivation in the acreage where they stood.

Perkins, an intelligent man with sound judgment, had not
only invested in this particular piece of property in order to grow
cotton on its surrounding acreage, but also for another reason. He
planned to use the platformed summit of the tallest mound as a
family cemetery plot, as its ancient builders likely had done. This
ideal location, on high ground far removed from the river but
conveniently situated in proximity to the Perkins' home on Williams Bayou, would protect future generations of Perkins' family
graves from the Mississippi River's flooding. Establishing this
family cemetery showed, too, William's intention to reside at the
Mound Plantation for the remainder of his life.

---

versity of Mississippi, 1926), 93. Hough later created another drawing, incorrectly oriented, of the mounds on Perkins' property. He also depicted an apparently smaller fifth mound on a neighbor's property.

The "Perkins" mounds

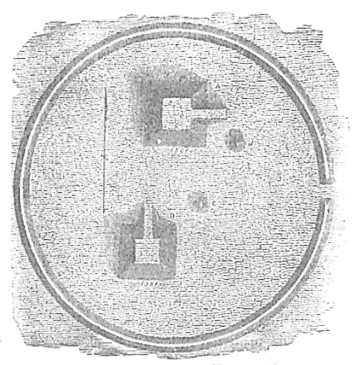

Figure A (aerial view, looking north).[27] Squier and Davis sketch of the Indian Mounds on William Perkins' property. Notice the distinctive circular embankment (described by Squier and Davis) surrounding the mounds. The top mound in Figure A (right hand mound in Figure B) is the taller of the two. The mounds alone would have occupied about half an acre for the larger mound and about two-fifths of an acre for the second largest.

---

[27]Drawing from Squier and Davis, *Ancient Monuments*, figure 22, 116-117. See also, Stephen D. Peet, *The Mound Builders: Their Works and Relics*, (Chicago: Office of the American Antiquarian, 1892), 176.

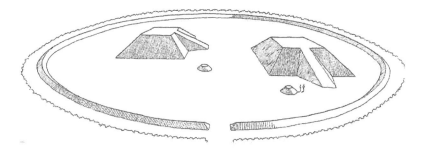

Figure B (looking west). Drawing courtesy of William Morgan.[28]

The Indian Mounds near Choctaw Bend and Williams Bayou.
1884 map (looking east), showing the Mississippi's serpentine
path. Notice the location of the mounds in relation to Williams
Bayou (Williams B. on the map). This is the only map found by
the author that references the Indian mounds located on William
Perkins' land.[29]

---

[28]William N. Morgan, *Prehistoric Architecture in the Eastern United States*,
(Cambridge: MIT Press, 1980), 75.

[29]"Mississippi Digital Map Library, Mississippi 1884, Memphis to Natchez," *U.
S. GenWeb Archives Mississippi*, accessed March 25, 2010,
http://usgwarchives.org/maps/louisiana/statemap/1884msrvymemnat.jpg.

The great Temple Mound at Winterville, Mississippi. This Indian
mound is an example of the type found on the William Perkins
plantation. Located in Washington County not far from the Perkins mounds, it stands fifty-five feet high, nearly three times
higher than any mound on the Perkins land. The two people
standing to the left provide a perspective as to its scale. Photo
taken by author July 2010

Later, in 1846 Hough, having completed his investigation
at the Mound Plantation, journeyed to Madison Parish, Louisiana,
where he conducted his second and final survey for Squier and
Davis. On the banks of Walnut Bayou southeast of Tallulah,
Louisiana, seven miles from the Mississippi River, he investi-
gated seven large mounds on land first cleared in 1827.[30] Despite
their great distance from the four intriguing Perkins mounds in
Mississippi, a link existed between the two sites.

---

[30]Squier and Davis, *Ancient Monuments*, xxiii.

It was no accident that Hough carried out this second investigation in Madison Parish. The mounds there were located approximately thirty miles from the plantation of Dr. Joseph Pugh, William's son-in-law. Pugh would have been aware of their existence, passing them as he traveled back and forth from Madison Parish to his other home in Madison County, Mississippi. While investigating the mounds on William's plantation, Hough likely received information from William concerning the Madison Parish mounds. With his work completed in Bolivar County, Hough embarked for Louisiana to document this second group of mounds. The results of his efforts likewise appeared in the Squier and Davis book but may have gone unreported had he not visited the Mound Plantation.

* * * * *

Created in 1836 and named after Simon Bolivar, the South American patriot, Bolivar County today is bounded on the north by Coahoma County, on the east by Sunflower County, and on the south by Washington County. It reaches its westernmost limit at the Mississippi River. Devoid of cities at its inception, Bolivar County included geographic features like Williams Bayou and Deer Creek that provided the only early map references to the location of the Perkins property. In 1828 a mapmaker had accurately designated the same area as a *swamp*. Despite revealing a wild landscape during its infancy, the county still possessed unlimited agricultural potential. Though in 1840 Bolivar County produced 274,155 pounds of cotton, its total paled in comparison to the 14,842,153 pounds grown that same year in more established Madison County. By the time of William's first Bolivar County land purchase in 1842, the region, still a wilderness expanse, encompassed 1,440 largely uncultivated square miles. While Madison County counted a population of 3,853 whites and 7,424 slaves in 1841, recently established Bolivar County reported a mere 423 whites and 712 slaves as of January 1841, for the taxable year 1840.[31]

---

[31]Mississippi, State Archives, Various Records, 1820-1951, State Census Return Madison County, 1841, image 18, and the 1841 Madison County Tax Roll, Box

The county's undeveloped nature also carried over into other areas. In 1850 Bolivar still claimed no teachers or schools, even though in May 1851 the county listed 104 educable children between six and eighteen years of age.[32] Rich planters were thus compelled to hire private home tutors to educate their children or send them off to other counties where schools already existed. The near total absence of roads meant William's $500 carriage would do him little good. Stores would not open until years later. (However, by October 1838 Peter Wilkerson operated a tavern within the county's borders.) Later, a hamlet, Bolivar, sprang up north of the lake of the same name, being the only such town of any size at that time. Even as late as 1856, Bolivar and Washington Counties, still relatively unpopulated, appeared as nearly blank areas on maps, in stark contrast to the more occupied and developed Madison County (Map 2).

However, over the next fifteen years, the climate and soil (some of the most fertile in the world) in this Mississippi Delta region, attracted slaveholding planters from not only Mississippi but also from other slave states. Initially, as most newcomers like Perkins realized before their arrival, cleared land did not exist, and preparing the soil for cultivation by removing forests and thick growths of canebrakes and draining swamps would require huge outlays of capital and an abundant supply of slave labor. As a result, only rich planters needed apply in Bolivar County, for only they, with their large gangs of slaves, could afford the attendant costs of establishing a plantation in this embryonic and daunting region.

By mid century Bolivar County recorded 395 whites, two free mulattoes, and 2,180 slaves. Possibly obscured in those figures is the fact that in the eight years since January 1842 when

---

3718, image 120. For Bolivar County see 1841 State Census Returns, Box 10449, image 5 and County Tax Rolls 1840, Box 2490, images 1-8, accessed October 30, 2011, *Family Search,* https://www.familysearch.org/search/image/index#uri=https%3A//api.familysear ch.org/records/collection/1919687/waypoints. For a summary of Bolivar County's population over the years see Appendix F.

[32]"Mississippi Enumeration of Educable Children, 1850-1892, Bolivar," accessed January 28, 2013, *Family Search,* https://familysearch.org/pal:/MM9.3.1/TH-1-14208-37344-78?cc=1856425&wc=10917670.

William made his first land purchase, the county had more than doubled its overall (black and white) population (1,135 to 2,577). During that same span, the slave numbers showed an astonishing three-fold increase (712 to 2,180). For every white in 1850, there were approximately 5.5 slaves, who accounted for eighty-five percent of Bolivar County's inhabitants. Few counties across the *entire* South could boast a greater percentage of blacks in the total population. The county continued to maintain this racial imbalance well into the Civil War years and beyond.

Yet, during this early period, Bolivar County's white population actually had decreased modestly, from 423 in 1841 to 387 in 1845. In 1853 its 418 whites still numbered less than in 1841.[33] In broader terms the lack of an overall white increase from 1842 to 1853 defies the expectation that the population growth of both *whites* and slaves would rise during a county's embryonic period.[34] So, why had Bolivar County shown a decrease in its white population during this twelve-year span? The answer can be found in the exclusivity Bolivar's environs demanded of its settlers. Bolivar, unlike other counties, demanded a high level of initial investment to create an ideal cotton-growing environment, a plateau available to only a privileged, moneyed few as we have seen. Consequently, though slave numbers increased, gradually fewer whites owned those slaves during Bolivar County's infancy. (Another reason, though unsubstantiated, is the fear of sickness and disease may have discouraged additional white families from settling there. See below.) Only later in the decade of 1850s did the county's white population begin to increase steadily.

The wealthy - in both property and slaves - entrepreneurially skilled planters ("pioneers with means" as one writer referred to them) who populated early Bolivar County constituted a small minority of the state's population. But, because most were well bred, articulate, refined in background, and well educated (Bolivar's literacy rate among its white population in 1850 was

---

[33]Mississippi, State Archives, Various Records, 1820-1951, 1841 Census Return Box 10449, image 5, State Census Return 1845, image 2, and State Census Returns 1853, Box 4887, image 2, accessed October 30, 2011, *Family Search,* https://www.familysearch.org/search/image/index#uri=https%3A//api.familysearch.org/records/collection/1919687/waypoints.
[34]Early Wilkinson County was another exception.

98.4%), they wielded tremendous economic and political power, not only in Bolivar County but also statewide.[35]

The county's eventual prosperity, however, contrasted to a degree with that of other nascent Mississippi counties. In those counties as wealth emerged, due to successful cotton crops, a moneyed planter elite then arose. Whereas, the early planters who arrived in Bolivar County (like William) brought an already established level of wealth with them to their new plantations - their wealth became the foundation for the county's prosperity. Accordingly, those early, affluent planters who settled Bolivar County in the decades of the 1840s and 1850s grew into an important developmental component of the pre Civil War culture and economy there and also across the expanding Delta region.

And nowhere was white dependence on slave labor greater than for the planters in this fertile Mississippi Delta region. With that dependence also came the affluent masters' expectations of huge profits from their cotton crops. Combined, these factors explained, in part, the extraordinary production levels and profits Bolivar County cotton planters generated during the next fifteen years. As a result, for enslaved blacks, their masters' increased economic gains only further solidified the oppressive slave system.

A list of William's neighbors resembled a roll call of Mississippi's privileged societal and slaveholding elite, a developing slavocracy, all convinced of their racial superiority: Former state representative and early Bolivar County resident General William Vick, of the family for whom Vicksburg was named, resided just north of William Perkins, and claimed 131 slaves in 1850 (Map 3).[36] At Stop Landing next to the Mound Plantation lived William C. Kirk of Waxhaw settlement in South Carolina with thirty-six slaves. Peter B. Starke owned twenty-three slaves on his estate

---

[35]Seventh Census, 1850 Agriculture, Bolivar County, Mississippi, Table IX, *Adults in State Who Cannot Read and Write*, 454. Neighboring Washington County in 1850 reported only one illiterate white.

[36]Seventh Census, 1850, Bolivar County, Mississippi, Slave Schedules, s. v. "William Vick," images 20-22, *Family Search*, accessed August 2, 2011, https://www.familysearch.org/pal:/MM9.3.1/TH-266-12117-18357-72?cc=1420440&wc=6145239.

Map 2
An 1856 map showing Madison County with several small cities,
including Livingston and Canton and, for comparison, the deso-
late tracts of land in Washington and Bolivar Counties. Williams
Bayou, the location of the Perkins plantation in Bolivar County, is
shown in the upper left.[37]

near the Mound Plantation on Lake Bolivar. Later, he became a
Mississippi state representative and senator, then a general in the
Confederate Army. Charles Clark, who arrived in Bolivar County
in 1850, owned the famous Doro Plantation north of Mound

---

[37]"Mississippi Atlas Map 1856." *Mississippi County Maps and Atlases,* accessed
September 8, 2010,
http://www.familyhistory101.com/maps/ms-maps.html.

Landing and claimed approximately 121 slaves by 1860.[38] Clark eventually emerged as Mississippi's Civil War governor. Just south of the Mound Plantation lived other members of the county's planter elite. The former Mississippi Secretary of State in 1841, and one of Bolivar County's original landowners, Lewis Galloway, owned property adjoining William's land and claimed 133 slaves in 1850.[39] Near Galloway was William's former neighbor in Madison County and future (1853) Bolivar County Justice of the Peace Hilliard (Hilead) Christmas, owner of ninety-seven slaves in 1850.[40] Another neighbor, Jefferson Wilkerson, held ten slaves in 1850 and approximately fifty-eight slaves in 1860.[41] West Point graduate and future Confederate general Leonidas Polk, a cousin to President James K. Polk, owned a 2,880-acre plantation purchased in 1855. Located south and west of Deer Creek in southwestern Bolivar County, it was managed by his son Alexander Hamilton Polk, owner of at least 150 slaves in 1860.[42] The Perkins family's close friend and one of the first merchants of Vicksburg, William R. Campbell, resided just across the county line in Washington County with his 118 slaves

---

[38]Eighth Census, 1860, Bolivar County, Mississippi, Slave Schedules, s. v. "Charles Clark," 25-27, accessed September 21, 2011, *Ancestry.com*.

[39]Seventh Census, 1850, Bolivar County, Mississippi, Slave Schedules, s. v. "James Garret Galloway," (Lewis Garret Galloway's first name appears as James in the index), images 14-16, accessed August 2, 2011, *Family Search*, https://www.familysearch.org/pal:/MM9.3.1/TH-266-12117-15931-52?cc=1420440&wc=6145239. Curiously, in the slave schedules, Galloway declared a nine-year old male slave to be *both* a fugitive and a manumitted slave. Such slaves were usually listed as one or the other, but not both. The boy's very young age is also unusual for such a designation.

[40]Ibid., images 13-14, accessed August 2, 2011. Hilead's surname is spelled 'Chrissmass' in the Slave Schedules. In 1938 a former slave, Taylor Jackson, recalled in an interview that Christmas "was mean to his folks [slaves]." *Slave Narratives: A Folk History of Slavery in the United States from Interviews with Former Slaves, Arkansas Narratives*, Pt. 4, (Washington, D. C.: Work Projects Administration, 1941), II, 22.

[41]Eighth Census, 1860, Bolivar County, Mississippi, Slave Schedules, s. v. "Jefferson & Jeff Wilkerson," accessed September 21, 2011, *Ancestry.com*.

[42]Eighth Census, 1860, Bolivar County, Mississippi, Slave Schedules, s.v. "H. Polk, Hamlin Polk, Hamelta Polk," accessed September 28, 2011. Ft. Polk, Louisiana, is named after General Leonidas Polk. Coincidentally, the author underwent his advanced individual infantry training there in early 1967.

in 1850.[43] A Washington County pioneer, Campbell also owned vast tracts of land in Bolivar County.

At first, most of Bolivar County's early planters lived in log cabins, but later these gave way to finer, stately residences associated with the refined Southern planter class. A visitor to the Mound Plantation in 1861 wrote that it was "an excellent house" and "has a very pretty location, one of the best plantations in Bolivar County."[44] Another writer described the Perkins plantation home as it appeared some twenty-five years later, in the late 1880s:

> She [Perkins' daughter Jane] has a pleasant residence on the banks of Williams Bayou, well shaded by large trees, and her home is well furnished, the walls being hung with family portraits. It is a beautiful place of residence, and now a strong new levee has just been completed along the riverfront. . . .[45]

This well-off, well-educated, well-housed, privileged slaveholding caste, the dominant force then in the county's social and economic fabric, eclipsed those Bolivar slaveholders who claimed but a few slaves and also the slaveless farmers who attempted to scratch out a living on their own small plots.

Scattered throughout the county, but living in stark contrast to Perkins and the county's other moneyed slaveholding planters, were the sixteen Bolivar County slave owners in 1850

---

[43]Seventh Census, 1850, Washington County, Mississippi, Slave Schedules, s.v. "William Campbell," images 5,6, accessed August 2, 2011, https://familysearch.org/pal:/MM9.3.1/TH-267-11055-71343-72?cc=1420440. Though Campbell and his wife Margaret owned a substantial number of slaves, they contributed $30 between December 1850 and January 1851 to the American Colonization Society to help repatriate freed blacks to Liberia.
[44]Diary of Milton Westfall, March 7 and June 8, 1861. Mississippi Department of Archives and History, Westfall, Milton S., Diary, 1861, Reference # Z 0724.000 S. Photocopy in author's possession.
[45]*Biographical and Historical Memoirs of Mississippi*, 586-587. The date of the book's publication (1891) and the manner and detail in which information regarding the Perkins family is presented indicates that the unknown author actually interviewed William Perkins' surviving daughter, Jane Perkins Curry Moore, and then based his family memoir on her recollections.

who held five slaves or less and the twenty-seven other heads of household who claimed none at all.[46] They, too, attempted to earn a living by raising primarily cotton. However, these men and their families generally owned lesser amounts of land (in some cases a quarter section - 160 acres or less) and possessed a far smaller amount of capital than their affluent neighbors. In this agrarian subculture, often the wives and children or other members of their extended families performed much of the farm labor. In many cases the lesser slaveholders could be seen working daily in the fields alongside their few slaves. Moreover, some of these small scale farmers who lacked their own cotton gins incurred an additional expense when they paid a fee to wealthier planters like William for the use of their, in many cases, new and efficient steam powered gins. For these forty-three Bolivar County farming families, the opulent plantation lifestyle of the Perkins clan was something to be envied and aspired to.

As time passed, the sudden acquisition of wealth in the South's cotton producing regions allowed for a newly-rich caste of planters, many of whom did not possess the more genteel qualities of some of these early Bolivar County men. A Northern observer traveling through the South and particularly Mississippi in the mid 1850s provided the following critical evaluation of these noveau riche planters:

> Of course, there are men of refinement and cultivation among the rich planters of Mississippi, and many highly estimable and intelligent persons outside of the wealthy class, but the number of such is smaller in proportion to that of the immoral, vulgar, and ignorant newly-rich, than in any other part of the United States. And herein is a radical difference between the social condition of this region [Mississippi] and that of the seaboard slave States,

---

[46]Seventh Census, 1850, Bolivar County, Mississippi, Slave Schedules, images 1-26, *Family Search*, accessed May 10, 2011, https://familysearch.org/pal:/MM9.3.1/TH-266-12117-16266-62?cc=1420440. See also Seventh Census, 1850, Bolivar County, Mississippi, Images 1-10, *Family Search*, accessed August 1, 2011, https://familysearch.org/pal:/MM9.3.1/TH-267-11882-27744-59?cc=1401638&wc=MM28-85D:n1586173744.

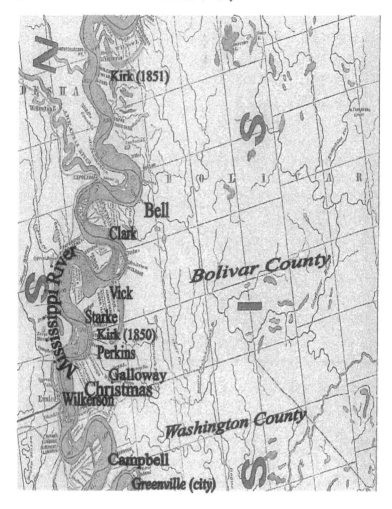

Map 3
An 1862 map of Bolivar County showing the location of the Perkins plantation and those of his neighbors situated along the Mississippi River. Located in Washington County is Argyle, the William R. Campbell plantation.[47]

[47]"Mississippi Digital Map Library," "Mississippi Map 1862," *US GenWeb Archives*, accessed March 25, 2010,
http://www.usgwarchives.org/maps/mississippi/statemap/msrtntola1862.jpg and
http://www.usgwarchives.net/maps/mississippi/#county.

where there are fewer wealthy families, but where among
the few people of wealth, refinement and education are
more general.[48]

On the other hand, the elevated social position of some
elements of Mississippi's privileged class could not mask the extreme acts of violence they meted out when punishing their slaves
for serious crimes. In Washington County, after deliberating in
council, "several highly respectable gentlemen," who shared
many traits common to their planter counterparts in neighboring
Bolivar County, burned a slave alive for murdering a female slave
on the Deer Creek plantation of a planter named Woolfolk (possibly T. G. Walcott). The execution occurred in "the presence of all
the negroes on that and several adjoining plantations, all of whom
seemed terrified out of their wits on viewing so awful a scene."[49]
The newspaper account pointed out that the public execution also
served a second purpose – to suppress any thought of rebellion or
misconduct "on the part of other desperate negroes in the neighborhood." The slave died cursing his judges, "vowing to take
vengeance on them when they met each other in - - - -." Significant, also, is the extralegal power the "gentlemen" assumed, collectively acting as judges, jury, and executioners.

Bolivar County's population data during this period shows
that the majority of its planters along with many of the county's
other white heads of household were born outside of Mississippi.
The 1850 population schedules illustrate that Bolivar's heads of
household were part of an ongoing general trend - the spread of
the Southern cotton culture from the upper South into the Southwest and the Mississippi Delta counties. Only fourteen of Bolivar
County's ninety-five heads of household hailed from Mississippi
in 1850, while sixty-four were born in other slave states.[50] These

---

[48]Olmsted, *Cotton Kingdom*, 158.
[49]*Vicksburg Sun* in *Macon Daily Telegraph*, April 15, 1860, 2.
[50]Seventh Census, 1850, Bolivar County, Mississippi, Images 1-10, accessed
August 1, 2011, *Family Search*. Several county residents were born in Northern
states while two came from Ireland, and one each from England and Germany.

men and their families had left Virginia, Tennessee, North and South Carolina, Georgia, Maryland, and Kentucky in favor of the tempting agricultural prospects in the Delta region.

The county's population growth over the years helped foster an intricate web of social relationships that soon emerged among its more affluent planters. Partly based on old friendships and partly a product of intermarriage between members of different local families, these associations became the social glue binding many of Bolivar County's residents to one another. Perhaps, too, a common Southern heritage facilitated the development of these connections. For example, the Perkins clan was particularly close to the Christmases, as both families had resided in Madison County on Persimmon Creek and because the Christmases were natives of Franklin, Tennessee, where William had grown up. Likewise, Perkins and William R. Campbell (of Kentucky) shared land investments in Bolivar County, and Perkins had also purchased acreage owned by Campbell. Both men enjoyed racing horses as well. Soon, the marriage of their children would bring the two families even closer. Neighbor Lewis Galloway was good friends with Perkins' Hardeman cousins in Hinds County, often visiting them and spending the night. Charles Perkins and two members of the nearby Kirk family (of South Carolina) would unite in a California goldfields adventure. Louisa McGehee Burrus, the wife of Bolivar County planter and probate judge John C. Burrus Sr., had grown up in Wilkinson County at the time William lived there, and later her family (the McGehees) owned property (and lived?) in Livingston, Madison County, near the Perkins plantation. Now, she and her husband resided in Bolivar County, not far from the Mound Plantation. Her husband John and his father Charles Augustus Burrus had both shared land on Thompson's Creek in Wilkinson County at the same time Perkins resided there in the late 1820s and early 1830s. Burrus' son, John Jr., later recalled his familiarity with the Perkins clan in Bolivar County during its early years. Both families would eventually send sons to Princeton University, but in different decades.

Because vast swamps and a dense living wall of primal forest made the county's inland area uninhabitable, many of these very wealthy families built their homes on or near the river (Map 3). These riverside (and for that matter all) Bolivar County resi-

dents quickly learned a basic truth; depending on its mood, the
Mississippi could be either the savior or the devil of the Delta region. On the one hand, yes, the river allowed planters to more
easily transport their crops to market. It also provided locals with
a vital link to and from the outside world while serving as a food
and irrigation source. Alternatively, what the Mississippi be-
stowed, it just as easily could swiftly and often disastrously de-
stroy, due to its renowned tendency for spring flooding. Thus, it
was incumbent upon those residing along the river to be especially vigilant during the flooding season.

County residents in the 1840s or before had recognized
the urgent need for a levee to protect against such inundations in
those exposed areas along the Mississippi's banks. In an attempt
to solve the problem, planters again resorted to slave labor. Initially, they erected small, private levees that held back the spring
floodwaters in most years. In the 1850s gangs of Irish laborers
were also brought in during the fall when slaves were occupied
picking cotton to construct more and better levees. However,
levee repair continued to be a work in progress for decades, continuing into the 1860s, and beyond, resulting all the while in additional, but necessary expenses for local residents. Later, the
county saw to construction of a larger, more consolidated levee
that afforded further protection.

An equally serious problem generated by proximity to the
river was that nearby swamps and bayous, some fed by the Mississippi, provided ideal breeding grounds for mosquitoes. Posing
a grim and often deadly threat of mosquito-borne diseases to Bolivar County's populace, these interconnected environmental
health risks defined the area for decades. As a result of this danger and other factors, the county's residents, whether black or
white, infant or adult, experienced a mortality rate higher than the
state average.

The 1850 census takers, in addition to taking a head count,
were required to provide detailed mortality figures for the preceding twelve months. Enumerators were asked to list the deceased
person's name, age, sex, color, status (slave or free), place of
birth, month of death, profession, cause of death, and number of
days ill. The thoroughness of these mortality schedules depended
on the individual enumerator, with information regarding black

mortality being generally less complete than white mortality. For instance, in some Mississippi counties, mortality lists include the names of deceased slaves, while in others slaves' names are not shown. Thus, many deceased slaves ended up appearing anonymously in two records, the mortality report *and* the Federal Census count (tallied every ten years). (D. B. Hudson, the Bolivar County census enumerator, provided no names for the county's 112 deceased slaves in 1850.)

Based on the state census of 1850 and the Bolivar County mortality data, the threat of death existed to a far greater degree in Bolivar County compared to most other counties in Mississippi. Deaths in the county's black and white populations by 1850 were more than three times the state average (as a percent of population) due primarily to an inhospitable climate, unhealthy living conditions, and the great amount of extraordinarily hard labor required of Bolivar County's slaves. Statewide, 1.4% of Mississippi's overall population died from June 1849 to June 1850. In contrast, *4.6%* of Bolivar County's population died during that same twelve-month span.[51] A closer look reveals that Mississippi's white mortality equaled 1.1% of the white population while slave deaths were nearly the same (surprisingly) at 1.7% of the slave population. In Bolivar County white deaths equaled 1.5% of the white population (*6 deaths out of 395 whites and 2 free mulattoes*), slightly higher than the state percentage. However, slave mortality in the county, as a percentage of its black population, stood at 5.1% (*112 slave deaths out of a slave population of 2,180*), exactly *three times higher* than the state figure in

---

[51]Seventh Census, 1850, Agriculture, Bolivar County, Mississippi, Table IV, *Births, Marriages, Deaths, Dwellings, and Families, 448-449*. Mississippi's population for 1850 (both blacks and whites) totaled 606,526, while Bolivar County counted 2,577 people. A comparison with the mortality figures in Washington County, Bolivar's neighbor to its south and Madison County, William Perkins' former home, reveals that rural Bolivar County's growing reputation for greater mortality was well deserved. From 1849-1850 Washington County, with an environment similar to Bolivar County, reported 210 deaths, or 2.5% of its overall population (higher than the state average). Inland Madison County, located in a far less austere setting than Bolivar County, recorded 232 total deaths, or 1.2% of its population for the same period. Yet, at the same time, Bolivar County's reported mortality of 4.6% of its total population almost doubled that of Washington County and was nearly four times higher than Madison County.

the period 1849-1850. Clearly, Bolivar County's elevated death rate among its slaves had been responsible for the county's inflated total mortality percentage of 4.6%.

Infant mortality, too, was particularly high, as 43 of the county's 118 deaths were children five years of age or younger, and all were black.

Nor did the birth rate offset the number of Bolivar's deaths. In the 1850 counting, just 62 births occurred, 9 whites and 53 slaves, while deaths for the preceding twelve months totaled nearly twice that figure.

As would be expected, the mortality schedule revealed that Bolivar County's people died from a variety of causes. The leading cause of death for the year recorded was cholera, which claimed 68 victims (58% of the total deaths), with most deaths occurring during two particularly virulent outbreaks in June 1849 and May 1850. Other causes of death were fever (probably malaria), worms (usually found in infants), drowning, typhus, dropsy (edema), consumption (tuberculosis), flux (dysentery), pneumonia, and croup.[52] Surprisingly, during this single year period, cases of yellow fever and malaria were not *specifically* mentioned. Nonetheless, Bolivar County had been and would continue to be considered less healthy than the state's interior uplands for years to come.

Medical attention and treatment in Bolivar County depended on a variety of sources and circumstances. Generally, because of their affluence, planters and their families had access to local physicians, but perhaps not with the immediacy they would have preferred. On his Madison County plantation, William Perkins had the good fortune to be able to rely on a family member, his son-in-law Dr. Pugh, to look after his ailing family and slaves (see the case of the tubercular Lucinda above). Most masters, of course, could not avail themselves of such a luxury.

---

[52]United States Census, *Mortality Schedule*, Bolivar County, 1850, *Family Search,* accessed 15 June 2012, https://familysearch.org/pal:/MM9.3.1/TH-266-11111-63227-12?cc=1420441. Care must be exercised in using these mortality documents, as one county's statistics overlap in that of the next county. For example, Attala County overlaps into Bolivar County and Bolivar's data appears in Carroll County. Check the county name on the mortality sheet prior to reading the data to avoid errors.

According to the 1850 Bolivar County census, only four physicians served the county's total white and black population of 2,577. (William Perkins' brother, Dr. Nicholas Perkins, visiting from Tennessee, was included in the census but omitted from my tally of Bolivar County's resident physicians.) Since Dr. Pugh still resided in Madison County, a local physician who fortunately resided between the nearby Galloway and Christmas plantations presumably treated the Perkins' family and its slaves.

On the other hand, another in the long list of tasks that occupied the plantation overseer was the health and welfare of the slaves. Overseers, who maintained daily contact with the blacks, were expected to watch for and report any signs of sickness or injury in the workers or their children. Masters, overseers, and even the slaves themselves might first attempt to treat minor maladies, but often physicians treated sicker slaves.

Slave owners were motivated to maintain the health of their slaves, perhaps in part due to humanitarian considerations. But, since his slaves represented both an investment and a means to profit, a master's concern for his slaves' health was more often than not motivated by primarily monetary factors.

Given that in 1841 William Perkins claimed eighty-one slaves (that number would more than double by 1850) and that his Mound Plantation was located in one of the unhealthiest areas of the state, his medical expenses for his slaves there may have been considerable. To illustrate this point, the records of a Hinds County physician prove helpful.

A Dr. Eckles billed William's brother, Daniel Perkins, on his Canebreak Place Plantation in Hinds County (generally, a healthier environment than Bolivar), for a variety of services during a twenty-seven month span, June 1, 1838, to September 26, 1840. Eckles' total bill for that period, which included charges for *168* house (slave quarter) visits (often several in one day), diagnoses, treatments, or prescriptions amounted to $607.35, no small amount in the 1830s.[53] Based on this figure, William, who owned

---

[53]Mississippi Probate Records 1781-1930, Hinds County, Estates (series 1) 1844-1855, no. 665-707, images 215-219,
https://familysearch.org/pal:/MM9.3.1/TH-1942-30881-22845-34?cc=2036959&wc=MMY2-7HS:409918074.

approximately three times as many slaves as his brother, could have paid more than $1,500 for the medical care of his slaves during the same period. While disease and treatment remained problematic in Bolivar County's early years, opportunities for religious worship were only slightly less so.

In 1850, according to a county historian, "a small Methodist Church was erected by private subscription of the adjacent planters."[54] However, the census of 1850 showed that Bolivar County counted a total of *three* churches, all Methodist, which suited William and Jane as both were of that faith.[55] Traveling preachers held services in all three churches and also at other locations.

These itinerant preachers in Bolivar County, by necessity, became men of many tasks - riding the rural circuit on horseback, often twenty miles per day, conducting services, visiting the sick, comforting mourners, and otherwise connecting with the community. These resolute missionaries of God typically preached two or three Sunday sermons to congregations at different sites, either in the county's early places of worship or on various plantations. Additionally, they often held midweek prayer meetings in Bolivar County's small communities. Services were held for whites, and on many plantations masters allowed their slaves to attend a separate service, some of which attracted large crowds of blacks.[56] One Northern minister preached to the black slaves (he referred to them as servants, carefully avoiding the use of the term slaves) at the Mound Plantation at least six times in 1861, noting that after one Sunday service "three or four [of Perkins' Negroes] have united [joined] with the Church."[57] When riding the circuit, preachers often visited several plantations in a single day, then lodged overnight with a local family, enjoying meals and sharing news and conversation with their generous hosts. Such visits also allowed these ministers to obtain a unique perspective on the pulse of the county's widely scattered residents. That these roving ministers continued spreading the word of God across the county

---

[54]Sillers, *History of Bolivar County*, 129.
[55]*Biographical and Historical Memoirs of Mississippi*, 586.
[56]Westfall Diary, January 20 and April 7, 1861.
[57]Ibid., April 14, 1861.

via horseback into the 1860s reveals that despite its wealth, Bolivar County remained rural in nature.

For the Perkins family by 1850, the growth of both Bolivar County and the Mound Plantation brought them a level of prosperity that perhaps exceeded their expectations formed eight years earlier at the time of William's first Bolivar County land purchase. Their productive Mound Plantation at mid century had become both the symbol and the reality of Southern wealth, landowning, slaveholding, and privilege.

Jonathan C. Kirk's Waxhaw Plantation residence near Rosedale north of Mound Landing. Photo probably post Civil War.[58] Courtesy of National Archives and Records

---

[58]"Photo Gallery," *Bolivar County GenWeb*, accessed July 11, 2010, http://msgw.org/bolivar/photogallery.htm. Kirk claimed thirty-one slaves in the 1860 census and was able to afford this stately home on the river. In *1850*, with William Perkins claiming 166 slaves, more than five times Kirk's number, we can only imagine the size and beauty of his Mound Plantation residence.

V

The Mound Plantation in 1850

Matilda, 18, and 2 children, Matilda, 16, and 1 child, Mariah, 19, and 3 children.

William Perkins describing 3 female
slaves and their six children he used as
collateral for a loan, November 30, 1842

In 1850 the document produced as a result of the Seventh Census of the United States was unique in several ways. It was the first to list *all* family members in each household by name, age, occupation, and birthplace, as well as the values of real estate and personal property (Appendix B). In addition, an accompanying *Production of Agriculture* portion provided detailed information concerning farm productivity. Moreover, a third feature, the census's *Slave Schedules,* while listing slaves anonymously, but by owner, included precise information on slaves' age, sex, and a designation as to whether the slave was (B) black or (M) mulatto (Appendix C, D, and E). Consequently, the data collected revealed a wealth of information regarding an expanding America at mid century, and more specifically the planters of Bolivar County.

Based on the data derived from these sources, a unique portrait emerges of William Perkins' family, his personal assets, plantation, and slaves. Perkins valued his Mound Plantation real estate at $40,000 (Appendix B).[1] By June 1850 he had 100% of his then 1,655 acres under cultivation, producing great yields of corn, sweet potatoes, and, of course, cotton.[2] No other planter in

---

[1] In today's currency its value would perhaps approach more than $570,000.
[2] The number of acres Perkins reported in the 1850 Federal agricultural census varies greatly when compared with Bolivar County records. In Bolivar County's Land Roll, submitted also in November 1850, Perkins reported ownership of 3,187 acres, a disparity of more than 1,500 acres compared to the Federal tally. Later in 1854, Perkins' total acreage of 2,658 acres still exceeded his Federal numbers in 1850, which may be reason to believe an error was made in the Federal counting.

A cotton plantation on the Mississippi. This picture, seen often in history texts, is probably very representative of the Mound Plantation. Located on the river and near the cotton fields, the various plantation buildings are shown to the right. In the background a passing steamboat appears, possibly bound for New Orleans. In the foreground slaves toil in the cotton field under the watchful eye of the mounted overseer while others guide a wagon filled with cotton bales. Illustration by William Aiken Walker. Courtesy of the South Caroliniana Library, University of South Carolina, Columbia, South Carolina

Bolivar County could claim such a high percentage. In the census's *Production of Agriculture* segment, William provided two separate sets of figures for his Mound Plantation. One set, in his name, disclosed production numbers for 800 acres, about half of the plantation's total.[3] The second revealed similar information for Perkins' remaining 855 acres, managed by his overseer William Paquinette and listed under his name. Paquinette, of course, did not own the land or its yield.

---

[3]Seventh Census, 1850, The Agricultural and Manufacturing Census for Bolivar County, Mississippi, reel 175, 115, 116. This census was enumerated on November 9, 1850, but it only included data for the year ending June 1, 1850.

Perkins chose to report the figures separately, thus establishing two separate enterprises, a customary practice of owners with unusually large estates whose slave force numbered in excess of 100. In Perkins' case it would have been both very unrealistic and inefficient to expect Paquinette to supervise well over 100 field hands and also escort them daily from their slave quarters to the fields and back again. Thus, William allowed Paquinette to manage a separate section of his sprawling plantation along with about one half of his slaves somewhat independently. Moreover, William most likely appointed a trusted black driver to oversee the slaves on his half of the plantation. Of course, such a creative management approach had hinged on William being able to employ a competent overseer and a reliable black driver.

Including the figures for Paquinette's portion, the total cash value for the 'farm' equaled not the $40,000 Perkins had declared in the population schedule, but instead $44,275. This figure exceeded the worth of every plantation in Bolivar County, allowing Perkins by 1850 to emerge as the county's wealthiest planter in terms of farm value.

These same agricultural records also reveal the Mound Plantation's near self-sufficiency, common to large Southern plantations at that time. "The planters who owned more than thirty slaves were the ones who achieved maximum efficiency, the most complex economic organization, and the highest degree of specialization within their labor forces," and Perkins' systemization and administration of the Mound Plantation was no different.[4] Perkins' entire plantation, for the year ending June 1, 1850, counted forty-eight mules, seventy milk cows, sixteen working oxen, 150 other cattle, forty sheep, and 380 swine, all valued at $5,685. The value of animals recently slaughtered was $1,600. Perkins (and Paquinette) estimated the worth of the plantation's farming implements and machinery at $6,000. Furthermore, the plantation's field hands had produced 15,000 bushels of Indian corn, eighty pounds of wool, 20,200 bushels of sweet potatoes (roughly three-quarters of the county's total and a staple of a

---

[4]Stampp, *Peculiar Institution*, 38.

An early cotton steamboat (similar to those that called at Mound Landing) on the Mississippi loaded with hundreds of bales of cotton.
http://www.cottontimes.co.uk/whitney02.ht

slave's diet), and 1,500 pounds of butter.[5] By assigning additional slaves to perform the multitude of other varied and essential tasks on the sprawling plantation, Perkins and Paquinette insured everything operated as smoothly as possible.

Also tallied and certainly of primary importance to William was his cash crop. His slaves produced 714 bales of cotton weighing 400 pounds each. (For simplicity, if cotton sold for ten cents per pound in 1849, a close approximation, the worth of his 714 bales would have equaled at least $28,560.) Though the Agricultural Census records do not provide figures regarding specific crop yields per acre, Perkins could expect his hands to produce about a bale an acre, the average figure cited for Delta cot-

---

[5]Since sweet potatoes are high in vitamins and minerals, they proved to be an ideal food for persons involved in heavy, muscular work.

ton, and more in a good year. The county as a whole produced 4,723 bales of cotton in the fiscal year ending in June of 1850.

Inasmuch as the 1850 cotton season was just beginning by the June 1 census cutoff date, William's 714 bales represented his crop from 1849. He may have retained part of this crop on his plantation until 1850, following some planters' customary practice of withholding a previous year's cotton from market in anticipation of receiving a more favorable price. In addition to revealing a plantation's agricultural output, the census also included data regarding the population and ownership of slaves, thus providing a further insight into the world of Bolivar County's slave-based economy.

In 1850 the census's Slaves Schedules revealed that sixty-eight (seventy-two percent) of Bolivar County's ninety-five heads of household were slave owners, holding a total of 2,180 slaves. Of the county's twenty-five white agents or overseers, thirteen represented absentee planters or those away on business or pleasure, while the other fifty-five owners were present on their plantations when the enumerator arrived. As a group the sixty-eight whites claimed as few as one and as many as 166 slaves, with the average being thirty-two slaves per owner.[6] Five slaveholders claimed more than 100 slaves: Perkins, Martin, Mrs. Brown, Vick, and Galloway. Countywide, an elite fourteen held 1,269 slaves or fifty-eight percent of Bolivar's total. This group of slightly more than a dozen slaveholders, combined with their counterparts in other Delta counties, represented the driving force behind the region's rapidly increasing cotton economy. Admired and respected by their neighbors, they typified the entrepreneurial planter-aristocrats of the antebellum South.

Precise evidence of William's increased affluence and prestige emerges from the pages of Bolivar County's Slave Schedules. Perkins, by 1850, held more slaves than he had ever previously reported. The enumerator's entries of his anonymous

[6]Seventh Census, 1850, Bolivar County, Mississippi Slave Schedules, images 1-26, *Family Search*, accessed May 10, 2011, https://familysearch.org/pal:/MM9.3.1/TH-266-12117-16266-62?cc=1420440. When searching for Perkins, see "Austin Alexander" (Alexander was Perkins' neighbor), as neither William Perkins nor William Paquinette appear in the *Family Search* index.

slaves provide mute testimony to the number and hence overall value of these human chattels. In addition to gaining slaves through natural increase (childbirth), William had apparently purchased additional hands during the decade of the 1840s, having anticipated a need for added field labor with the acquisition of his vast Bolivar County acreage.

At first glance the 1850 Slave Schedules reveal William Perkins held eighty-one slaves, forty-four males and thirty-seven females, a significant decrease from the 117 slaves he owned four years prior.[7] However, on the page previous to William's name and his slave ownership data appears the name of William Paquinette, and inscribed in small handwriting above it the words *agent for W.P. Perkins,* signifying Paquinette as the plantation overseer.[8] Then appearing below Paquinette's name a startling revelation appears: An additional *eighty-five* slaves belonging to William, but shown for Paquinette's portion of the plantation, are enumerated (Appendix C, D, E). Combining this second group with the previous eighty-one, William owned, as of November 1850, a staggering 166 slaves. (The Slave Schedule also shows that none of William's slaves were currently fugitives/runaways, nor had he manumitted any slaves at the time of the counting.)

The reader should not be misled by the fact that eighty-five of William's slaves are listed under overseer Paquinette's name as Perkins' agent. In noting the slaves in this manner, the census enumerator was following an established protocol when reporting slave ownership on a 'shared' plantation or for an absentee or, in William's case, an ill master.

On November 9, 1850, as the initial counting of the Perkins' slaves began, William lay in bed in the main plantation house near death attended by his family. As a result, D. B. Hudson, a Bolivar County citizen and the local census taker, possibly guided by Paquinette on 'his' portion of the plantation, counted as many of the slaves as possible that day. Three days later, on No-

---

[7] Ibid., images 17-18 and Bolivar County 1846 Tax Rolls 1846-1858, Box 9845. For the number of slaves per slaveholder in 1846, see images 1-16. For Bolivar County's total number of slaves under sixty years old in 1846, see image 18.
[8] Ibid., 1850, image 16. There are various spellings in the sources consulted for Paquinette: Pacquinette, Pacquinett, Paquinett, and even Pagwinett.

vember 12, Hudson returned and completed the job, listing the remaining slaves under William's name.

Southerners measured status in society by counting their slaves, and accordingly William Perkins ranked at the head of the local list, as he claimed more slaves than any other Bolivar County slaveholder.[9] Perkins' slave tally filled nearly four full columns in the Slave Schedule, more than doubling his count in the 1840 census, and underscored William's need to split his plantation into two manageable parts.

Of William's 166 slaves, there were eighty females and eighty-six males. Fifty-three of the 166 were children 10 years or younger, William's future field hands, blacksmiths, teamsters, cooks, and house servants. (Natural increase was a significant part of a slaveholder's profit margin.) Just fourteen slaves were 50 or older, the oldest being a 70 year old female. The remaining ninety-nine slaves fell into the *older than 10 but less than 50* category.[10] The average age for male slaves on the Mound Plantation was 19.8 years, an exceedingly low number. Generally, with most of a plantation's male slaves performing jobs as field hands, the very young average age of this key group meant William could expect excellent productivity and potentially increased profits over the next decade or longer. While the female slaves averaged 25.1 years of age, twenty-seven of the those shown had reached the optimum children bearing age, that is, between the ages of 18 and 35. (By 1842 three of William's female slaves raging in age from sixteen to nineteen had already produced six children.)[11] Furthermore, the average age of Perkins' entire slave work force proved to be just 22.3 years.[12]

Housed on the plantation in the slave quarters - approximately thirty-five to forty separate, rudimentary, dirt-floored,

---

[9]In 1860 Bolivar County resident Miles McGehee claimed 234 slaves, but this was after William's plantation and slaves had been divided among his heirs.

[10]Seventh Census, 1850, Bolivar County, Mississippi Slave Schedules, images 16-18, *Family Search*.

[11]*Bolivar County Deed Book B*, FHL, microfilm roll 886085, 393, November 30, 1842. Matilda, sixteen, one child, Mariah, nineteen, three children, and another Matilda, eighteen, two children.

[12]One study estimated the average life expectancy of a twenty year-old prime field hand in the period 1830-1850 at thirty to thirty-five years.

one-room cabins, each a cauldron of squalor, with some clustered
near Paquinette's portion and others near the Big House - William's slaves represented a huge investment, while their labor was
indispensable to his financial security. At an average 1850 price
of perhaps $1,000 per slave (less for women and children), Wil-
liam's slave property equaled nearly $165,000.

As Perkins was aware, success or failure of a cotton plantation depended on the overall health and birth rate of its slaves as
well as the size and quality of its cotton crop. To that end, a responsible master's financial interests were best served by judi-
ciously caring for his slaves in much the same manner as he
would care for his valuable livestock. We have no evidence as to
how the slaves under William Perkins' (or Paquinette's) control
fared, but regardless of their treatment, Perkins as a slave master
may have sought to view himself in the best possible light, a
common means of rationalization amongst slaveholders. Dove-
tailing with this philosophy, Perkins had very likely adopted the
steadfast, paternalistic belief that his enslaved Negroes fared
much better living on his plantation than they would have if other
masters owned them or had they remained in 'primitive' Africa.
He never understood the moral indefensibility of slavery.

William's ownership of 166 slaves placed him in an elite
category occupied by not even one percent of his fellow Southern
slaveholders. (Only 1,733 of 345,000 slaveholding families nationwide owned 100 or more slaves in 1850.) His paper worth in
real estate, slaves, and cotton stood at nearly $238,000 in 1850
currency. Though we have no accurate way to measure William's
return on his investment, it may have equaled or surpassed the estimate of one Mississippi planter in 1855 who calculated a planter
earned eight percent on his capital from the sale of cotton alone.[13]
However, the luster of these impressive numbers for William and
other Southern planters undoubtedly obscured the possibility that
plantation slavery, though it produced great wealth across a predominantly agricultural South, was becoming an economic dead
end that would eventually leave the South sinking in the wake of
the North's Industrial Revolution.

------

[13]Stampp, *Peculiar Institution*, 409.

Under normal circumstances a slave's life would remain almost as anonymous to historians as his 'appearance' in the slave schedules and mortality reports. But, in various Bolivar County documents containing records of William's business transactions, especially those where he secured loans with slaves, the names of dozens of his slaves appear. Listing slaves in most cases by first name only, William often provided (to the recorder) their color and age, though the latter was not always accurate. Occasionally, he revealed which slaves were married and the name of the spouse.

The following, Slaves as Loan Collateral, is an example of one such document. It shows William in May 1848 securing a new $12,416 loan listing nearly the same "fifty-one Negro slaves and their increase [children]" previously mortgaged to the Commercial Bank of Natchez in November 1842.[14] In this instance William omitted the slaves' color but included their ages:

---

[14]While William's slave May appeared on both the 1842 and 1845 collateral document, his name is conspicuously absent on the 1848 document for a reason discussed below.

Slaves as Loan Collateral, May 1848. In this original document, the recorder listed the names and ages of the fifty-one slaves William Perkins used as loan security.[15]

[15]*Bolivar County Deed Book C*, FHL, microfilm roll 886086, 441. Another "collateral" document dated February 15, 1845, found in *Bolivar County Deed Book C*, FHL, microfilm roll 886086, 6, 7, 10, and 11 provides names, ages, color, and the relationships of many of these slaves shown in William's May 1848 list:

A closer look at the page reveals additional information regarding several of William's slaves mentioned in Chapters II and III. One of the two Charlottes and one of the three Louisas may be the two slaves Jane Perkins' father Charles Stewart sold/gave to William in 1824 and 1826. The slave Sandy (column 1) is Sandy Jones, one of the dozen slaves William had gifted to his son Charles in 1840. Using other documents, it is possible to identify Sandy's wife Patience and their two grown children, Wake and Simon (columns one and two). Wake's wife, Matilda, is also shown along with their two children (Sandy Jones' grandchildren), Sandy II and Sophia (or Sophy) Jones, under columns one and two.

An additional fifty-three slaves, including several unnamed slave children from the Perkins plantation, appearing as collateral in two other of William's debts, (to neighbor James H. Cousar and to Joseph Hough), can also be identified (chart below).[16] With the inclusion of this group, more than 100 of the 166 slaves on William Perkins' plantation have thus been named.

Escaping the anonymity of the slave schedules, these slaves, due to the meticulousness of white owners and businessmen, emerge momentarily and unintentionally from the loan collateral lists. As a result, a limited glimpse into their lives and also the restrictive institution of which they were a part is revealed. Their names, marital status, and even color bring 'life' to an existence from which there was little chance of escape. However, in choosing to do just that, run away, one of William Perkins' slaves unwittingly brought his story, as brief as it is, to light.

Aaron, age 26, was married to Little Charlotte (24). Henry Ford (46) and Sidney (female, 36) both mulattoes, were married. Tom (34) was married to Varny (?) 26, the sixth slave listed in row three, and both were copper colored. George (26) was married to a mulatto, Louisa (24). Light-skinned Andy (44) was probably married to light-skinned Margaret (22). Joe Ready (36) and Nelly (28) were husband and wife. Green (26) and the mulatto Matilda (22) were married. Joe Short was copper colored. Old Nancy's surname was Sims.
[16]Ibid., 6, 7, 10, 11.

Name	Color	Age	Name	Color	Age
William	mulatto	25	Bill	black	26
wife:Daphney	black	23	wife:Louisa?	black	?
Mary		6	Ellen		5
?evin		4			
Sandy		2	Anthony	black	23
Edward		1/2			
			May (male)	copper	35
Stephen	black	50	wife:**Nancy**	light	30
wife: Polly	black	45	**John**		10
Dinny?		14	__?__		8
Stephen		12			
Lot		10	Bob Adams	dark	26
Eliza		6	wife: Jane		23
Moses		4	unidentified children		
unreadable	mulatto	22	John Nick	copper	25
wife:Fanny	black	22	wife:Louisa		25
*Ellen		4	unidentified children		
Simon	copper	19	Mariah, wife of Joe Short		24
			unidentified children		
Jesse	black	34			
wife: Lucinda		28			
M_?__		11	unidentified child		
Nathan		8	Henry Baily	mulatto	26
Churchill		6	wife: Charlotte		25
Lucky		4			
Jesse		2	unidentified child		
Sophy		1/2			
			Morris	light	22
Aggy	copper	45	wife:Elizabeth		18
Dan___?	mulatto	25	Becky		32
Daniel		10	Morning?	fem.	25
P__?__		8	Louisa	black	18
			Nancy	black	20
Clary	female black	28	Henry Hannah?	yellow	17
Thompson	light	17			
Bob	copper	25			

32 slaves   21 slaves, and at least **9**
                              unidentified children

Additional *named* slaves of William Perkins, February 1845[17]

---

[17]Ibid.

PUBLISHED BY WELD & CO.,

68 CAMP STREET,

NEW ORLEANS,

THIRD EDITION OF THE

COTTON-PLANTATION RECORD AND ACCOUNT BOOK;

No. 1, for a Plantation working 40 hands or less, $2 50.
No. 2, 	"	"	80	"	"	$3 00.
No. 3, 	"	"	120	"	"	$3 50.

By THOMAS AFFLECK.

An 1851 advertisement for a cotton plantation organizational log. On the left-hand page - *Daily Record of Cotton Picked* - space is provided for the names of forty slaves. Next to each name, the plantation overseer or owner entered the amount of cotton picked each day. On the right hand page - *Daily Record of Passing Events on Plantation During the Week* - entries would include information on weather, slaves' health, or crops. Perkins, through the years, would have maintained just such a record.

As early as 1842, or possibly before, William Perkins owned May, a copper-colored, male slave. May stood "5 feet 10 or 11 inches high," and because of his size, age, and the fact that he "was stout through the shoulders," Perkins probably used him as a field hand on his plantation. Two traits made May unique. He required water while eating, as he had a tendency to hiccup, and his "good" front two teeth showed a distinctive space between them. By February 1845 May, then thirty-three, and his wife Nancy, a light-skinned thirty-year old, had two children, John age ten and another child age eight.[18] Probably between February 1845 and May 1848 William Perkins either sold or traded May to a neighbor, James H. Cousar, in the process perhaps separating the slave from his family. (Far from strangers, Perkins and Cousar had done business in the past; in 1845 William had pledged four of his slaves as collateral in a loan from Cousar.) Presumably a troublesome slave, May showed raised scars on his back caused by the whip. It is unclear whether the whipping(s) had occurred while he lived on the Perkins plantation or under his new master Cousar, or both.

Near the approximate time of the transaction in 1850, Cousar resided at Stop Landing, close to the Mound Plantation, so this proximity may have eased May's transfer from Perkins to Cousar. However, by 1852, Cousar, with May and his other slaves in tow, relocated to Victoria, still in Bolivar County, but farther north. May's resettlement most likely caused the slave additional anguish, as the distance to the Perkins plantation (and any family he had there) now increased to at least a dozen miles. Consequently, after laboring on Cousar's plantation for at least four years, May in 1852 rebelled against his new owner and ran away, leaving his family behind in Bolivar County.

Pursued by slave catchers, the fugitive fled to Ozark County, Missouri, another slave state, more than 330 miles from Cousar's plantation. May's unexplained and remarkable success in traveling undetected (until he reached Ozark County) for such a great distance through unfriendly slave states defied all odds. From Ozark County, May's trail then grew cold. Possibly he had

---

[18]Ibid. May and his family are shown above on the February 1845 chart. That year Perkins erroneously listed May's age as "about 35".

moved on, heading north, anticipating freedom once he arrived in a free state.[19] On November 27, 1852, Cousar placed a notice in the *Jefferson* [City] *Inquirer* (in Cole County, Missouri, 400 miles from Bolivar County). Offering a $100 reward for the then forty-year old fugitive, Cousar described May as "copper colored" and promised to "give the above reward for his [May's] confinement in jail, so that I can get him."[20]

The result of May's freedom attempt is unknown. But, unless he somehow reached Canada, his eventual capture and return to slavery would have been the most likely outcome, further accentuating the hopelessness faced by runaways from the Deep South in their efforts to reach freedom despite an active Underground Railroad. The entire episode also serves as another stark reminder of the harshness of plantation slavery, not only on the Perkins and Cousar plantations but also across the entire South. And, if somehow May's escape attempt had been *successful*, he

---

[19]May was possibly unaware of the recent, more stringent federal Fugitive Slave Law of 1850. Its threat of heavy fines for whites harboring or abetting escaped slaves even in free northern states made many unwilling northerners and their institutions responsible for participating in the apprehension of runaways. As a result of this new law, Canada became the only true haven for escaping slaves like May.

[20]*Jefferson Inquirer*, November 27, 1852, found in Franklin Riley, *School History of Mississippi*, (Richmond, Virginia: B. F. Johnson Publishing, 1905), 162. This scenario and May's description are based on the fugitive slave notice Cousar placed in the *Jefferson Inquirer*, November 27, 1852, seeking May's return. The author contends this May is the former Perkins' slave for a number of reasons. First, May is a highly unusual first name for a male slave. Second, May's age in 1852 equates with his actual age then, based on Perkins' records appearing in *Bolivar County Deed Book B*, page 393. Therein, Perkins shows May, a thirty-year old slave, on a document dated November 30, 1842. Ten years later, in 1852, May would have been forty, as Cousar stated in his newspaper notice. May's name is also absent from Perkins' 1848 collateral document shown and discussed above suggesting he was no longer in Perkins' possession. The proximity of the Cousar plantation to the Mound Plantation, along with the mutual familiarity of Cousar and Perkins, also weighs heavily in this scenario. Lastly, May's unique copper color, *noted by both Cousar and Perkins*, combined with the other factors outlined above, provides additional strong circumstantial evidence as to his identity as Perkins' slave.

could never have been reunited with his enslaved family in Mississippi. Ironically, the diligence of each slaveholder in documenting May's existence through a business transaction and a wanted poster resulted in a story that would have otherwise remained untold.

At approximately the same time as the episode of May unfolded, three other Perkins' slaves also emerged from the anonymity of slave life. Their tale began when Charles Perkins, and coincidentally two other members of the Cousar family, decided to transport them to the California goldfields.

VI

Charles Perkins in the Goldfields

"Perkins, C., and servant"
New Orleans Picayune, June 26, 1849,
reporting that Charles Perkins and his
slave sailed for Panama

By late June 1849, the size of the Perkins family had increased to nine with the births of two sons, Noland S. and James W., born in 1841 and 1847 respectively. While Noland, James, Daniel, William Jr., and their still unmarried sister Jane resided with their parents on the family plantation, the oldest son Charles Perkins, heeding the call later championed by Horace Greeley, had gone West.

Charles, despite his rural Mississippi upbringing, had graduated from the College of New Jersey (Princeton) in June 1848.[1] Thousands of miles away and five months earlier, James Marshall had unsuspectingly stumbled on gold in the American River near Coloma in northern California's Sierra Nevada Mountains. The news quickly spread, and soon Charles Perkins heard the phrase that excited the nation, then the world, "Gold in California!"

As a result, twenty-two year old Charles planned to join the rush to California in June of 1849. Rather than remain in Mississippi and enjoy the comfortable lifestyle of a planter's son, he now faced a challenging test of his early manhood. It is unknown whether Charles' father, William, had expected his son to make his own fortune and thus encouraged this California adventure, or if he had reluctantly acquiesced to his son's gold seeking dream.

---

[1] A year prior to his graduation at the college's Centennial Anniversary Celebration on Tuesday, June 29, 1847, Charles and other students were asked to deliver "orations." Charles, a junior then, spoke that evening on "Why America Has No National Literature." John McClean, *History of the College of New Jersey from Its Origin in 1746 to the Commencement of 1854*, (Philadelphia: Lippincott, 1877), 367, accessed July 4, 2010,
http://books.google.com/books?id=qEdAAAAAIAAJ&pg=PA367&dq=charles+s+perkins+the+college+of+new+jersey&hl=en#v=onepage&q&f=false.

No matter what his motive, Charles may have viewed his journey as an opportunity to independently reap a fortune from a rich claim. He also possibly recognized that if successful he could return proudly to the family plantation having proven himself in the rugged West by demonstrating the highest qualities of his illustrious family pedigree. Charles might naturally have had such feelings and ambitions. But, as the family's oldest son, he was the first of the new generation of this rich, privileged, and influential Southern family so no one knows what family dynamic might have existed. What is certain, though, is that Charles was not seeking the capital to establish his own plantation once he returned. He already had inherited twelve slaves, and just prior to leaving for California, he had purchased 480 acres in section twenty-nine of the Mound Plantation from his parents.

On June 15, 1849, Charles prepared to board one of the southbound passenger steamers regularly plying the Mississippi. Though he had visited his first destination, New Orleans, at least once before, this time it would serve merely as a connection point, the initial leg of a prolonged sea passage, via Panama, ending half a continent away in San Francisco.[2] From there he planned to continue his journey by horse and wagon inland to the goldfields, swarming now with thousands of others (their collective historical destiny later would be termed forty-niners) who had arrived in the seventeen months since Marshall's discovery.

Because of his advantaged plantation upbringing, Charles had not been exposed to the sort of Spartan existence he would soon encounter in the rugged Sierras. He could claim little work experience with a pick and shovel. There would be no bevy of servants, relaxing summer evenings on the front porch overlooking the meandering Mississippi, or a luxurious room in the majestic, domed St. Charles Hotel like that which he had occupied during a visit to New Orleans in December 1847. However, young Charles brought certain advantages uncharacteristic of most forty-niners in the goldfields.

Accompanying him was another Perkins, nearly Charles' own age, but despite their common surname the two were not related. Aware of the benefits of slave labor, Charles had selected

---

[2]*San Francisco Weekly Christian Advocate*, August 5, 1852, 150-151.

one of his father's 166 slaves, a trusted and favorite black field hand, Virginia-born Carter Perkins. At nineteen Carter was young, strong, and sufficiently intelligent to withstand the rigors and repetitive nature of prospecting in the Sierra's Mother Lode country.[3] A peculiar feature of this relationship centered on its symbiotic nature. In the diggings both master and slave would be working *side by side* with Charles benefiting from his slave's labor. While Carter had little choice in emigrating, he might have hoped for an opportunity in the goldfields to experience a slight and unique measure of 'freedom' and also a welcome respite in a more appealing climate from the grueling routine of Mississippi cotton field labor.

While the use of slave labor in the goldfields during the Gold Rush's early years was uncommon, rarer still was the prospector who had earned a diploma from a prestigious college like Princeton and at the same time possessed technical knowledge of minerals and soil. Charles brought these other unique advantages to California as a result of two mandatory college courses in geology and mineralogy taken in his senior year (just twelve months earlier). As a result, he knew better than most prospectors where to find gold and stake a claim.[4] Armed with Carter's labor and this specialized knowledge, along with liberal amounts of mettle and self-confidence, Charles stood a good chance of success.[5]

---

[3]Cornelius Cole, "Essays," *Cornelius Cole Papers*, Department of Special Collections, University of California, Los Angeles, III: Box 29, Folder 2, 7. Copies are in the author's possession. Cole, a Sacramento attorney, referred to Carter as "an intelligent young fellow." These essays are Cole's unpublished reminiscences of his life. Recorded decades after the events therein occurred, the portions relating to the Perkins matter, while fairly detailed, leave gaps in the overall story. In addition the years clouded Cole's memory and caused him to make occasional omissions and errors. However, among the Essays are Cole's legal documents from 1852, which are very accurate contemporary sources.
[4]*Catalogue of Students of College of New Jersey*, (1847-1848), 8, accessed June 1, 2011,
http://books.google.com/books?id=SS1LAAAAYAAJ&pg=PA82&dq=charles+s+perkins+the+college+of+new+jersey&lr=&cd=2#v=onepage&q=geology&f=false, scroll to p. 114.
[5]Further evidence of Charles' intelligence can be gleaned from John Williams, editor, *Academic Honors in Princeton University, 1748-1902,* (Princeton: Princeton University, 1902), 50. Charles, as a member the college's Cliosophic (Debating) Society, was selected in 1847 (his junior year) along with two other

On that mid-June departure day, contrasting scenes played out on different parts of the plantation. Numerous times over the past several years at the Mound Landing, William Perkins had overseen the loading of his cotton aboard paddle wheelers, similar to the one currently before him, likewise bound for New Orleans. Now, as Charles prepared to board, William may well have reflected on the generational significance of the moment. His father (and Charles' grandfather), Daniel, had similarly departed his family's comfortable Virginia plantation at age nineteen, while in a parallel scene in 1818 he (William), approximately Charles' age, had left the family home in Tennessee to make a new life in Woodville, Mississippi. Meanwhile, on another part of the plantation in the slave quarters, the sad and anxious family and friends of Carter Perkins had earlier offered him their good-byes before setting out for their day's work in the fields. Unlike Charles' family, Carter's relatives could expect no letters from California as all including Carter were illiterate. Already filled with anticipation regarding their journey, Carter and Charles might have been even more eager to leave Bolivar County that June than would normally be expected. A seasonal outbreak of cholera had recently struck resulting in the deaths of dozens of the county's slaves.[6]

Prepared for their great adventure, despite any uncertainties lingering in their minds, both slave and master, not partners to any extent but reliant on each other nonetheless, boarded the vessel with their baggage. Earlier, in a large, carefully packed trunk, next to his clothing and toilet articles, Charles might have placed a small, framed daguerreotype of his family, a letter of introduction from his second cousin and bank president William Hardeman, and for protection a pocket pistol, perhaps a derringer.

Presently, the paddle wheeler eased slowly away from Mound Landing, beginning the first segment of an epic journey, a journey that from our vantage point of more than 160 years was nothing less than a part of the great American experience. As a

---

Mississippi students and an Irishman to debate the four members of the rival American Whig Society team. Only eight of the junior class's top students were chosen to compete in these much-anticipated contests that culminated the academic year.

[6]*Mortality Schedule*, Bolivar County, 1850.

part of their adventure, Charles and Carter would soon encounter in California eager, adventurous, often young men from every corner of the world, from every layer of society, and every level of culture, most intent on striking it rich.

A day or two later the pair arrived in New Orleans. Carter may have marveled at the biggest and busiest city he had ever seen, while Charles booked passage on a Panama-bound ship, the dual-masted brig *Octavia*. According to contemporary newspaper ads, "this fine, fast [eighty-two foot] sailing coppered and copper fastened brig [built in 1836] . . . has comfortable cabin accommodations, and the steerage is fitted up so as to handsomely accommodate a limited number of passengers. . . ."[7] Booking a departure for Saturday, June 23rd for Chagres, Panama, Charles paid nearly $150 for his cabin and significantly less for Carter's space in the cheaper steerage compartment. Because Charles was traveling with Carter, one additional item required his attention before sailing.

In 1849 United States law required slave owners traveling with their slaves in coastal waters to complete a specific transport document prior to leaving. At the New Orleans Custom House, Charles submitted paperwork (now lost) swearing that Carter had not been *imported* to the United States since January 1808 when Federal law had first banned the importation of slaves. Instead, Charles declared his intent to merely transport the American-born Carter from one location to another, i.e. New Orleans to Panama, then on to San Francisco. (Perkins, of course, had no way of knowing that in 1849 he was at the forefront of a great many Southern masters who, enroute to California aboard every sort of vessel in the next few months and years, would complete similar customs declarations for their slaves.) With this final task completed, both master and slave, anxious to get underway, prepared for the *Octavia's* departure.

---

[7]*New Orleans Picayune*, June 23, 1849, 1 and *New Orleans Commercial Bulletin*, June 21, 1849, 3, column 7. While Charles sought passage to California, life went on in New Orleans. Preceding the *Octavia*'s ad in the *Bulletin* on June 21 was an announcement for a slave auction to be held at 12 o'clock on June 23rd for, "Very Valuable Slaves, Carpenter, Cabinet Maker, Baker, and Butcher," all "fully guaranteed."

As it turned out, according to the June 28 edition of the
Picayune, the *Octavia* was delayed three days. It finally sailed on
Tuesday evening, June 26, with one of her sixty-eight named passengers recorded simply as "Perkins, C., and servant." Without
fanfare the two Perkins men, products of such different worlds,
now became united in the historical record.

Just four days earlier, on June 22, 1849, William Lloyd
Garrison's antislavery newspaper, *The Liberator*, coincidentally
declared:

> It is frequently asserted by those who oppose the Wilmot
> Proviso [a failed bill that would have banned slavery in
> any territory acquired from Mexico as a result of the
> Mexican War] that slavery cannot exist in California, un-
> less established by law, and that a positive prohibition is
> unnecessary. That is asserted in the face of the fact that
> slaves have already been taken to that territory by South-
> ern men who are writing for more. . . .[8]

In early July Charles Perkins and Carter arrived at their
destination, Chagres, Panama. In order to avoid the long and dangerous voyage around Cape Horn, Charles chose to first canoe
with a native boatman and other passengers up the Chagres River
then trek the remaining way across the Isthmus through its dense
jungle, amidst chattering monkeys and colorful parrots. Even with
a guide, this leg of the journey still remained a hazardous undertaking at the time. Once on the Pacific side, he hoped to catch
some San Francisco-bound steamer to complete this much shorter
route to his destination. Based on their eventual arrival date in San
Francisco (early October), it appears Charles and Carter experienced an inopportune delay in Panama.

The scarcity of northbound steamers combined with an
estimated 6,000 eager, competing Argonauts also awaiting California-bound vessels caused delays for everyone. These unexpected slow downs, revealed the tidal wave of humanity bound for
California even in this, the early phase of the gold rush. The pause

---

[8]"The Liberator, Slavery in California," *The Liberator Files*, June 22, 1849, accessed July 7, 2011, http://www.theliberatorfiles.com/slavery-in-california/.

An ad in the New Orleans *Commercial Bulletin* for the Brig *Octavia's* voyage on June 23, 1849, to Chagres, Panama

may have delayed Charles and Carter for four to five weeks or longer.[9] Soon, competition in Panama among these travelers naturally drove up prices for the limited number of tickets on outbound ships, making the hold up all the more annoying.

At this same time, the *Panama Star and Herald* reported a speculation in fares to California. Steerage tickets for the August steamer "change hands freely, and today $270 to $300 is the price asked for them. Cabin tickets are less in demand, though they are in market at $400."[10]

Perkins' delay may have been made slightly more palatable, though, by the advertised fact that the *Octavia's* agent in Panama guaranteed passage through to San Francisco at the lowest

---

[9]"Complete Story, Slave Case," *Naglee Family Collection*, BANC MSS C-B 796, Box VII, (folder) MR552, June 6th, 1852, University of California, Bancroft Library, Berkeley, California. Attorney Cole, during an interview in June 1852, learned Charles and Carter came to California by way of the Isthmus. For information on the delays in Panama in July 1849 see (no author), *Santa Cruz County, California. Illustrations descriptive of its scenery, fine residences, public buildings, manufactories, hotels, farm scenes, business houses, schools, churches, mines, mills, etc. . . . With historical sketch of the county*, (San Francisco: W.W. Elliott, 1879), 86.

[10]*Panama Star and Herald*, August 11, 1849, 2.

possible rates and allowed passengers one dollar per day while in the Isthmus.[11]

Weeks later on approximately October 1, 1849, Charles and Carter, perhaps on board the steamship *California,* passed through a picturesque Golden Gate surrounded by green hills, then waited for the ship to drop anchor in a crowded San Francisco Bay.[12] Cluttered with a fleet of similar, but abandoned vessels, their crews now seeking gold inland, the harbor assumed an even more curious appearance with the slender masts of scores of these idled ships rising skyward. Some ninety-seven days had passed since Perkins' New Orleans departure and his arrival in a bustling San Francisco.

Though such thoughts would never have entered Charles' mind, possibly during the long sea voyage Carter reflected on the family stories he had heard of his early African ancestors. They had unwillingly experienced their own ocean journey, the harrowing trans Atlantic middle passage from Africa to an American port, in the dark dungeon that was the hold of a slave ship. While Carter's journey differed markedly from the middle passage of his captive relatives, he, too, faced a similarly uncertain future upon arrival at an unfamiliar destination.

The California that tempted Charles Perkins and thousands of others in 1849 was likewise entangled in the ongoing

---

[11]*New Orleans Picayune,* June 23, 1849, 1 and the *Commercial Bulletin's* ad above.

[12]*Advocate,* August 5, 1852, 150-151. The *Advocate's* article, written nearly three years later, reported among other details the approximate date of Perkins' arrival, on or about October 1, 1849. Various sources show the San Francisco arrival date for the *California* from Panama as October 11, 1849. One primary source voyager indicated, however, it arrived as early as about October 1, having stopped in Acapulco on the trip north: See Julius Pratt, "To California by Panama in '49", *The Century,* 41: (November 1890-April 1891), 911. (Pratt was delayed approximately four weeks in Panama, from April until May 1849, due to a dearth of California-bound ships.) This author could locate no other vessel arriving in San Francisco from Panama during the early October time period. The *Senator,* however, is reported to have arrived anywhere from October 5 to October 27 from Panama. The *California's* published passenger list containing some 230 names did not mention Charles Perkins or his "servant." Because the *California's* capacity approximated 500 passengers, it is very likely that Charles and Carter (if they were aboard) had been compelled to travel with the remaining 270 unnamed travelers in the cheaper steerage.

slavery question that had characterized America for more than 200 years, dating back before the arrival of the second Nicholas Perkins in Virginia. This increasingly incendiary controversy had easily transcended the Great Plains, the Rockies, and the nation's expanding boundaries and surfaced in a mineral-rich land on the Pacific shore thousands of miles from the nearest Southern plantation. Though California had not yet achieved statehood, pro and anti slave factions existed within her borders in 1849. For the most part, these men co-existed in the goldfields reasonably well. Their numbers, however, changed with the arrival of each steamer or wagon train. Conversely, in the political arena, battles would soon be waged to determine the essence, slave or free, of California's state constitution.[13]

In San Francisco Perkins and his slave may have checked into a local hotel that first night to enjoy a warm bath, comfortable bed, and a hot meal. (Carter undoubtedly occupied a less hospitable space somewhere, separate from his master's room.) Eager to begin prospecting, Charles resisted any notion of a prolonged stay in the city, and the two "sloped soon after they landed."[14] Unexpectedly, Charles learned that steamboats had just begun making the passage from San Francisco to Sacramento. This new water link from the bay to the interior fortunately allowed Perkins to avoid a longer and disagreeable overland wagon or horseback ride, thus making this, the second to final leg of his journey, more bearable.

Nearly four months had elapsed since Charles Perkins and Carter had departed the Mound Plantation, but now their arrival in the small, but thriving city of Sacramento in early October 1849 meant the journey was almost complete. Since Marshall's gold discovery, Sacramento had begun to benefit from its ideal location as a steppingstone to the gold country and also as a waypoint on the Sacramento River for large ships. Known at first as the Embarcadero, Spanish for "landing place", the city counted approxi-

---

[13]One of the many Southerners opposing California's admittance as a free state was Mississippi and Wilkinson County's U.S. Senator Jefferson Davis.

[14]*Sacramento Daily Union*, June 3, 1852, 2. The meaning of the verb 'sloped' in this context is either 'left' (slipped away) or possibly the writer's play on words meaning, 'headed for the slopes' of the Sierra Nevada Mountains, i.e. the gold country.

mately 1,000 people in October 1849 according to one forty-niner. As gold fever raged, Sacramento's location allowed its population to increase dramatically, from the initial 1,000 to three or four times that by June 1850.[15] Controlling his understandable impulse to get to the 'diggins' Perkins, before leaving, must have taken the time to outfit both he and Carter at one of the city's many general stores, perhaps at Watson's Miners Store at the corner of Third and K Streets near the wharf.[16]

Soon, Charles "had met with great success in digging for gold in an obscure camp in El Dorado County," the same county in the Sierra Nevada Mountains in which James Marshall's electrifying discovery had occurred in 1848.[17] As it turned out, Perkins had chosen well for El Dorado County, with a population recorded in 1850 of more than 20,000 inhabitants, became one of the most prosperous of California's gold mining areas.

While Charles prospected in the Sierras, one of his Tennessee cousins faced a challenge of a different sort, but in the California political arena. Forty-two year old Peter Hardeman Burnett had just recently begun his campaign for governor of California. Born in Nashville in 1807, Burnett and his family moved to Franklin, in Williamson County, Tennessee, in 1811. There they remained until 1817 occupying a farm about four miles south of Franklin and not far from their Perkins relatives.

Charles Perkins and Burnett could point to common ancestors. Burnett's mother, Dorothy Dolly Hardeman, was the daughter of Thomas Hardeman and Mary Harden Perkins. Going back farther in the Perkins family tree, both Burnett and Charles were descended from Constantine and Ann Pollard Perkins of Henrico County, Virginia, their great, great grandparents. Both men also shared a common lineage before that, at least as far back as Nicholas Perkins I.

Undoubtedly, the Perkins and Burnetts interacted in Franklin given their proximity and common heritage. Charles' grandfather, Daniel P. Perkins, and Burnett's grandfather, Thomas

[15]Letter, Albert Brown, June 10, 1850, transcribed at
http://www.yubaroots.com/nuggets/goldrush.htm.
[16]*Placer Times*, October 20, 1849, 4, column 1.
[17]Cole, *Essays*, III: Box 29, Folder 2, 7.

J. Hardeman, belonged to the same Franklin Masonic Lodge. (Charles' father William would have been sixteen when the Burnetts arrived in Franklin, while Daniel P. Perkins may have met the young Peter Burnett on any number of occasions.) It is almost certain that Charles was aware of the family connection he and Burnett shared. (Burnett mentions his Perkins heritage in his autobiography.) Charles may have been unaware, though, of his cousin's presence in the state until he either read newspaper accounts or heard about Burnett's campaign.

When Burnett returned to Sacramento on October 23, 1849, Charles and Carter were probably already in the goldfields. However, Burnett began a campaign speaking swing lasting from October 23-29, taking him to the mining towns of Mormon Island, just outside out Sacramento, and Coloma and Placerville in El Dorado County. Inasmuch as Charles had just begun prospecting in that some county at that very time, it is highly probable the two met in one of these austere mining locations. If the two men got together in the goldfields, (for perhaps a rustic dinner or a shot of whiskey in some tented 'restaurant/hotel') any conversation regarding the slavery question between Burnett, who advocated the exclusion of blacks from California despite his proslavery feelings, and his cousin, the slaveholder Perkins, would have been an interesting one.

By December 1849 Burnett had won the election and assumed the duties as California's first civilian (territorial) governor. While Perkins may never have benefited from his relationship with Governor Burnett, it never hurt to have an influential family member in such a position of power, especially for a twenty-two year old 2,000 miles from home.[18]

---

[18]Much of this information regarding Peter Burnett can be found in his autobiography, *Recollections and Opinions of an Old Pioneer*, (New York: D. Appleton and Company, 1880), particularly pages 1-7, and 347. Like Charles, Burnett had come to California in search of gold (but in 1848). After enjoying modest success in the goldfields, Burnett worked for John Sutter Jr. selling land in the new town of Sacramento. Later, as governor his advocacy of excluding blacks from California went against the state's proslavery faction. (He also demonstrated an openly racist attitude toward Chinese and Native Americans.) While Charles Perkins remained in the goldfields, Burnett resigned his position as governor in January 1851 having alienated many in the state with his political stances on

If Charles and Carter remained in the diggings that winter of 1849-1850, they most likely experienced some very difficult months. Rain, beginning in late December, fell almost constantly in nearby Placer County and undoubtedly in El Dorado County. At the higher elevations it turned to snow, blanketing the mountains.[19] The flimsy canvas tents the miners called home offered little protection from the severe weather of the Sierras. Perhaps, though, Charles had opted, as many miners were doing, to winter in Sacramento where the weather was milder and the accommodations less austere. Near the end of February 1850, as spring approached, the weather turned warmer, and news of the rich gold discoveries made the previous fall spread among the miners. A general stampede then occurred into the area of Placer and El Dorado Counties, as eager gold seekers sought to regain the time winter had stolen from them.[20]

Several months later Charles must have conveyed to his family back home news of his success in California. As a result, Charles' cousins Albert Green (A. G.) Perkins and W. B. Perkins, and two neighbors from Bolivar County, brothers Jonathan Cousar Kirk[21] and Stephen Kirk, decided to join Charles in the goldfields.

---

various issues. Burnett eventually became a partner in San Jose's first law firm, living in that city for many years before moving to San Francisco in 1863. He is buried in the Mission Santa Clara Cemetery in Santa Clara, California, just a few miles from the author's home. In San Jose a middle school bears Burnett's name. See the *Placer Times*, October 27, 1849, 2, column 1 for a report of Burnett's candidacy.

[19]R. J. Steele, *Directory of the County of Placer for the Year 1861*, (San Francisco: C.F. Robbins, 1861), 26-27. The writer of this historical sketch of Placer County wintered there during the memorable winter of 1849-1850.

[20]Ibid., 27. The areas in the Sierra Nevada foothills where miners like Perkins staked their claims tended to be free of the oppressive heat and humidity found in Mississippi during the summer months.

[21]*Biographical and Historical Memoirs of Mississippi,* 2: 729. (Firebird Press published this particular volume.) A native of Waxhaw Settlement, South Carolina, Jonathan Kirk had arrived in Bolivar County on horseback between 1842 and 1845, the same time that William Perkins was establishing his plantation there. Kirk resided in 1850 at Stop Landing just north of the Perkins plantation on the Mississippi River (Map 3 above). Later, in 1851 upon his return from California, Kirk purchased land above Rosedale, and there he established his Waxhaw Plantation. Like the Mound Plantation, his 2,000-acre Waxhaw estate fronted the river. A convenient landing made it easier to connect with the Perkins

On Saturday, May 11, 1850, the four, along with 183 other passengers, boarded the steamship *Alabama* bound for Chagres. Then docked at the wharf at the foot of Girod Street, she would sail from New Orleans at 9 a.m.

Five other men, all blacks, traveled with the two Perkins men and the Kirk brothers. The Kirks each escorted a slave (and possibly a third) from the Perkins plantation. Two of these slaves, Robert Perkins and Sandy Jones, were born in Tennessee and North Carolina respectively. Though Robert and Sandy were twice as old as Carter Perkins, both men had worked as blacksmiths on the Mound Plantation and possessed the strength and stamina necessary to carry out the difficult tasks of gold miners.

The six-foot tall Robert, listed as Robbin on the ship's official Manifest of Slaves completed by Jonathan Kirk, left a wife and five children behind.[22] A forty-year old according to the customs document, Robert and young Carter Perkins may have been related, possibly as brothers, cousins, or as father and son. Or, as was often the case in many Southern master-slave relationships, they were unrelated and had assumed (or had been given) their master's surname.

William Perkins had acquired Robert and Carter in 1844 or earlier as part of his purchase of thirty slaves from his deceased brother's estate. Both slaves had resided on Daniel Perkins' plantation since at least 1839, possibly sharing the same slave cabin, which supports the notion they were likely related.[23] Soon, if all

---

family and others who lived in southern Bolivar County. The writer described Kirk as, "generous, whole-souled [whole hearted], and straightforward to a marked degree," (729).

[22]*Advocate*, August 5, 1852, 150-151, and *Outward Slave Manifests 1812-1860*, United States Customs Service Records, Port of New Orleans, Louisiana, (Outbound) Slave Manifests 1847-1850, microfilm M1895, Roll 25, November 1847-June 1850, s. v. " May 10, 1850, Steamer *Alabama*." Kirk failed to indicate on the document that he was transporting Robert as the agent for the slave's owner.

[23]In the Daniel P. Perkins estate documents, an unpaid doctor bill reveals that in July and August 1839 a Dr. Eckles made five separate visits to Daniel Perkins' plantation to provide treatment for slaves Robert/Robin and Carter (both were listed consecutively on Eckles' bill). While no last names are indicated, the two slaves referred to are undoubtedly Robert and Carter Perkins, given the proximity of their names in the doctor's bill and the fact that Carter and Robin are unusual names for slaves. See Eckles' bill at Mississippi Probate Records 1781-1930,

132   Charles Perkins in the Goldfields

went according to plan, these two Perkins slaves would be re-united in California.

Another black, fifty-year old Sandy Jones and the oldest of the five, traveled in the custody of Stephen Kirk. Sandy was the slave William Perkins had gifted to Charles years earlier. At five feet eight inches, Sandy was not quite as tall as Robert Perkins, but like Robert he had left behind in Bolivar County his wife Patience (perhaps fifty years old also) and two sons, Simon and Wake, both married men with families.[24]

Three other slaves were also making the trip to the gold-fields. Jonathan Kirk accompanied Isaac, a five foot six inch, thirty-year old, presumably Kirk's own slave from his Mississippi plantation. A. G. Perkins escorted two additional blacks, forty-seven year old Willis, the shortest of the five slaves, and Andy, age forty-five, five feet two inches and five feet six inches tall re-

Hinds County, Estates (series 1) 1844-1855, no. 665-707, images 215-216, accessed November 11, 2012, *Family Search*, https://familysearch.org/pal:/MM9.3.1/TH-1961-30881-22528-37?cc=2036959&wc=MMY2-7HS:409918074.
[24]*Advocate*, August 5, 1852, 150-151. See also *Bolivar County Deed Book C*, microfilm roll 886086, 441, May 2, 1848. Robert Perkins's age varies only slightly in the records used. However, Sandy Jones' age varies greatly depending upon the source consulted. In the *Advocate*, August 5, 1852, pages 150-151, Sandy's birth year is shown as 1793, making him fifty-seven when he arrived in California, far too old to be used effectively in the goldfields. The slaves themselves responded to the census taker's questions in the California state census of 1852, which shows Sandy's age as forty! See California State Census, 1852, San Francisco County, s. v. "Robert Perkins," p. 34, line 31, accessed January 15, 2011, *Ancestry.com*. (All respondents, blacks included, in the 1852 *California* census appear showing name, age, birthplace, and last residence.) Even the meticulous William Perkins in four separate legal documents shows the master's difficulty in keeping track of his slaves and their ages. Sandy Jones appeared as a forty-year old and Patience as thirty in *Madison County Deeds, Book G*, microfilm roll 886078, 614, February, 1840. Two years later, Sandy was still shown as forty while Patience was forty-two (*Bolivar County Deed Book B*, microfilm roll 886085, 393, November 30, 1842). In February 1845 just three years later, Sandy was now forty-eight and Patience was forty-five (*Bolivar County Book C*, microfilm roll 886086, 11). In 1848 William recorded Sandy's age as forty-six and Patience's age as forty-eight (*Bolivar County Deed Book C*, microfilm roll 886086, 441, May 1848)! And finally on a customs document completed in 1850, Stephen Kirk listed Sandy's age as fifty. Regardless of his exact age, Sandy probably held the distinction of being one of the few working black grandfathers in the diggings.

spectively.[25] Perkins declared on the customs form he was transporting Andy, not as his owner, but as the agent for another. This statement, when combined with Andy's age and his name, could mean he was one of William Perkins' slaves; the light-skinned Andy (age forty-four in 1848) married to Margaret, and mentioned in several of Perkins loan collateral documents.[26]

Noteworthy are the ages and marital status of these five slaves. Four of the five were at least forty years old. Their advanced ages seem to defy the logic and wisdom of bringing younger slaves to the goldfields. However, more mature slaves would possibly be less troublesome and less likely to run off especially, if like Sandy, Robert, and Andy, they were married. Moreover, masters and slaves both realized an escape would effectively eliminate any chance the slaves could ever rejoin their families in Mississippi.

Arriving in Chagres the Perkins and Kirks, with their slaves, were delayed slightly but eventually managed to board a sailing vessel, the *Sarah*, on June 5, 1850.[27] The Kirks and A.G. Perkins found space in the ship's more comfortable cabins (see the *Sarah's* passenger list below), but the slaves and possibly W. B. Perkins made the journey in the oppressively hot steerage compartment. Sailing around the Cape (the longer route), the group

---

[25]*Outward Slave Manifests 1812-1860.*

[26]*Bolivar County Deed Book B,* November 30, 1842, 393, *Book C,* February 15, 1845, 11, and May 2, 1848, 441.

[27]In reporting the *Alabama's* departure from New Orleans in May, the *New Orleans Picayune* noted two unnamed "servants" traveling with A. G. and W. B. Perkins while the other three slaves were not listed at all next to the Kirks' names. The *Picayune* reported 187 passengers including servants on board. The author's recount of the names on the list revealed only 184 travelers. Presumably, the disparity meant that three of the Perkins-Kirk slaves had gone unrecorded in the newspaper. However, slaves Isaac, Willis, and Andy do not appear in any other sources after their mention in the New Orleans customs documents. Nor did Robert or Sandy mention them later when they spoke about their voyage to California. W. B. Perkins likewise disappears from the historical record after the *Alabama* arrived in Panama. No mention is made of him being aboard the *Sarah* or in California. The unanswered question is what became of Willis, Andy, Isaac, and W. B. Perkins?

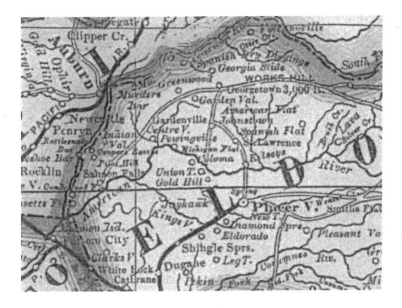

Map 4
In this 1883 map, El Dorado County, California, and Marshall's
gold discovery site at Coloma (near the map's center) are shown.
Charles Perkins and Carter mined in El Dorado County until approximately October 1850. The town of Ophir, where the three
slaves later worked from November 1851 to May 1852, lies in
Placer County in the upper left corner. (The railroad shown on the
map did not exist in 1852.) Library of Congress, Rand McNally.

arrived in San Francisco on August 19, seventy-five days later.[28]
     The sight of several blacks disembarking the *Sarah* in
1850 may not have elicited as much notice or surprise among
whites standing on the wharf that day as it would have in 1849
when Charles and Carter arrived in San Francisco. With the gold
discovery, California's black population, both slave and free, had
been increasing steadily, from a few dozen in 1848 to 600-700

---

[28]Louis Rasmussen, *San Francisco Ship Passenger Lists*, (Baltimore: Clearfield,
2002), II: 19. Whether or not A. G. Perkins knew or was related to Peter Hardeman Burnett, California's governor, is uncertain. Governor Burnett visited San
Francisco on August 21, 1850, just two days after Perkins' arrival (coincidence?),
staying at the city's St. Francis Hotel.

living in the Mother Lode in 1850. By 1852 more than 2,000 blacks lived in California.[29] (The white population, of course, also rose, but at a much faster rate.)

Some weeks later, in the gold country near Mormon Island, approximately thirty miles northeast of Sacramento (in Sacramento County) on or near the American River, Jonathan Kirk and A. G. Perkins staked their claim. Eager to find gold, they put the slaves to work almost immediately.[30] Having taken ill sometime during the journey to California, Stephen Kirk remained in Sacramento or San Francisco.

The results of the prospecting efforts of Kirk and A. G. Perkins (with their slaves) remain unknown. Most probably they did not enjoy the same measure of success as Charles Perkins, for they lacked his specialized knowledge of soil and minerals acquired at Princeton. As these new arrivals worked their claim, Charles Perkins with Carter was busy developing a new site in the gold country in hopes of further increasing his already substantial profits.

---

[29]Rudolph Lapp, *Blacks in Gold Rush California*, (New Haven: Yale University Press, 1977), 49, 50.

[30]Seventh Census, 1850, California, Sacramento County, s. v. "A. G. Perkins, Lines 35, 36," accessed July 25, 2011, *Family Search*, https://familysearch.org/pal:/MM9.3.1/TH-266-11073-66750-33?cc=1401638. Their names appeared on a census page next to other miners listed in the Mormon Island area. Just two "dwelling houses" below that of A. G. Perkins and Kirk in the November 1850 census record for Sacramento County was 'J. Stanford' of New York. This is Josiah Stanford, one of the Stanford brothers, who would soon forgo gold mining, open a store in Mormon Island, and later another in Sacramento on K Street with his brothers. One brother, Leland, later became governor of California. Given the proximity of Josiah to Perkins and Kirk, it is very possible the three men interacted as they panned for gold. Once Stanford's store opened at Mormon Island, its availability of goods made it an immensely popular establishment for supply-hungry miners like A. G. Perkins and Kirk. Thus, the possibility of additional contacts between the three men exists.

The Manifest of Slaves showing the names of slaves Robbin
(Robert Perkins) and Isaac bound for "San Francisco via Chagres"
on board the steamer *Alabama* dated May 10, 1850. Note John C.
Kirk's signature at the bottom right.[31]

Meanwhile, by October 5, 1850, some sixty-four miles
from Mormon Island, Charles and Carter Perkins had begun working a different claim, this one in Yuba County. Located just north
of Placer County and close to their old diggings in El Dorado
County, the Yuba region offered the pair new opportunities in
their search for gold. They may have worked the Yuba River, pan-
ning near Long Bar twenty miles east of Marysville. By this time
Charles, now twenty-three years old, and Carter twenty (but
shown as nineteen in the census), could be termed experienced
miners having spent close to a year in the goldfields.

Not only did Charles work side by side with his black
slave, but in the goldfields they also lived together. Described as
miners in the 1850 census, Charles and Carter shared a "dwelling
house" (tent) with fifteen others. The enumerator erroneously recorded the surname 'Black' for Carter, the only Negro in the

---

[31]*Outward Slave Manifests 1812-1860.*

group, without designating him a slave.[32] The fact that a Negro slave, Carter, shared a tent with whites (including eight born in slave states) and his master illustrates how the rough and tumble life of Sierra-Nevada miners, far from the restrictive atmosphere of Southern plantations, could weaken previously established social barriers. Undoubtedly, these men did not accept Carter as an equal, but this unique cohabitation between a slave and whites would have been virtually unheard of in the South.

Another sheet from the *Alabama's* Manifest, also dated May 10, 1850, showing Sandy (Jones). S. J. Kirk (bottom, lower left) is shown as an *agent* for the slave's owner (Charles Perkins).

---

[32]Seventh Census, 1850, California, Yuba County, s. v. "C. L. Perkins," (The "S" representing Charles' middle name in the enumerator's handwriting appears to be an "L"), Lines 18, 20, accessed July 25, 2011, *Family Search*. In the United States Census of 1850 for California (a free state) there were no slave schedules. Enslaved blacks like Carter thus appeared *by name* in a census for the *first* time in their lives.

The *Sarah's* passenger list, excluding the 166 unnamed steerage passengers, as it appeared in the *Alta* on August 20, 1850, upon its arrival in San Francisco. Note the names of A G Perkins and two names later the incorrect middle initial and spelling of what should be S J Kirk. J C Kirby is most likely Jonathan C. Kirk.

     In either October or November 1850, Jonathan Kirk and A. G. Perkins turned Robert Perkins and Sandy Jones over to Charles Perkins.[33] Specifically, the transfer occurred after the Yuba County census (October 5, 1850) but before the November 30 Sacramento County tally, as neither of the two slaves appears in either census record. For the next five or six months, Charles would benefit from the labor of not one, but three slaves. At some point his cousin, A. G. Perkins, may have joined him in Yuba County.

     On November 30, 1850, the Kirk brothers aborted their brief stay in California and began their return journey to Mississippi. Though Jonathan Kirk would have preferred to remain in California, Stephen's worsening illness dictated they make an early departure. Leaving A. G. Perkins and Charles Perkins behind, the two brothers left on the Panama-bound steamer *Oregon*. Both understood that by returning home they were denying themselves a great opportunity to acquire wealth in the goldfields.[34]

---

[33]*Advocate*, August 5, 1852, 150-151.

[34]Curiously, both Kirk brothers appear on the steamer *Oregon's* passenger list on November 30, 1850, the same day Jonathan Kirk was counted in the Sacramento

Sadly, Stephen Kirk would never see Mississippi again, as he died aboard ship in sight of New Orleans shortly before its arrival on January 10, 1851. He was buried at Stop Landing, Mississippi, on the property of relatives there, next to the Perkins' plantation.[35]

* * * * *

Meanwhile, as Charles sought to add to his already considerable earnings in the goldfields with the additional labor provided by Sandy and Robert, daily life in Mississippi continued for the Perkins family that late summer and fall of 1850. With the county's continued absence of educational facilities, Charles' younger brothers even now were either tutored in the Perkins' home or attended school outside of the county. The Perkins' oldest daughter Jane, still single, remained on the plantation. William had recently learned that the Canton Masons Lodge had "demitted" Charles, a member since 1848, for non-attendance.[36] In August 1850, with Jane and the children visiting in Tennessee, William Perkins had gone downriver, then inland, to visit his Hardeman relatives.

On the morning of August 23, at his cousin Ann Hardeman's plantation just a few miles south of Jackson, he began the return journey to Bolivar County and "his residence on the river."[37] William felt compelled to return home to personally oversee, as was his custom, the upcoming cotton harvest.

County census. Peter E. Carr, *San Francisco Passenger Departure Lists*, (San Bernardino, California: The Cuban Index, 1991), 1: 48.

[35]Sillers, *History of Bolivar County*, 461. On their return voyage, the Kirks journeyed across the Isthmus, boarded a steamer for Havana, then once in Havana they booked passage on the *Pacific* for the journey to New Orleans. The total elapsed time for this shorter route was forty-two days from San Francisco. Find the Kirk's arrival in New Orleans online at "Passengers Arriving at the Port of New Orleans January 1, thru July 7, 1851," *Louisiana Secretary of State*, accessed May 27, 2011, http://www.sos.louisiana.gov/tabid/248/Default.aspx. Click on 'passenger text' and scroll down to find the Kirk brothers (incorrectly shown as D. C. and S. A. Kirk) listed alphabetically on the *Pacific* on January 10, 1851.

[36]Charles had joined the Canton Lodge as a twenty-one year old. He had retained a residence in Canton until sometime in early to mid 1849.

[37]O'Brien, *An Evening*, 223.

On the Mound Plantation, a beehive of activity soon prevailed, as the fields, beginning to turn white with cotton, signaled the beginning of the picking season. That fall the crop must have been considerable given that even though William owned 166 slaves, he still required additional help with the harvest. Ann Hardeman noted that on a fine fall day she "started ten hands up to cousin Wm P.'s [Perkins] to pick out cotton."[38]

Apart from these domestic and plantation matters, William Perkins and other Mississippians during 1850 wrestled with several sectional issues that had grabbed the nation's attention and were then being discussed and debated in the press, on plantations, at dinner tables, and in Mississippi cities like Jackson, Vicksburg, and Greenville. Earlier, Pennsylvania Congressman David Wilmot in his memorable and controversial proviso had proposed that Congress *ban the spread of slavery into the territories acquired from Mexico*. Though it was defeated in 1846 and again in 1847, the proviso remained stuck in the craw of many Southerners, arousing alarm and resentment. In turn, items linking the expansion of slavery and California (acquired from Mexico) appeared in local Mississippi newspapers.

William may have read the *Jackson Mississippian's* article of April 1, 1850, titled, "California, the Southern Slave Colony." Defying Wilmot's suggestion and written before California attained statehood, the article requested that citizens of the slave-holding states desirous of migrating to California send their names, number of slaves, and departure date to Southern Slave Colony, Jackson, Mississippi. The organizers hoped to settle 5,000 whites with their 10,000 slaves in the richest mining and agricultural regions of California and "to secure the uninterrupted enjoyment of slave property."[39] Though Perkins left no record of his stance on this expansion issue, it is logical to assume that as a dedicated slaveholder he would support any opportunity for slav-

---

[38]Ibid., Wednesday, October 9, 1850, 225. In rare instances like this where slaves journeyed to another plantation, some had the opportunity (albeit brief) to converse with other slaves apart from their own plantations and exchange news or perhaps pass verbal messages from friends or relatives who remained behind.
[39]Hubert Howe Bancroft, *Western American History*, (New York: Bancroft Company, 1902), 23: pt. 6, 313, fn. The article also appeared in Sacramento's *Placer Times* on May 1, 1850, so Charles Perkins may have also read it.

ery to extend its boundaries. This grand colonizing scheme was soon thwarted, though, under the terms of the Compromise of 1850.

Later that year in September, with the passage of the Compromise of 1850, a division in the Southern states again developed between those satisfied with the Compromise and those who opposed allowing California to enter the Union as a free state without any reciprocal action regarding a new slave state. According to a contemporary observer in Mississippi and later a Bolivar County resident, the feelings in the Southern states both for and against the compromise measures ran highest in Mississippi and South Carolina.[40]

Many Mississippians feared that allowing a free California to enter the Union would upset the existing balance between free and slave states, so important in the Senate where bills regarding slavery must eventually arrive for a vote.[41] As a result, Mississippi's so-called "fire eaters" or ardent secessionists, pursuing their hard line feelings, issued a radical call for the establishment of a "separate slaveholding Confederacy." For nearly a year, the sectional debate and pro and anti secessionist rhetoric dominated Mississippi politics (calls for disunion were also heard in Georgia and later South Carolina), while the Perkins family most certainly also struggled with this controversy. Months later in 1851, in a defeat for secessionism, Mississippi's Unionists had prevailed, pushing the secessionist threat temporarily aside, at least until another sectional controversy erupted.

During the sixteen months since Charles had left for California his family's only contact with him had been his letters from the goldfields. However, when their neighbor Jonathan Kirk returned from California unexpectedly in early January 1851, the

---

[40]Frank A. Montgomery, *Reminiscences of a Mississippian in Peace and War*, (Cincinnati: The Robert Clarke Press, 1901), 8-9.

[41]Votes in the Senate had increasingly taken on a sectional bias, as Senators from the antislavery North and proslavery South tended to vote according to their views on slavery. The 'compromise' portion provided for a tough new Fugitive Slave Law to assist slave owners in capturing runaways in the North. In addition, Utah and New Mexico would allow the slavery question there to be decided by popular sovereignty (a vote of the people) – another effort to placate the South.

Perkins family may have received verbal news of their son via
Kirk and certainly any letters Charles may have entrusted to Kirk
to convey to his family. Both parents anticipated the day that their
oldest son would rejoin them in Mississippi. For William Perkins
that happy day would never arrive.

By late October 1850 with Charles still in California, William Perkins battled a serious illness. Ann Hardeman noted in her
diary on October 25, "My bror [the Canton banker William Hardeman of Madison County,] & wife went up on the River to see
cousin Wm P. Perkins - who is very ill accompanied by Dr [J. J.]
Pugh, his wife [Perkins' daughter Ann] & two children Joseph [J.
Jr.] and the youngest Sally Jane [one year old]."[42] Once they realized the seriousness of William's condition, the Hardemans remained at the Mound Plantation for several more days. William's
brother Nicholas and his wife Mary, recently arrived from Tennessee, joined the family in a bedside vigil. Charles, 2,000 miles away
in California, would remain unaware of his father's illness for several weeks.

William suffered from dengue fever, a viral illness trans-
mitted by a mosquito bite.[43] Swarms of the pests filled the sloughs
and bayous in the bottomlands on and near the Mound Plantation
where William had possibly been bitten. (As William lay ill and
bedridden, a dengue outbreak was being reported in Vicksburg,
downriver from Bolivar County.) By early November William's
condition continued to deteriorate.

On Saturday, November 9, 1850, the Federal Census
taker, D. B. Hudson, called at the Mound Plantation. He dutifully
recorded the Perkins family members, including the ailing William, along with William's visiting brother and sister-in-law.[44]
Hudson next contacted Paquinette, the overseer, and managed to
complete a partial count of eighty-five of the 166 slaves on the
Perkins plantation, indicating he would return on Tuesday the
twelfth to complete his tally of the remaining slaves.

---

[42]O'Brien, *An Evening*, 225.
[43]Ibid., 226.
[44]Appendix B. The Pughs, present at William's bedside in Bolivar County then,
would be counted in the Madison County, Mississippi, census enumerated on
December 1, 1850.

Later that same day, in the chilly evening hours between nine and ten with his family at his bedside and with maybe a fire burning in the fireplace, William Price Perkins passed away, the deadly fever having claimed yet another victim. Cousin Ann Hardeman noted that William had been a very dear friend of her two brothers.[45] The noted Methodist Reverend Lewell Campbell of Vicksburg who "attended cousin Wm. P. Perkins in his last illness preached his funeral on Wednesday [the thirteenth] and [he] was buried on Friday [the fifteenth]" in the family cemetery on the picturesque summit of "one of the three [actually four] Indian mounds" in the middle of the Mound Plantation cotton fields.[46] Back in the 1840s, when he had selected the cemetery's location, William had no way of knowing that he would be the first to be interred there.

On November 6, just days before his death William, still tending to business from his sickbed, had reduced by one the number of slaves he owned. On that day a very weak William reached out to his six-year old grandson: "In consideration of the love and affection" he bore for Joseph J. Pugh Jr., William then legally signed off on the transfer of Grandville, a ten-year old, copper-colored, Negro boy, to Joseph Jr.[47] With the best of intentions, William had formally presented a death bed gift to his beloved grandson while at the same time effectively separating the slave from any family he may have had in Bolivar County. Grandville's life would now be spent with the Pugh family in Madison County or farther away at their other home in Louisiana. For William, even in his last hours, slaves remained property to barter, sell, use as collateral, or gifts.

With William's passing the Mound Plantation came under the direction of Mrs. Perkins. Later, when he returned from California, Charles assumed the duties of head of household and plantation manager. During the first months of this transition period, Jane may have relied heavily on the management experience of overseer Paquinette. However, not long after William's death, the

---

[45]O'Brien, *An Evening*, 226. A little more than a month later William's older brother, Harden Perkins, died in Alabama at age fifty-nine.

[46]Ibid. See also *Biographical and Historical Memoirs of Mississippi*, 586.

[47]*Bolivar County Deed Book D*, microfilm roll 886086, 84-85.

Pugh family temporarily moved in with Ann's grieving mother, not only to console her, but also to assist in running the plantation until Charles returned. Anne Hardeman wrote on November 24, 1850, that the Pughs had planned their move there from Madison County soon after William's death: "Dr. and Mrs. Pugh called on their return home from Chocktaw [sp] Bend the residence of her late Father they expect to move up there after the first of Jan."[48] The Pughs and their children subsequently remained with the widowed Mrs. Perkins at the Mound Plantation well into the spring of 1851.[49]

Following William's death Mrs. Jane Perkins assumed the role of administrator of the estate. A group of commissioners, though, controlled the actual distribution of real and personal property according to William's wishes.[50] Each of William's living heirs (his wife and children) received a part of the inheritance, while Jane oversaw the interests of her minor children, Noland S. and James W. Records show that parts of the divided Mound Plantation lands were known as Southland Plantation, specifically those allotted to heirs Charles Perkins, daughter Jane, and Daniel Perkins.[51] Though no legal record from 1850 exists to support this supposition, William most likely willed his 166 slaves to his wife Jane and/or to his children. By 1860, however, documents reveal that the slaves indeed had been divided among several of the Perkins children.

William Perkins, for his entire life, had enjoyed the benefits of a refined Southern slaveholding heritage and the planter lifestyle existent for generations in his family. Slavery had been a focal part of his life from his childhood in Virginia and Tennessee until his death in Mississippi. The buying and selling of slaves and

---

[48]O'Brien, *An Evening*, 227.

[49]"Mississippi Enumeration of Educable Children, 1850-1892, Bolivar," accessed August 1, 2011, *Family Search*, https://www.familysearch.org/search/collection/show#uri=http://www.familysear ch.org/searchapi/search/collection/1856425. The three children between six and eighteen years of "Dr. Pugh" are listed next to the two minor children of "Mrs. Perkins."

[50]*Bolivar County Deed Book F*, FHL, microfilm roll 886087, 219-220, February 7, 1857.

[51]Ibid.

the daily operation of a plantation utilizing slave labor were second nature to him. The lessons learned from his stint in the military under Colonels Benton and Pillow and General Jackson lent order and stability to his life and consequently to the several plantations he had managed for thirty years. He was the consummate parent, planter, entrepreneur, and slaveholder responsible in taking care of both his family and his financial obligations. William, despite his wealth and prestige, seems to have preferred a life out of the public eye, avoiding politics altogether except for a brief stint with the Bolivar County Board of Police. He did not shy away, however, from using the courts/legal system to his advantage. Respected by family and community, William now rested in the very soil that had helped bring such prosperity to his family. He had left Jane and the children in a very comfortable financial position with his land holdings in various counties, more than 160 slaves, a fine house, and vast cotton fields on his 2,000 or more acres in Bolivar County. In death, as in life, William had always been a good provider.[52]

* * * * *

Unaware of his father's passing in Mississippi that November, Charles Perkins, with his three slaves, continued working his claim in the goldfields. Up to this point, Charles' exact relationship with Carter in California is unknown. Given the vague

---

[52]Jane Perkins, in November 1852, accumulated paperwork she would eventually need to file a widow's land claim for William's War of 1812 service. On November 17, 1852, a Wilkinson County justice of the peace attested to Jane's statement of William's service as a sergeant in Captain McEwen's Company during the War of 1812 and also to the fact that William and Jane had been legally married in Mississippi since 1818. Almost three years later, in March 1855, Congress passed "An Act in Addition to Certain Acts Granting Bounty Land to Certain Officers and Soldiers Who Have Engaged in the Military Service of the United States." The widowed Jane Perkins thus received title to 160 acres of land based on William's rank and length of war service. Possibly acting on the advice of son Charles who may have visited the area during his time in California, Jane selected 160 acres in Franklin Township, Elk Grove, California. Located approximately seventeen miles south of Sacramento in the flat and fertile Sacramento Valley, the acreage Jane selected resembled land in Bolivar County. Jane had no thoughts of creating a Mound Plantation west, though the area is conducive to cotton growing even today. Instead, she chose to assign (sell) the land warrant, a common practice of land grant recipients.

legal status of a slave residing in a free state, Carter could well have used this uncertainty to perhaps modify in some way the master-slave relationship more to his advantage. Charles also may have dangled the promise of emancipation before Carter, either in Mississippi or upon their October arrival in California, to ensure Carter's loyalty. He may have been motivated to do so (or at least considered it) almost immediately upon their arrival, because in November 1849 California, in anticipation of its admission to the Union, adopted its first constitution, *as a free state*. This decision inserted another dynamic into not only the master-slave relationship between Charles and Carter but also between other forty-niners and their slaves statewide. Carter's youth and unmarried status -- two characteristics of a potential runaway – perhaps also weighed on Perkins' mind. Likewise, with Charles and his slave spending weeks, months, and now a year working side by side - a first for any Perkins master with his slave – a less authoritarian relationship on Charles' part may have evolved. One slaveholder lamented, "Negroes in California are not the same that they are at home by a long gap."[53] The question arises also as to the nature of conversations Charles and Carter must have had as they panned for gold and sat around innumerable campfires during their months together in the gold country.

Anther outside factor may also have influenced Charles' thinking. Certainly, living with Carter among large numbers of antislavery white northerners (seven whites from free states shared their dwelling, according to the 1850 census) had to have some effect on Charles. This is not to say he felt pangs of conscience regarding slaveholding, but instead Charles may have sensed 'pressure' from the antislavery men he encountered. Thus, this unique California gold rush world Perkins and his kindred gold-field slaveholders experienced may have emerged as a force compelling them to restructure relationships with their slaves. Not long after Robert and Sandy joined him in November 1850, and upon hearing of his father's death, Charles appears to have made plans for his three slaves once he left California.

---

[53]Stacey L. Smith, "Remaking Slavery in a Free State: Masters and Slaves in Gold Rush California," *Pacific Historical Review*, 80: No. 1, (2011), 48.

During his time in California Perkins, by April 1851, had accumulated a great amount of gold dust due in large part to the efforts of Carter (eighteen months in the goldfields), Robert, and Sandy (six months mining labor for Charles). At some point Charles had received the news of his father's death five months earlier.[54] Later that April Perkins planned for his return to Mississippi. Prior to leaving the goldfields, he turned the slaves over to a local twenty-six year old doctor, John N. Hill of Missouri (a slave state), *perhaps* with an agreement that they would work for Hill for a specified amount of time and then he (Hill) would set them free.[55]

Hill and Perkins may have met earlier when Charles first arrived in California. Hill appears in the 1850 census (enumerated late, on February 4, 1851) at Mosquito Canyon in El Dorado County, the same county where Charles and Carter had first begun prospecting soon after their arrival.[56] The fact that Charles left in Hill's custody his three slaves worth more than $1,000 each in Mississippi indicates that he and the Doctor must have developed a strong bond of trust in the months since they became acquainted.

Shortly thereafter on May 1, 1851, Charles Perkins, now in San Francisco, boarded the Panama-bound steamer *Union*, the first step of his long return voyage to Mississippi.[57] Charles' grand adventure had proven successful. He was returning to Mississippi wealthier, having conquered hardship in the rugged goldfields, and proving he was every inch a 'Perkins' man in the tradition of his father and grandfathers. The only untoward event of his nearly two-year long exploit had been the unexpected death of his father. Leaving California behind Charles undoubtedly reflected on his

---

[54]Cole, *Essays,* III: Box 29, Folder 2, 7.

[55]*Advocate*, August 5, 1852, 150-151 and the *Sacramento Daily Union*, June 3, 1852, 2.

[56]Seventh Census 1850, California, El Dorado County, s. v. "John N. Hill," line 12, *Family Search*, accessed May 1, 2011, https://familysearch.org/pal:/MM9.3.1/TH-267-11119-93268-15?cc=1401638. All those listed on the census sheet with Dr. Hill are miners, so the counting was done in the goldfields.

[57]Carr, San *Francisco Departure Lists,* 2: 65, s. v. "Perkins, C. S." on the list of passengers. Several weeks later on July 4, 1851, on a different voyage the *Union* went ashore 300 miles south of San Diego resulting in a total loss.

recent accomplishments while also anticipating the new challenges ahead - assuming the twin roles of plantation owner and head of the Perkins family, hefty responsibilities for a man in his early twenties.

With their former master now departed, the three slaves set to work for Dr. Hill. Since Charles had transferred the three to Hill in April 1851, just weeks after the Doctor had been counted in the El Dorado County census, they may have worked for Hill there on his claim in Mosquito Canyon.[58] Any money the three may have generated during their time in the goldfields had always gone to either the now-departed Kirks or Charles Perkins. Now, Dr. Hill became the latest beneficiary of their labors. Some seven months later, though, the three men experienced an unbelievable, life-altering event.

On November 15, 1851, Dr. Hill freed Carter, Robert, and Sandy. Later, in notes written during his first interview with the slaves, attorney Cornelius Cole recorded, "Hill then *told* them [the slaves] to go, that their time was out [italics mine]."[59] Ominously, should any white authorities later question the former slaves' freedom, their lack of any supporting documentation to that effect would place them in serious jeopardy.

The three former slaves soon settled in Placer County near the Auburn Ravine and the bustling town of Ophir, California. Located approximately thirty miles northeast of Sacramento, Ophir in 1852 had emerged as the county's most populated town (Map 4). Its 500 citizens made use of the bank, three express companies including a Wells Fargo office, eight retail stores, three hotels, four saloons, two bakeries, and a drug store. Given the success Robert, Carter, and Sandy were about to achieve there, the three must have found the city to their liking.

The strong possibility exists that soon after their emancipation Robert Perkins and Sandy Jones, both family men, were

---

[58]Weeks before Hill took charge of the three slaves, a very astute Federal Census taker recorded Hill's presence in El Dorado County. To the last column on his sheet the enumerator added the following novel heading: *"average value of each miner's daily product."* Most men, including Hill, responded they were earning $5 per day. Some reported $2 per day. Seventh Census, 1850, California, El Dorado County, s. v. "John N. Hill," line 12, *Family Search.*
[59]Cole's notes, Naglee Family Collection.

motivated by the hope they could accumulate enough money in California to eventually purchase the freedom of their enslaved families in Mississippi. Soon, they acquired a four-mule team, harness, and wagon worth nearly $700, deriving the capital for these expenditures from prospecting.[60] In the ensuing months and with winter approaching, the trio began hauling freight to supplement their mining income. Providing that the color of their skin did not pose a barrier to business opportunities, the three blacks' chances for success apart from mining would have been good with "four and six horse teams constantly running between this place [Ophir] and the city [Sacramento?] bringing up commodities sufficient to satisfy all the possible wants of our inhabitants."[61] As experienced blacksmiths, Robert and Sandy may also have earned money using those special skills learned on the Perkins plantation.

According to a later edition of the *Placer Herald*, the winter of 1851-2 was one in which "miners . . . were generally very successful and many new diggings were discovered in the vicinity [of Ophir]. . . ."[62] Because it was located at a lower elevation on the fringes of the Sierras, Ophir often received less snowfall than diggings elsewhere, thus allowing hearty prospectors to occasionally work through the winter. Robert, Carter, and Sandy may well have taken advantage of this good fortune to further increase their earnings. Records later indicated that by May 1852 they had more than $650 in gold dust in their possession.

Since Dr. Hill had emancipated them in November, the former slaves appear to have adjusted quite well to this oddly unfamiliar, yet joyous world of personal freedom. However, as the months passed and as the three blacks began growing accustomed to their independence (and having money in their pockets), the California Assembly and Senate in Sacramento debated a controversial bill that, if passed, would jeopardize not only these three freed men but also hundreds of the now approximately 2,000 other blacks statewide.

---

[60]*Advocate*, August 5, 1852, 150-151, and Cole, *Essays*, III: Box 29, Folder 2, 8. The *Advocate* reported the three men paid taxes on $500 for the wagon and mules.
[61]*The Weekly Placer Herald* (Auburn), September 18, 1852, 4.
[62]Ibid.

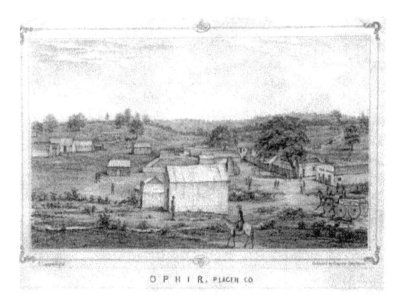

O P H I R, PLACER CO

Early view shown on a California Pictorial Letter Sheet of Ophir,
Placer County, California, where Robert and Carter Perkins and
Sandy Jones lived and worked as free men from November 1851
until May 1852. Ophir was reduced to ashes in an August 1853
fire and is now long extinct. Courtesy of the Bancroft Library,
University of California, Berkeley

VII

The Fugitives

If a man aid a male or female slave of the palace, or a male or female slave of a freedman to escape from the city gate, he shall be put to death.

Code of Hammurabi

Thou shalt not deliver unto his master the servant which is escaped from his master unto thee: He shall dwell with thee, even among you, in that place which he shall choose in one of thy gates, where it liketh him best: thou shalt not oppress him.

Deuteronomy 23:15-16

By 1852, admitted as a free state under the terms of the Compromise of 1850, California had been part of the Union for two years. Nonetheless, California's pro and antislavery factions remained at odds and the state legislature, also divided along sectional lines, reflected the equally divided Congress in Washington, D. C. Though California's constitution had outlawed slavery, the institution remained a simmering legal problem fueled by the contradiction that slaves resided there on free soil. Furthermore, California's antislavery constitution never addressed the problem created by the presence of those slaves brought by their masters into California *before* its adoption.

As a result in January of that year, a transplanted, twenty-eight year old, proslavery lawyer from Nashville, Tennessee, Henry Crabb, introduced to his fellow California assemblymen a strongly worded fugitive slave bill.[1] Part of his motivation in doing so may have been linked to his frustration in seeing some slaves previously brought into California by their masters success-

---

[1] Crabb represented San Joaquin County (near Sacramento) in the state Assembly. His family had roots in Nashville, and it is possible the Crabb family was acquainted with the Perkins clan in Tennessee. Crabb's father was a local judge and also a trustee of Cumberland College from 1816 (while William Perkins was enrolled there) until 1827. Henry Crabb practiced law in Vicksburg, Mississippi, from 1847 to 1849 while Charles Perkins resided in close by Madison County during part of that same period. Crabb appeared in the 1850 California census not far from Sacramento, in Stockton.

fully sue for their freedom.[2] Crabb's bill would supplement, but not duplicate, the Federal Fugitive Slave Law that applied only to slaves who escaped across state lines into free states. His bill gave white men broad powers in returning blacks deemed slaves to Southern states. Specifically, one key provision *denied testimony to accused fugitives* at their hearing before a magistrate. Section 4 of the bill declared that anyone held to labor in any state or territory of the United States then brought to California prior to her admission "*shall be held and deemed a fugitive from labor*" if the individual refused to return to the state where he owed service (in other words a return to slavery).[3]

The phrasing of Section 4 described Carter, Robert, and Sandy's situation exactly. Each had entered California prior to its admission on September 9, 1850. Carter had arrived in 1849 while Robert and Sandy entered California in August 1850.

After the bill's passage in the Assembly, the state Senate, "in session until long after candlelight," debated and then passed it by a fourteen to nine vote on April 9, 1852. (The new law would take effect on April 15). The vote that night yielded two results. It served to jeopardize the already precarious and legally questionable status of the state's slaves and alleged fugitive slaves, while at the same time it empowered their masters.

A few newspapers went on record regarding this unique California statute. The *Advocate*, referred to the law as both "unjust" and "unconstitutional."[4] San Francisco's *Daily Alta California* labeled it an "objectionable law", then commented, "The major portion of it is a useless and infelicitous attempt to re-enact the [Federal] Fugitive Slave Law passed by the last Congress [of 1850]." Continuing, the paper declared, "But to the last section [four, see above] there is the most pertinent and strong ground of complaint. The effect of it is to virtually establish slavery in this State for one year from the date of its passage. . . ." Anticipating an imminent legal struggle in some future test case over the law's

---

[2]*Daily Alta California*, April 2, 1851, 2, "County Court." A slave, Frank, brought into California by his master was set free because he (the slave) did not fall under the provisions of the Federal Fugitive Slave Law.
[3]S. Garfielde and F. A. Snyder, compilers, *Compiled Laws of the State of California*, (Benicia, California: S. Garfielde, 1853), 231-233.
[4]*Advocate*, June 10, 1852, 118.

provisions, the paper also predicted, "there can be no doubt that the section [four] of the proposed law would not be able to stand the test of an adjudication by the Supreme Court. . . ."[5]

On April 14, 1852, the day before the law took effect in California, Charles Perkins, having safely returned to Bolivar County in the summer of 1851, visited Jackson, Mississippi. Aware that prime field hands were then selling for more than $1,000 in Mississippi, Charles had evidently changed his mind on any arrangement he may have made with his three slaves - he now intended to initiate a legal process to recover them. Perhaps Perkins had received word within weeks of the California Assembly's opening debate on the bill, back on February 7, 1852, and he may have viewed it as the means to reclaim his slaves should the bill become law. Charles may have also been influenced in his decision to pursue this matter because his father had used the courts successfully on at least two occasions, in the case of the slave girl Lucinda and in the U.S. Supreme Court hearing with his cousin William Hardeman.

In Jackson Perkins appeared at the office of the brilliant jurist Judge William Yerger. A Tennessee-born slaveholder of sixty-five slaves in 1850, Yerger had graduated from Cumberland College in Nashville. No stranger to the Perkins family, Yerger had previous ties to the Perkins clan in Franklin, Tennessee, and then in Mississippi.[6]

Charles, however, had not called upon Yerger merely for a social visit. Using his family's close ties to the judge, he obtained a document from Yerger naming Albert G. Perkins of Sacramento City his true and lawful attorney. To lend additional authority to the matter, Charles had opted not just for any magistrate, but instead he had sought out Justice Yerger, a distinguished jurist seated on Mississippi's High Court of Errors and Appeals (Supreme Court), to complete the power of attorney paper.

---

[5] *Weekly Alta California,* April 10, 1852, 2, column 3. In an earlier article, printed on February 18, 1852, the *Alta* had labeled the bill "a useless incumbrance [sic] upon the Statute Book."

[6] In addition to being acquainted with William Perkins, the Judge also knew Ann Hardeman, William's cousin, who lived near Jackson, and Perkins' son in law Dr. J. J. Pugh of Livingston. Yerger and Pugh had served on the same railroad planning committee in Jackson.

The document authorized Charles' cousin, Albert Green (A. G.) Perkins, to "sue for and use all legal means to recover possession of the following named slaves . . . Carter, Sandy, and Robin [Robert] from any person or persons in whose possession or employment said slaves may be."[7] Based on this phrase, it is evident Charles remained unaware that the three blacks were now free and worked for themselves. At the same time, Charles Perkins could never have imagined his efforts to reclaim his human "property" would stir up a legal hornet's nest in California.

Meanwhile, a month earlier in March 1852, Harden Scales, age thirty-six, and his younger brother Thomas, twenty-three, left their Davidson County, Tennessee, home near Nashville bound for the California goldfields. Unmarried, both men worked as farmers and resided at the family plantation with their parents and several siblings. Their mother, Sarah Price Perkins Scales was a cousin to William P. Perkins, making Charles Perkins their cousin as well. (The Scales family connection to the Perkins clan resembled that of the Perkins-Hardeman families in that intermarriage between Scales and Perkins folks dated back several decades to Virginia, then Tennessee.) Whether the Scales brothers originally planned to search for gold or if Charles Perkins had asked their help in recovering his three slaves in California is uncertain. Not nearly as affluent as their Perkins Mississippi cousins (their father Robert Scales claimed forty-six slaves in 1850), the two brothers may have relished the opportunity for adventure and money through work of any kind. In any event by late April, they had arrived in San Francisco from New Orleans, via Panama.[8]

Nearly five weeks later, just before midnight on Monday, May 31, 1852, Harden Scales, along with Placer County's first Sheriff, the tall, muscular, hard drinking, Alabama-born Samuel Asten, "usually cool, collected and good natured - afraid of no

---

[7]Power of Attorney, C. S. Perkins, April 14, 1852, *In re Perkins* Case File (California State Archives, Sacramento), copy in author's possession.
[8]*Advocate*, August 5, 1852, 150-151. An H. Scales and another Scales (Thomas?) appear on the *Winfield Scott's* passenger manifest of April 28, 1852, when it arrived in San Francisco. See Rasmussen, *Ship Passenger Lists*, III: 167, 171. Harden Scales' given name was Giles, but apparently he preferred Harden.

man,"[9] arrived at a darkened cabin near Ophir, Placer County. Accompanying them were Constable James Ross, John Hubank, a miner named Woods, A. G. Perkins, and probably Harden's brother Thomas Scales. With the two Scales brothers and Perkins' cousin A. G. Perkins involved, the slaves' apprehension now became a family affair, with potentially as many as four Perkins relatives participating in the arrest that night.[10] Sheriff Asten may have welcomed their assistance, reasoning that a show of force, six or seven armed men arresting three, might prevent any resistance the blacks might offer. Based on the legal demand of Charles Perkins, their task was to arrest Carter Perkins, Robert Perkins, and Sandy Jones now deemed fugitives under the recently enacted California Fugitive Slave Law.

Bursting into their cabin, Asten and the others surprised the three sleeping men. A. G. Perkins provided Sheriff Asten with positive identification of the trio. After binding two of the three prisoners securely and under cover of darkness, Sheriff Asten and the others hurried the blacks away by a circuitous route to avoid contact with any of their friends. Forcing the third black to drive and using their (the blacks') own wagon and team, the disparate group set out for Sacramento.

Prior to leaving the cabin with the three prisoners, Harden Scales confiscated the blacks' money and gold dust and gave it to A. G. Perkins. A subsequent claim filed on their behalf to recover this property attested to the prosperity they had enjoyed since Hill released them in November 1851. Later, on Sunday June 6, it was noted in a jailhouse interview with the three that at the time of their arrest, "Sandy had in his private purse $230 in [gold] dust and Robert a little more than $200 of his own" along with $426 in gold dust in the 'company' purse. Also, "they all have money due them at & about Ophir" for work they had provided on credit.[11] Later, a final accounting revealed their total loss had increased

[9]"Pioneers of Placer County," in the *Placer Herald*, October 9, 1937, *Placer County Gen Web*, accessed September 22, 2011, http://www.cagenweb.com/placer/pioneers.htm.
[10]'Hubank' may actually have been Eubank, and maybe a Perkins relative from Hinds County, Mississippi.
[11]*Advocate*, August 5, 1852, 150-151 and Naglee Family Collection, MR 552.

dramatically. Confiscated and never returned were $1,000 in gold and money, four mules and a wagon valued at $1,200 and $1,000 in other property, a total of $3,200.[12]

Bound for Sacramento, Sheriff Asten and Constable Ross accompanied the group for some ten miles until Tuesday morning. At that point, they reached the Sacramento County line where Asten's jurisdiction ended. Asten and Ross then returned to Ophir leaving Harden Scales, Woods, Perkins, Hubank, and perhaps Thomas Scales to complete the journey.[13] By Tuesday evening the blacks and their captors had arrived in Sacramento, having taken the better part of a day to travel the thirty-five miles from Ophir.[14]

Upon arrival, A. G. Perkins and Scales seemingly would have been very anxious to immediately convey the slaves to Sacramento's legal authorities. Instead, they took the unusual step of first paying an evening call to Dr. E. M. Patterson. A fifty-two year old Nashville, Tennessee, slaveholder, Patterson had lived in California for only a few months. Married in Williamson County, Tennessee, in 1826, Patterson most likely was familiar to the Perkins and Scales families residing there. Since Dr. Patterson was the first person Perkins and the Scales men sought out in Sacra-

---

[12]Cole Papers, Department of Special Collections, University of California, Los Angeles, District Court 6th Judicial District, *Perkins, Perkins, and Jones v A. G. (Green) Perkins*, June 7, 1852. In retelling this episode years later, Cole alleged someone in the arresting party burned the freedom papers Dr. Hill had provided. Cole, *Essays*, 9. However, his recollection of the event is so fraught with errors that this may or may not be true.

[13]Naglee Family Collection, MR 552.

[14]In the 1980s non-fiction film titled *Minority Pioneers, A Western Anthem*, an actor portrayed an apparently actual 1850s California gold miner. According to the film, the miner, Tom Moore, had previously lived in Ireland and New York before arriving in California in an unspecified year. Moore's age is also unknown. During the course of the film "Moore" stated he had *taken over a claim previously worked by three slaves whose master had reclaimed them.* Believing this to be a reference to the Perkins slaves, the author in the ensuing years attempted unsuccessfully to locate a copy of the film, a transcript of its dialog, and a list of the sources consulted. The author also attempted to locate, again without success, a diary Moore supposedly had written during his time in California. The closest reference to Tom Moore appears in the 1852 Yuba County, California, census (the same county where Charles Perkins had prospected and near Placer County where the slaves were arrested). In that record the name of a twenty-four year old miner, Thomas Moore, previously from *Ireland* and *New York*, appears.

mento, it follows that they, too, were well aware of him, and that perhaps one or more of the slaves had been injured during the arrest and were now in need of medical attention.

Following this meeting with Dr. Patterson, Perkins, Scales, and their captives made an additional stop before conducting the blacks to the K Street station house between Second and Third Streets. Perkins called on the local justice of the peace, a twenty-nine year old, two-year resident of Sacramento, Virginian B. D. Fry. (Fry, a proslavery man and sympathetic to slaveholders, had ruled in favor of a master just weeks earlier in a similar case. In that hearing the master, under the terms of the new fugitive slave law, had used Fry's court to reclaim a slave he had brought to California in 1849.) Now, in an unusual evening 'judicial hearing' before Fry, the three blacks were undoubtedly mere spectators as they sat and listened to Perkins' 'evidence' against them. Under California's recently enacted fugitive slave law, they were not allowed to testify. Afterwards, Fry ruled that because (upon demand of their master's agent) "they [the three blacks] have refused to return to the said state of Mississippi," they are remanded to the custody of A. G. Perkins to convey them to C. S. Perkins.[15] As a result, Robert, Carter, and Sandy were then escorted to the city jail where they would await transport to San Francisco and eventually to the Mound Plantation.

---

[15]Statement of B. D. Fry, June 2, 1852, *In re Perkins* Case File (California State Archives, Sacramento). Fry erroneously wrote that the slaves were brought before him on May 31st instead of June 1st. Birkett Davenport Fry (1822-1891) was a descendant of a notable Virginia family. Fry's great grandfather Joshua Fry co-created with Thomas Jefferson's father the famous Fry-Jefferson map of Virginia shown in Chapter I. Joshua Fry was also the same (Colonel) Joshua Fry who commanded the Virginia regiment in Pennsylvania in 1754. Fry's second in command a young Virginian, Colonel George Washington, initiated a skirmish with the French near Great Meadows (Ft. Necessity), the first engagement of the French and Indian War. Justice of the Peace B. D. Fry later fought for the Confederacy in the Civil War, was wounded four times, participated in Pickett's Charge at Gettysburg, attained the rank of general, and later became a prisoner of war. On June 27,1852, just four weeks after ruling in the Perkins hearing, "Capt" B. D. Fry organized the Sacramento Sutter Rifle Corps, a local military group. In 1856 Sheriff Asten and Judge Fry would participate as officers in the "army" of the slavery advocate William Walker in his attempted military expedition to Nicaragua.

Subsequent to the proceedings in Fry's courtroom, Harden Scales unwisely "fell into a condition of hilarity before he, his brother, and A. G. Perkins began their long return journey with their unwilling charges."[16] Because of this delay, word of the incident quickly spread to Sacramento's black population and eventually reached Mark Hopkins, a local antislavery storekeeper and later one of the "Big Four" in California railroad history.[17] In turn, Hopkins contacted attorney Cornelius Cole, whose office over 52 K Street was next to Hopkins' own brick office/store, and asked him to look into the matter.[18]

Cole, twenty-nine, had journeyed overland to California arriving in July 1849, just months before Charles Perkins and Carter. (Coincidentally, he too had mined in El Dorado County, the same county where Charles Perkins had staked his first claim.) A New Yorker, Cole had studied law in the office of one of the nation's leading antislavery advocates and later President Lincoln's Secretary of State, William H. Seward. In his own words Cole was not a pronounced abolitionist but was opposed to slavery on political and sentimental grounds.

Responding to Hopkins' request, Cole visited the three alleged fugitives in the jail located across the street from his K Street office on Sunday June 6, and perhaps also the day prior. There, he listened attentively as they related the complete details of their ordeal to him. The trio explained they came from Greenville, Bolivar County, Mississippi, (naming the nearest city to the

---

[16]Cole, *Essays,* III: Box 29, Folder 2, 11. Cole never explained whether the "condition of hilarity" was due to Scales' drunkenness or ill-timed boasting.

[17]In *Memoirs of Cornelius Cole* published in 1908, Cole recalled that Hopkins learned of the slaves' predicament through his (Hopkins') colored servant, 94. However, in his *Essays* found in the Cole Papers, III: Box 29, Folder 2, 11, Cole wrote "information regarding the case was given to the colored people of the place [Sacramento] and was communicated to Mark Hopkins and by him to me."

[18]Occupying the buildings at 56 and 58 K streets was the dry goods store of the Stanford Brothers (including Josiah, formerly of the Mormon Island area near Sacramento). The last of the brothers, Leland Stanford, arrived in Sacramento in July 1852. Stanford University in Palo Alto, California, is named after Leland Stanford's son. Nearby, at 92 K Street in Sacramento, was the store (opened in May 1852) of wholesale merchant George Hearst, the father of future American newspaper magnate William Randolph Hearst.

Justice of the Peace Birkett Davenport (B. D.) Fry (in his later years) of Virginia who presided at the first hearing of the three alleged fugitive slaves in Sacramento. Photo from the National Archives

Mound Plantation (even though Greenville is located in Washington County) and their master William P. Perkins was now deceased. Robert, Carter, and Sandy next described how they had worked in the goldfields for Perkins, the Kirks, and Dr. Hill and then obtained their freedom. The three concluded with an explanation of the circumstances of their recent arrest.[19] (In Cole's notes of this interview, there is no mention of any freedom papers or the burning of any such papers as he later mentioned in his *Essays* written decades later. Such an omission raises further doubt as to their existence. Since no other source except an aged Cole referenced any freedom papers, and since none were ever produced by

---

[19]Naglee Family Collection, June 6, 1852. This information is derived from Cole's notes of the interview he conducted with Robert, Carter, and Sandy in their cell in Sacramento just days after their arrest in Placer County. Cole may have begun his interview on June 5 according to the date he first entered on the original. His notes *ended*, however, with this sentence: "These facts were related to me on Sunday, June 6, 1852, in the station house in this city."

August 1852, the question arises as to their existence in the first
place.) After listening to their story, Cole obtained their powers of
attorney, witnessed by their jailer Samuel Deal; their X signatures
on the document bore silent testimony to their predicament, three
illiterate, now penniless black men, alleged fugitive slaves, held at
the mercy of both the prejudicial April 15th law and their abduc-
tors, Perkins and Scales. Cole next filed for a writ of *habeas corpus*. Slightly more than seven weeks after its passage, the California Fugitive Slave Law was about to face its first legal challenge.

    While Cole set to work for his new clients, free blacks in
Sacramento also swung into action. It seems that Cole, prior to his
meeting with the slaves, had penned a letter relating what he already knew about the case to his former law partner James Pratt. A
local black then delivered the letter to Pratt in San Francisco. On
June 3 Pratt replied to Cole, writing that the [black] "man who
brought me a letter wanted me to put something in writing which
he might use in your city [Sacramento] to aid him in raising
money [for the defense]."[20] Thus, within just three days of the
arrests of Carter, Robert, and Sandy, Sacramento blacks, not content to stand idly by, had initiated the first steps of an eventual organized black response to what they perceived as a flagrant injus-
tice. Soon, this black activism would spread to an already-primed
San Francisco black community.

    As Cole prepared for a hearing on the writ he had filed, he
received an encouraging letter from a prominent white reverend,
S. D. Simonds, editor of San Francisco's *Weekly California Christian Advocate*. On June 8 Simonds wrote wishing Cole success in
his efforts to free the three blacks. Then he added several sen-
tences that revealed the extent of the organization and concerted
efforts of blacks in both Sacramento *and* San Francisco to assist in
the defense of the three "fugitives":

> The colored people here [San Francisco] have been ap-
> plied to by a committee of a meeting held in Sacramento
> for aid. They write here they [the Sacramento black com-
> mittee] have feed [compensated] lawyers and paid court

---

[20]James Pratt to Cornelius Cole, June 3, 1852, in Cole Papers, Box 2, Folder
1851-1859, transcribed copy in author's possession.

expenses to the amount of 400 to 500$ and are now straitened [depleted] for fund[s]. I make no doubt that all necessary help can be had here. I . . . desire you to make a statement to me of what amount and for what purposes money will be wanted. . . . Push the case to the last point.[21]

Simonds, a resident of San Francisco, and Cole of Sacramento both realized that due to their limited size the black communities in their respective counties faced huge difficulties in raising the necessary defense funds. In San Francisco County, only 284 blacks over twenty-one were counted in the California census of 1852 while Sacramento had tallied just 218. Thus, only 502 blacks in those two locales might have been able to donate to the defense fund. Of those, an unknown number, not designated as such in the state census, were nonetheless slaves who would have been prevented from making any donations at all.

Cornelius Cole (1822-1924) Wikipedia.org

[21]S. D. Simonds to Cornelius Cole, June 8, 1852, Cole Papers.

Though Cole and Simonds possibly remained unaware of
it at the time, rumblings of organized Negro activism in California
had appeared in a published statement just one week after the implementation of the state's Fugitive Slave Law. At a hastily called
meeting of the colored citizens of San Francisco held on April 22,
1852, its chairman, J.H. Marrs, speaking on behalf of the city's
blacks, declared:

> Resolved, That we are a law-loving and a law-abiding
> people, but at the same time we feel it to be our duty
> that we owe to ourselves, to posterity, and to our down-
> trodden and oppressed brethren, to resist every attempt
> made to carry out the late fugitive slave law of this state.[22]

Uttered weeks before Perkins, Perkins, and Jones were
arrested in Placer County, this statement is remarkable for its resolute and defiant tone in a state drastically divided over the slavery
issue and because its authors were black men.

In Sacramento at 10 a.m. on Tuesday, June 8, 1852, thirty-
two year old Sixth District Court Judge Lewis Aldrich entered his
courtroom, seated himself, gazed at the large gallery, and prepared
to hear arguments in the Perkins *habeas corpus* proceeding. Aldrich, a proslavery Floridian according to Cole, would be called on
to decide, hopefully without bias, the fate of Cole's clients.[23] The
Alta, sensing the public's anticipation and the case's significance,
ran a brief article under the heading, "Testing the Constitutionality
of the Fugitive Slave Law."[24]

---

[22]*Daily Alta California*, April 28, 1852, 2.
[23]Aldrich was actually born in Rhode Island, a free state, but had resided in Florida during the 1840s where he had served in the Florida House of Representatives
(1846-1847). In 1848 he was elected to the Florida Senate. Corinna Brown Aldrich, Ellen Brown Anderson, James M. Denham, and Keith L. Huneycutt Aldrich,
*Echoes from a Distant Frontier: The Brown Sisters' Correspondence from
Antebellum Florida*, (Columbia: University of South Carolina Press, 2004), 181.
In 1854, he formed a law partnership in San Francisco with former Mississippi
Senator and Governor Henry Foote. Aldrich later married Foote's daughter. It
was Henry Foote who had dared not cross-examine witnesses against his client in
the 1835 Livingston, Mississippi, slave insurrection scare.
[24]*Daily Alta California*, June 12, 1852, 2.

That morning in the crowded courtroom an abundance of legal talent appeared for both sides attesting to the importance of the case. Not one, but three attorneys, represented each side. (Those hiring Charles' lawyers had spared him no expense.) Judge Aldrich undoubtedly recognized one of the opposing counsel, former judge Tod Robinson, his predecessor on the bench, seated with his clients Scales and A. G. Perkins.[25] Across the aisle sat Cole, who also later referred to Justice of the Peace Fry as a "pronounced pro slavery man," while lamenting his clients' recent hearing before him.[26] Besides Cole, the black community had engaged two other local attorneys as his co-counsel, Joseph Winans and James Zabriskie. Both had successfully represented blacks in previous cases prior to the enactment of the April 15th statute.[27]

No record exists as to the impression this trio of white lawyers made on A. G. Perkins and Scales, but if nothing else the two Southern men realized these antislavery attorneys would not allow the blacks to return to bondage unchallenged. Moreover, Scales and Perkins may well have been utterly surprised at the involvement of the local black community in assisting the defense.

Reflecting on the heightened tensions regarding the case, Cole recalled that the "large [Sacramento] courtroom was pretty well occupied by his [Harden Scales' proslavery] sympathizers many of whom were well armed for a possible conflict."[28] (Did local blacks dare attend as a show of support in such a tense and hostile environment?) During a lull in the proceedings a "large man" named McCandless (possibly a thirty-five year old Irishman, W. McCandless) personally threatened Cole with violence on account of the case. As Judge Aldrich commanded order in the

---

[25]Robinson, one of the three attorneys arguing the case on behalf of Charles Perkins, was a highly respected slaveholding lawyer originally from North Carolina, but more recently of Brazoria County, Texas. In January 1851 Charles' cousin, Governor Burnett, had selected Robinson to fill the vacant judge's seat in Sacramento. Judge Robinson held the position until August 1851 when he returned to private practice. His replacement, Judge Lewis Aldrich, now presided over this *habeas corpus* hearing.
[26]Cole, Essays, III: Box 29, Folder 2, 10.
[27]*Placer Times*, (Sacramento) May 27, 1850, 2, "The Slave Case." Zabriskie and Winans won the slave's freedom in this case reported by the *Times*.
[28]Cole, *Essays*, 12.

courtroom, Cole received assistance from an unlikely source,
forty-year-old B. F. Mauldin, a former client but "by no means an
antislavery man" (Mauldin came from Maryland, a slave state). He
appeared unexpectedly at Cole's side "to repel anything like a
forcible interruption to the proceeding."[29] The *Pacific* later reported the incident hoping that the case would be decided on its
merits while declaring, "We learned with regret that an effort at
intimidation and threats of personal violence were made against
Mr. Cole. We trust no such threats will be executed."[30]

During the two days of the hearing, Aldrich listened attentively to arguments from counsel, but ultimately he ruled on June
11 in favor of the absent Charles Perkins, again assigning custody
of the prisoners to A. G. Perkins and Harden Scales for transport
to Mississippi.

Just hours after Aldrich announced his decision, one ob-
server, attorney G. E. Montgomery, noted in his journal that Judge
Aldrich seemed weak and intimidated by the pro Southern mob.[31]
Montgomery noted Aldrich

> had decided on Tuesday [early in the hearing] that evi-
> dence could not be introduced under the writ, but that the
> case must stand or fall upon the return of the Justice [Fry].
> This grave error shut out proof which they [defense coun-
> sel] alleged they possessed, that the blacks were brought
> here under a contract to labor, and had performed that
> agreement, and had been discharged by their owners
> [Charles Perkins and later Dr. Hill] accordingly.[32]

Cole noted that while he didn't think Aldrich was intimidated, he agreed with Montgomery that Aldrich "would not allow
any inquiry into the merits of the case and refused to go behind the

[29]Ibid., 13.
[30]*Pacific* (San Francisco), June 11, 1852, 2.
[31]G. E. Montgomery, "The Lost Journals of a Pioneer," *Overland Monthly and Outwest Magazine*, (San Francisco, 1886), VII: 180. Noted writer Bret Harte edited the *Overland Monthly*.
[32]Ibid.

certificate of Justice of the Peace Fry."[33] Cole then remarked that Judge Aldrich in so doing had restricted the hearing as much as possible. Such a constraint had prevented Cole from presenting among other evidence the freedom documents (if they existed) that Dr. Hill had allegedly given the slaves at the time of their release in November 1851.[34] Cole later briefly summarized the hearing in a letter to his former mentor William H. Seward on June 14 closing with: "This state [California] has hitherto been more Southern in sentiment than South Carolina."[35]

Newspapers both in and outside of California reacted in the aftermath of Aldrich's decision. Locally, The *Pacific* declared that "Contrary to our statement of last week these colored men affirm that they did work for their master or his agents the full amount of time which was originally agreed on."[36] The *Sacramento Daily Union* editorialized, "The decision of the Court gives very general satisfaction in the community."[37] Nationally, the New York *National Antislavery Standard*, the official newspaper of the American Antislavery Society, wrote that as a result of the case, "the pro slavery party [in California] have [sic] received, from the decisions of the Courts, all the encouragement they could desire."[38] The *New York Tribune* on July 16 noted, "Considerable feeling was manifested when the [Aldrich's] decision was announced, but it passed off much more quietly than was anticipated."[39]

With seemingly no additional obstacles in their way, A. G. Perkins and Harden Scales now planned to usher the three blacks to San Francisco and quietly book passage on the *California* to Panama, the first leg of the return journey to Bolivar County. The tenacious Cole, however, would not be deterred. He filed

---

[33]Cole, *Essays*, III: Box 29, Folder 2, 13-14.
[34]For details of the legalities of the Perkins slave extradition matter, see Ray R. Albin, "The Perkins Case: The Ordeal of Three Slaves in Gold Rush California," *California History*, LXVII: No. 4, (December 1988), 214-227.
[35]Cole to Seward, June 14, 1852, William Henry Seward Papers, (University of Rochester, New York).
[36]*Pacific*, June 18, 1852, 2.
[37]*Sacramento Daily Union*, June 15, 1852, 2.
[38]*National Antislavery Standard*, July 29, 1852, 39.
[39]*New York Tribune*, July 16, 1852.

for another writ of *habeas corpus* in San Francisco, intending to make this THE test case regarding the constitutionality of the recently enacted California Fugitive Slave Law.

The idea of testing the law's constitutionality had been in the works since at least June 3rd or before. On that date Cole had received a letter from the Brown, Pratt, and Tracy law firm in San Francisco. They wrote, "The sum of one thousand dollars is the least sum for which the constitutionality of the law can be properly tested before the Supreme Court."[40]

In San Francisco on June 14, 1852, just three days after Aldrich's ruling, Chief Justice Hugh Murray of the California Supreme Court examined the affidavit of Moses A. Jackson. An approximately forty-year old, literate, free mulatto or black (depending on the source consulted) laborer from Maryland, Jackson now resided in Sacramento. The nearly six foot tall, black-eyed, brown-haired Jackson had acted in concert with the Sacramento defense team and filed the document now before Judge Murray on behalf of Robert, Carter, and Sandy affirming that the three were imprisoned in the Sacramento station house against their will.[41]

In and of itself, this scene is extraordinary. The affidavit of a common black laborer in the most compelling California fugitive slave case of its time makes its way to the Chief Justice of the California Supreme Court. Presented on behalf of three illiterate blacks, twice deemed "fugitives" by two other California magistrates, it contained a testament that would ultimately impact the case dramatically. While we will probably never learn why the defense team allowed Jackson to become involved to this degree, nonetheless his declaration had a great impact on the final act of the Perkins case.

---

[40]Pratt to Cole, June 3, 1852.

[41]*In re Perkins* Case File (California State Archives, Sacramento), Affidavits of Moses A. Jackson (issued by the California Supreme Court), copies in the author's possession. For Jackson in the 1852 California census, see Sacramento County, s. v. "Masis [sic] A. Jackson," 132, accessed July 25, 2011, *Ancestry.com*. The census shows Jackson as a forty year old, but other documents reveal that he was born in 1810 or 1811. Jackson's address is found in Samuel Colville, *Sacramento Directory For the Year 1855*, (Sacramento: James Anthony & Co, 1855), 47.

Jackson may have been a former slave himself, hence his desire to aid Carter, Robert, and Sandy. Born in Maryland, a slave state, to slave parents who were born there as well, Moses Alexander Jackson by 1850 resided as a free man. In New York City, he lived with his wife, Virginia-born Elisabeth, twenty-six, and also literate, and their four young children. Identified as mulattoes (in an 1880 census, Jackson is listed as black), the family lived on the income Moses earned cleaning clothes. The possibility exists that Moses somehow had gained his freedom (a runaway?) and moved to New York. Sometime between 1850 and 1852 Jackson had journeyed to California and now found himself involved in the legalities of the Perkins case.[42]

Meanwhile in Mississippi Charles Perkins, hoping for the prompt return of his slave property, remained unaware of these recent proceedings in California. Soon enough he would learn that his efforts to recover the slaves had resulted in a sudden turn of events, and an extraordinary third hearing, this one before the Supreme Court of California. For the second time in two months, a justice of a state high court had become involved in the Perkins matter; Justice William Yerger's role had been ancillary, Chief Justice Hugh Murray's would be central.

After examining the papers filed by Cole and Jackson's affidavit stating Jones and the two Perkins men were being held against their will in Sacramento, Justice Murray issued three separate arrest warrants, one for each of the three blacks, ordering their appearance before the Supreme Court in San Francisco on July 5.[43]

---

[42] Seventh Census, 1850, New York, New York County, Ward 8, s. v. "Moses Jackson," line 25, accessed June 20, 2011, *Family Search*, https://familysearch.org/pal:/MM9.3.1/TH-267-11783-137511-28?cc=1401638. Jackson and his family had lived in Canada (a haven for slave runaways) apparently in the late 1840s. In migrating to California, Jackson left his family behind in New York. In 1855 he continued to reside, apparently alone, in Sacramento.

[43] Arrest warrants ordered by Justice Murray for Robert Perkins, Carter Perkins, and Sandy Jones June 14, 1852, *In re Perkins* Case File (California State Archives, Sacramento), copies in author's possession.

Important Fugitive Slave Case.

The first cause under the Fugitive Slave Law
of the last Legislature is now on trial in this
city before Judge Aldrich, of the 7th District
Court. Three negroes claimed as the property
of Mr. Perkins of Mississippi, were brought before Justice Fry on Thursday last, when he
gave Mr. Perkins a certificate in accordance
with the statute, authorising the capture and
extradition of the negroes. Thereupon the negroes sued out a writ of *habeas corpus*, return-
able before Judge Aldrich, and the fugitives
were brought before him on Monday.

The only question for the decision of the court
is, whether the Fugitive Slave Law conflicts
with either the Constitution of the State or that
of the United States. Upon a preliminary question being raised, the court refused to admit
testimony behind the certificate. The cause
was argued by Messrs. Robinson, Edwards and
Rosborough for the claimant, and by Messrs.
Winans, Zabriskie and Cole for the fugitives.
The judgment of the court will be rendered tomorrow. When the case is concluded, we shall
publish it in full.

Sacramento Daily Union, June 9, 1852, relating details of the Perkins Case nine days after the blacks' arrest. It, however, provides a
slightly incorrect timeline regarding the days on which the events
occurred.

In the gloomy pre-dawn hours of June 18, less than three
weeks after their first arrest, Carter Perkins, Robert Perkins, and
Sandy Jones, escorted now by Hardin Scales, filed aboard the
steamer *California*, docked in San Francisco (Ironically, it was the
California that may have brought Carter to San Francisco in October 1849). Earlier, A. G. Perkins had signed a power of attorney
document transferring custody of the three slaves to his cousin
Scales, thus allowing Scales to legally deliver the trio to Mississippi. At this point, unexpectedly for Scales and possibly the three

blacks, the legal system that had recently condemned the blacks to slavery interceded on their behalf in the form of San Francisco Constable James Harding.

Between the hours of four and five a. m. Constable Harding, acting on Justice Murray's writ recently obtained by Cole, boarded the steamer *California* just prior to her scheduled departure at six a.m. and dramatically arrested Cole's three clients. He then transferred them to the city jail on Broadway Street pending a hearing before the California Supreme Court, scheduled for July 6.[44]

Within days the San Francisco press reacted. Typical of the divided local public opinion regarding Harding's action, which also reflected the *nation's* divided sentiments on the slavery issue, were the *Pacific* and the *Herald*. The *Pacific* referred to the arrest as a "rescue" and later declared, "Because these Negroes are in arrest under the so called 'Fugitive Slave Law' it is easy to fall into the mistake of calling them Fugitive Slaves."[45] In contrast, the *Herald* condemned the arrest as a "very senseless and mischievous" attempt to disturb the recently enacted state Fugitive Slave Law.[46]

While newspapers and the public debated the matter, California continued the process of conducting its own census. With its tremendous population increase since the Federal Census in 1850 due to the Gold Rush, the state had authorized a special counting for 1852. Among those tallied in San Francisco on July 2, 1852, while awaiting their Supreme Court hearing were Robert, Sandy, and Carter (ironically misidentified as Charles Perkins in

---

[44]On the same day as the arrest of the three slaves, the June 18, 1852, edition of the *San Francisco Herald* ran an ad proclaiming "Negro for Sale." But, blacks were not the only people to feel the sting of racial prejudice in California. In May 1852 at Foster and Atchinson's Bar in Yuba County, members of a meeting passed a resolution denying Chinese the right to hold claims and requiring all Chinese to leave.

[45]*Pacific*, July 2, 1852, 2 and July 9, 1852, 2.

[46]*San Francisco Herald*, June 19, 1852, 2. The (Stockton) *San Joaquin Republican*, June 23, 1852, 1, offered another view of the episode: "We believe the law of the state [the California Fugitive Slave Law] to be constitutional, and that a refusal to make such provisions as the law contains would be unjust and oppressive. We fully endorse the views of the *Herald*." Crabb, the law's author, represented *San Joaquin County* in the California Assembly.

the census). Peering through the bars of their jail cells, the census taker, perhaps misunderstanding the accents of these Southern blacks, 'heard' the men say they were from "Boula" County, Mississippi, instead of Bolivar County. He correctly listed Robert and Sandy as blacksmiths and Carter as a farmer. The census document also revealed that despite the fact that all three men were born in the United States, by law slaves did not qualify as citizens. In column 10 of the census sheet, "Number of citizens of the U.S. over 21 years," their boxes remained unmarked.[47]

Two days later, San Francisco held a gala July 4th parade celebrating America's independence and *freedom*. The participants assembled on Broadway Street, and during their march passed directly in front of the city jail where the slaves remained imprisoned. As they heard or saw the marchers (among them the Supreme Court justices who soon would decide their case) and revelers celebrating this glorious day in American history culminating in a fireworks display above the city, what thoughts crossed Robert, Carter, and Sandy's minds? Did the three blacks grasp the irony of the entire situation?

In the days following their arrest and the hearings before Justice Fry, then later Judge Aldrich, Carter, Robert, and Sandy encountered an exceedingly different kind of white man than they had known in Mississippi; whites willing to take up the gauntlet on their behalf in their quest for freedom. Bolstered by these enthusiastic antislavery whites, the trio may have been equally surprised at the vigorous involvement of the free black community.

The three blacks eagerly anticipated their next court hearing, but the stress of the situation and their weeks behind bars had begun to take a toll. Cole's partner, Pratt, reported that, "We have had considerable trouble with the negroes. They [are] vacillating from one lawyer to another and the result is we alone are in the case."[48] Had the trio had access to the *Pacific* and had they been literate, their fears would not have been eased. Referring to the impending Supreme Court hearing, the *Pacific* declared:

---

[47]Coincidentally a white man, Jackson Moses, not to be confused with the Sacramento black man Moses Jackson, served as their jailer. His name appears above theirs in the 1852 census.
[48]Pratt to Cole, July 1, 1852.

> This, then, is the court of last appeal. By its decision will
> be determined the *Constitutionality* of the Slave Law,
> and the right of these men to their freedom. This case is
> a most important one; far more important than any
> other that has yet come before the Court for decision.[49]

Delayed for several weeks, arguments finally began in San
Francisco on July 29, 1852, before the California Supreme Court
in the first case to test the constitutionality of the state's recently
enacted Fugitive Slave Law. While it was later cited as *In re Perkins* (2 Cal. 424), most observers then referred to it simply as the
Perkins Case. Only two justices presided at the hearing, both from
slave states, Chief Justice Hugh Murray of Missouri and Alexander Anderson of Tennessee. Arguing the case for the blacks was
Harvey Brown, assisted by Cole, while Tod Robinson again represented Charles Perkins' interests. Because the attorneys for the
three apparently had no documented evidence that their clients
were free by contract, they argued instead against the constitutionality of the law under which the blacks were being held. With arguments for both sides completed by July 31, the waiting process
for the court's decision began.

A ruling did not emerge quickly. The court's already slug-
gish process of decision-making was further delayed from August
15 on due to Chief Justice Murray's "indisposition", which created
added suspense among interested observers. On August 30, 1852,
though, the court finally reconvened, to announce its long-awaited
judgment in the Perkins matter.

Prior to the judges' pronouncement, E. Norton, another of
the blacks' lawyers, moved for a re-argument in the matter. Norton
contended that a full bench of three justices rather than just Murray and Anderson should hear the case. Justice Murray rejected
Norton's motion explaining that since he and Justice Anderson
were in agreement, a new hearing would not be necessary.

With that, the two concurring justices announced their
ruling, upholding the constitutionality of the law under consideration, one of the more pronounced proslavery judgments ever af-
firmed in a free state. Each asserted that slaveholders could not be

---

[49]*Pacific*, July 2, 1852, 2.

deprived of their slave property because of the due process and just compensation clauses of the Fifth Amendment. "The judgment of the court is that the writ be dismissed and the slaves . . . be remanded . . . to jail . . . and . . . delivered to the master or his agent."[50] Having enjoyed freedom from November 1851 until the end of May 1852, Robert, Carter, and Sandy must have been devastated by the ruling and its enduring result - the cruel certainty of a lifetime of servitude awaiting them back on the Mound Plantation.

Conversely, for Charles Perkins the court's decision meant that he had finally won the custody of his three slaves. Eclipsing Perkins' personal triumph, at least on the California stage, was the fact that Court's decision had validated the April 15th law while simultaneously presenting California's proslavery forces with a resounding victory.

In the ensuing weeks as Robert, Carter, and Sandy, slaves once again, languished in the San Francisco jail awaiting transport to Mississippi, newspapers not only in California but nationwide carried the story and the Court's ruling. Locally, the San Francisco *Alta* printed without comment a review of the case focusing on the facts and the court's decision (below). Several days later, the *Sacramento Daily Union* followed with a reprint of the *Alta's* article. The *San Joaquin Republican* on September 4 devoted just two lines to the judgment. The Court's finding also appeared in the *New York Times* and the Vicksburg, Mississippi, *Weekly Whig*. The *National Era* of Washington, D. C., on October 14, 1852, reprinted the *Alta's* story. The *Liberator* reported, ". . . the worst decision has been made that ever disgraced a judicial bench. The State [California] is now perfectly open to slavery."[51] In May 1853 The *Thirteenth Annual Report of the American and Foreign Antislavery Society* in New York recounted the Perkins case and then related the stories of two other "fugitive" blacks arrested and

---

[50]*In re Perkins*, 2 Cal. 438, (1852), 442. Coincidentally, as it reported details of the Perkins case, the *Advocate* also ran front-page excerpts from Harriet Beecher Stowe's new novel indicting slavery, *Uncle Tom's Cabin. Advocate*, August 12, 1852, 156.
[51]*New York* Times, October 4, 1852, 3. *Vicksburg Weekly Whig*, October 6, 1852, 4, 3. National *Era*, October 14, 1852, 4, column 5. *Liberator*, October 20, 1852, 1.

apparently returned to slavery under the terms of California's Fugitive Slave Law.[52]

In this three-month long legal steeplechase, the state's prejudicial Fugitive Slave Law and the proslavery officers of the court proved to be the primary insurmountable hurdles for the three blacks and their attorneys. Unnoticed by most observers (except perhaps those appearing on behalf of the three blacks) was the fact that during their ordeal Carter, Robert, and Sandy had confronted proslavery Southerners in positions of power from the time of their arrest until their remand to Scales as a result of the Supreme Court ruling. The arresting officer, Sheriff Asten, B. D. Fry, the Sacramento Justice of the Peace, Tod Robinson, the slaveholder and opposing counsel, Lewis Aldrich, the District Court Judge for Sacramento, and both of the Supreme Court Justices in San Francisco all hailed from or had lived in slave states. (Even Dr. E. M. Patterson, who may have treated one or more of the three blacks soon after their arrest, was a slaveholder.) All more than likely supported the state's Fugitive Slave Law.

It could be contended, but impossible to prove, that the presiding magistrates' proslavery Southern backgrounds predisposed them to judge the three blacks on the basis of their skin color. While the two Supreme Court justices may have simply been following the law, a reading of their opinion raises serious doubts about their *impartiality*. The language includes demeaning references to the petitioners.

For example, Chief Justice Hugh Murray in the court's decision wrote, "the increase of the free Negro population has for some time past been a matter of serious consideration with the people of this State [California], in view of the pernicious consequences necessarily resulting from this class of inhabitants" [blacks]. He then added, "I am satisfied [with] the desire to purge

---

[52]Open Library.org, accessed December 11, 2011, http://www.archive.org/stream/thirteenthannual00amer#page/40/mode/2up, 40-41.

the State of this class of inhabitants who, in the language of a distinguished jurist, are 'festering sores upon the body politic'. . . ."[53]

If undeclared racial discrimination had indeed played a role in the slaves' previous two hearings before Fry and Aldrich, these two Southern high court magistrates had surpassed that level, placing their prejudice in black and white for all to read. Charles Perkins could not have bought a more 'favorable' pair of judges. With the Supreme Court's decision, the three slaves and their attorneys might have finally understood their fate may have been a foregone conclusion each time they appeared before a Southern judge whether his name was Fry, Aldrich, Murray, or Anderson.

Meanwhile, and coincidentally, while reporting the Perkins Case, The *San Francisco Herald* also noted (without linking the two cases) the Missouri Supreme Court's proslavery decision in the matter of a black slave, Dred Scott, *who had temporarily resided with his master on free soil and subsequently sued for his freedom.* Afterward, the Missouri high court's decision against Scott initiated a protracted legal battle that in 1857 resulted in the monumental United States Supreme Court proslavery ruling in *Dred Scott v Sandford.*[54]

The Dred Scott Case bears noting because of the sway the Perkins case exerted on several of its significant issues. "Key pieces of [the] Dred Scott [decision] appeared in the California Supreme Court's opinion *In re Perkins* several years before, in 1852" namely "applying the ideas expressed in the resolutions to determine the right of slave owner[s] to slaves brought into California."[55] In short, did slaves become free when entering, with the permission of their master, a state or territory where slavery is not tolerated? Both the California Supreme Court in the Perkins matter

---

[53]*In re Perkins*, 2 Cal. 438, (1852). The other Justice hearing the case, Tennessean Alexander Outlaw Anderson, had served as a U.S. Senator from that state.

[54]Historians view the United States Supreme Court decision in *Dred Scott v Sandford* as one of the contributing factors to the Civil War.

[55]Alfred L. Brophy, *Considering Reparations for the Dred Scott Case,* (Ohio State University Press, Columbus, 2008), 10-11. PDF file abstract, copy in author's possession, download at
http://papers.ssrn.com/sol3/papers.cfm?abstract_id=997900#%23.

Daily Alta California.

By F. GILBERT & Co.

F. GILBERT,   P. C. REALS,   E. CONNER.

TUESDAY MORNING, AUGUST 31, 1852.

Printing Paper Wanted.—A premium will be paid for white printing paper. Those who may have it in large or small quantities, will find ready sale for it by applying at the office of this paper.

To the Public.

We shall be obliged to continue the publication of the *Alta* upon the present style of paper, until the arrival of some of the clippers now over due, and throw ourselves upon the indulgence of our friends for a few days longer.

THE FUGITIVE SLAVE CASE.—Judges Murray and Anderson yesterday rendered the decision of the Supreme Court in the matter of the three slaves, whose case has been under delibera tion by that court for some time past. Their names are Carter Perkins, Robert Perkins, and Sandy Jones. Mr. C. S. Perkins, of Bolivar coun y, Mississippi, is the claimant, and arrived here in October, 1849, with the first named slave. The other two arrived here afterwards. They have been at work in the mines until the 31st of May last, when they were arrested at Ophir, Placer coun y, by the sheriff of that county, on the complaint of Mr. Perkins, who seeks to re-convey them to Mississippi, under the provisions of the act of the Legislature " respecting fu gitives from labor and slaves brought to this State prior to her admission into the Union," passed April 15th, 1852. They were taken thence to Sacramento city, and before Judge B. D. Fry, Justice of the Peace, where proof was adduced of their being the property of Mr. Perkins, and they were ordered into his custody. They then sought for a release, under writ of *habeas corpus*, before Judge Aldrich, of the District Court of that Ju dicial District, who held that they were legally restrained of their liberty, and remanded them into custody. Mr. Perkins then brought them down here, for the purpose of putting them on a steamer, when they obtained from Judge Wells, then hold ing a temporary appointment as Associate Justice of the Su preme Court, a second writ of *habeas corpus*, which brought their case bef re that tribunal.

The case was argued there a month since by Messrs. E. Nor ton, C. Cole and H. S. Brown, on behalf of the slaves, and by Judge Tod Robinson for the master. Judge Wells's term hav ing expired by reason of the return of Judge Heydenfeldt, the decision of the case was left in the hands of Judges Murray and Anderson, each of whom delivered opinions coming to the same conc usion. Both of the opinions are very lengthy, and we re gret that we have not the space to publish them, our present re stricted form preventing even the report of a digest of the same. The opinions are devoted exclusively to the discussion of th constitutionality of the law of the Legislature, and both Jus tices concur in the opinion that the law is constitutional and valid An order was accordingly made that the negroes be re delivered into the custody of the claimant.

The *Alta's* report of the California Supreme Court's decision, *In re Perkins*, which newspapers across America reprinted in the weeks following the case.

and later the United States Supreme Court under Justice Taney in
the Scott decision responded in the negative. Judge Anderson declared in the Perkins decision that a slave's temporary residence
on free soil did not alter his servitude, words also echoed by the
United States Supreme Court five years later in the Scott case. As
Cole later remarked, "Judge Murray enunciated the identical doc-
trine [in the Perkins matter] afterwards made famous by the judgment of Chief Justice Taney in the Dred Scott Case, namely that a
negro had no rights a white man was bound to respect."[56] Furthermore, according to *De Bow's Review*, a contemporary proslavery, pro Southern, pro secessionist journal, Reverdy Johnson, one
of the attorneys for Sandford in the Scott case relied on Judge Anderson's 1852 Perkins' opinion as authority.[57]

Given the passionate feelings in California that stemmed
from the Perkins case along with the legal issues involved, the
question arises why Cole and his co-counsel never petitioned the
United States Supreme Court to hear the Perkins matter. The answer cannot be attributed to a lack of attorney interest in pursuing
such an appeal but instead, it appears, to a lack of funds to carry
out such an undertaking.

On July 27, 1852, just two days prior to the California Supreme Court hearing, Cole received a short note from his co-
counsel Judge Harvey Brown destined to be the lead attorney for
any appeal. Brown closed with the following significant statement:
"It is a matter of great doubt as to what the result [of the Perkins
case] will be but if we fail here *we must go with it to the Supreme
Court of the U.S. without fail* [italics mine].[58] So the desire for an
appeal existed, at least on July 27. However, the reason for
Brown's failure to bring the matter before the United States Supreme Court may be found in a letter from Brown's law partner
James Pratt to Cole written weeks earlier. On June 3, 1852, just
days after the three slaves were arrested, Pratt wrote: "The truth is
[Harvey] Brown . . . is not willing to take hold of the dark [Negro]

---

[56]Cole *Essays*, III: 15.
[57]James Dunwoody Brownson De Bow, *De Bow's Review*, New Orleans, 1857,
XXIII: 100-101.
[58]Harvey Brown to Cornelius Cole, July 27, 1852, *Cornelius Cole Papers*,
UCLA, Box 2, Folder 1851-1859, copy in author's possession.

side of these cases without a handsome fee being paid in advance."[59] Thus, it seems that because sufficient funds could not be raised later in 1852, any appeal in the Perkins case to the Supreme Court in Washington, D.C. died unceremoniously in northern California.

Had the funds been forthcoming and had Brown succeeded in getting the Taney Supreme Court to hear the Perkins case, would the Dred Scott case ever have reached the High Court? The similarities in the two cases were startling, a major difference being, however, the role in the Perkins matter of California's own unique fugitive slave law.

What would the effect have been on the legal history of the United States had the Perkins case, with its central issue of a slave's status after residing in a free state, been heard first (instead of Scott) in the United States Supreme Court? Would a negative decision (for Brown, Cole, and the slaves) by the High Court in the Perkins matter have inflamed America's antislavery faction in 1852-53 as much as its Scott decision did later in 1857? Would such a negative ruling by the Taney Court in *Perkins* have been considered later as a factor leading to the Civil War, as was the Scott decision? Charles Perkins and others never realized how truly close this matter came to representing a landmark case in American antebellum law. Nonetheless, *In re Perkins, 1852* became a part of the legal and Constitutional history of California and the United States greatly eclipsed, however, on the national stage by its more famous counterpart *Dred Scott v Sandford*.[60] Significantly, a legacy of the Perkins case was that it managed to underscore the persistence of the nation's slavery conundrum as it extended into the Far West, to a free soil state two years after the Compromise of 1850.

Charles Perkins achieved some hometown/home state notoriety as a result of the case. The newspaper accounts that circulated across America repeatedly carried his name in connection

---

[59]Ibid., James Pratt to Cornelius Cole, June 3, 1852. Earlier, in 1850 law partners Cole and Pratt shared a San Francisco office at the corner of Montgomery and Jackson Streets in San Francisco.

[60]In 1858 in San Francisco, a judge cited both the Perkins case and the Scott case in his decision to *free* a fugitive slave.

with each phase of the proceedings. The *Vicksburg Weekly Whig* on October 6, 1852, printed an article in which it mentioned "Mr. C. S. Perkins of Bolivar County, Mississippi [just upriver from Vicksburg]" and each of the three slaves by name.[61] Perhaps, too, upon his return to Mississippi in July or August 1852, A. G. Perkins, as a first hand participant, had spread descriptions of the most recent events surrounding Charles's legal efforts to regain custody of his slaves. Ironically, despite his legal victory, Charles Perkins may never have seen his three slaves again.

Subsequent to the Supreme Court hearing, the slaves may never have returned to Mississippi. Since A. G. Perkins had departed San Francisco on June 26, it fell to Harden Scales to escort the three back to Mississippi.[62] Two separate sources provide sketchy, if unverifiable, accounts of the their possible plight. Cornelius Cole wrote, though he admitted having no reliable information on the subject, that in crossing the Isthmus of Panama "Andy" made his escape. Besides providing a wrong name for the slave, Cole also failed to mention the other two slaves.[63] Another source, a Marysville citizen, W. C. Ellis, wrote to Eastern friends on October 26, 1852, explaining that the slaves left San Francisco on the steamer *Cortez* and made their escape while in Panama.

A problem with Ellis's report is the timing. According to the *San Francisco Passenger Departure Lists* the *Cortez* departed San Francisco on October 20, 1852, for Panama. Neither the three slaves nor Scales were listed on the passenger manifest. (However, they may have been among the unnamed passengers in the ship's steerage.)[64] It would have been impossible, however, because of the time factor for Ellis, residing in northern California, to receive word six days later from Panama of the slaves' escape. The *Cortez* could not even have arrived in Panama by October 26. Nor could the ship have made a voyage to Panama prior to its October 20 departure because she had only arrived in San Francisco on her

---

[61] *Vicksburg Weekly Whig*, October 6, 1852, 4, copy in author's possession.

[62] Carr, *San Francisco Departure Lists*, 5: 4. 'A. Perkins' is shown departing San Francisco for Panama aboard the *Winfield Scott*, the same ship that had earlier carried the Scales brothers to San Francisco.

[63] Cole, *Essays*, III: 16.

[64] Carr, *Passenger Departure Lists*, 5: 11-12.

first trip from Central America on October 7, 1852.[65] Yet, Ellis in his letter stated with certainty the men had made their escape there.[66] Moreover, if the three had fled in Panama in 1852, they could not have risked returning to Mississippi until at least 1865 at the end of the Civil War because under Mississippi law they still would have been considered fugitives. A subsequent check in the 1870 and 1880 Mississippi Federal Censuses reveals no record for any of the three men.

For six months Robert Perkins, Carter Perkins, and Sandy Jones had enjoyed a short-lived taste of freedom and monetary success unattainable at that time to the millions of other enslaved blacks in the United States. Carter had spent more than three years away from Mississippi, and Robert and Sandy over two years. The three never realized that when they departed the Mound Plantation with their masters their exchange of heartfelt farewells with family and friends was for eternity. With their collective fates lost now to history, the three gained, however, a measure of immortality as a result of the men and legal system that sought to reenslave them.

---

[65]E. W. Wright, *Lewis & Dryden's Marine History of the Pacific Northwest,* (Portland, Oregon: Lewis & Dryden Printing Company, 1895), 69.

[66]Lapp, *Blacks in Gold Rush California,* 146. It is possible that Ellis correctly reported the escape, but that he had named the wrong ship. That same year, 1852, Colombia had abolished slavery in the Isthmus. Local freed blacks in the Isthmus made attempts to persuade American slaves to escape during the time they were passing through. If Carter, Robert, and Sandy had escaped while in Panama, they would have sought work to sustain themselves. In 1852 and 1853, the ongoing construction of a forty-seven and one-half mile railroad line across Panama resulted in the need for thousands of manual laborers. The three escaped and undoubtedly unemployed blacks quite possibly could have joined approximately 1,200 other Negroes and thousands of whites working on its construction. Due to diseases, primarily malaria, yellow fever, and cholera, thousands died, maybe 6,000 in all. Accurate mortality records differ, and there is no reckoning of the number of black deaths. Thus, the possibility exists that Carter, Robert, and Sandy may have remained in Panama, worked on the railroad and eventually died there. "Since a large percentage of the dead men had no known next of kin, no permanent address, often not even a known last name, it was decided to pickle their bodies in large barrels, then sell them in wholesale lots. The result was a thriving trade with medical schools around the world. . . ." David McCullough, *Brave Companions,* (New York: Simon and Schuster, 1992), 97-98.

Though Charles Perkins may never have realized it, his efforts to recover his three slaves had altered California's political and social landscape. An unexpected result of the case had centered on the emergence of the California black community and the surprising role it played in the matter. Beginning with the dual efforts of Sacramento's black committee and then San Francisco's blacks in raising defense funds, and aided by dedicated men like Moses Jackson, black activism in California found its roots in the Perkins case. Armed with this new resolve and bolstered by white support from lawyers like Cole, Winans, Zabriskie, and Brown (as long as his fees could be paid), the ability and willingness of the California black community to fight for their civil rights was no longer in doubt. Subsequently, black activism maintained a strong foothold in this free state despite its large proslavery element. Thereafter, blacks' freedom attempts in California ceased being individual struggles and instead garnered support from *both* the black and white communities.

The irony is inescapable. Charles Perkins, slaveholder and a staunch advocate of slavery who sought to recover his slave property, took action in April 1852 that as time passed would galvanize the California *antislavery* community, both black and white. Furthermore, four years after the Perkins case, Cornelius Cole joined the fledgling Republican Party (a party opposed to slavery's expansion, later the party of Abraham Lincoln), becoming one of its California founders in Sacramento. Years later Cole recalled how the Perkins" case fueled his own antislavery fire:

> The incident [*the Perkins case*] goes some way to show the character of a system [slavery] which I, as a member of Congress, afterwards assisted in overthrowing, and it is not impossible that my zeal in that movement may have been somewhat augmented by the recollections of the events [in the Perkins matter]. . . .[67]

---

[67]Cole, *Essays*, III: 16. Between 1856 and 1858, the Sacramento Republican Party leadership met in the office of Mark Hopkins and his partner Collis P. Huntington. In addition to Cole, Hopkins, and Huntington, the party's other leaders were Leland Stanford Sr. and Charles and Edwin Crocker. Cole edited the first Republican Party newspaper in Sacramento. He subsequently became a California Republican Senator in the United States Senate. Later, Hopkins, Stanford,

It also bears noting that in his absentee efforts to recover his slaves, Charles Perkins spent more money than the slaves were worth in Mississippi. Healthy male slaves at the time, especially those like Robert and Sandy who possessed blacksmith's skills, sold for perhaps $1,000-1,500 in 1852. While Carter, at age twenty-two, could be considered a prime field hand both Robert and Sandy exceeded forty years of age and faced far fewer years of productivity.

Also, from correspondence that Cole received during the several months he and other attorneys represented the three blacks, we learn that lawyer's fees even in 1852 were not cheap. In two letters to Cole from the San Francisco law firm of Brown, Pratt, and Tracy both written on the same day, June 3, 1852, Pratt wrote, "the colored men [of Sacramento] by paying a little each might raise at least the sum of five thousand dollars which would pay pretty well you know for the trouble [of defending the slaves]." In a second letter, Pratt reiterated, "there should be a fund raised of at least five thousand dollars. . . ."[68]

The fees Charles Perkins pledged to his bevy of attorneys (which opposing counsel Pratt referred to as "capital talent") in the hearings before Judge Aldrich and the California Supreme Court thus had to be considerable, and at least comparable (perhaps more so) to what the black community was doling out to the five lawyers representing the two Perkins men and Sandy Jones. Additionally, Charles most likely paid for some or all of the expenses A. G. Perkins and Thomas and Harden Scales incurred as his agents. Perkins also faced paying for the costs of the return trips for the three slaves and Scales to Mississippi. (It is unclear who benefited from the money/property taken from the slaves at the time of their arrest.)

In hindsight, would the always-practical William Perkins, had he been alive at the time, have advised his son early on to cut

---

Huntington, and Charles Crocker formed the "Big Four" of railroad fame. Since Leland's brother Josiah Stanford had lived in the goldfields next to A. G. Perkins in 1850 and given the close proximity of the Stanfords' business in Sacramento to Cole's office, did Josiah and Cole converse about the Perkins case during those days in June 1852 when it emerged as the city's *cause celebre*?

[68]James Pratt to Cornelius Cole, June 3, 1852, *Cornelius Cole Papers*, Box 2, Folder 1851-1859.

his losses, as his expenses were exceeding the value of the property to be recovered? The answer is probably no, because for both William and Charles it was always about property rights and that entrenched Perkins slaveholder psyche, a product of the Southern state mentality, that would not permit such a travesty - three perfectly good, profit-generating slaves released to freedom. (But, even if Charles may not have intended for Dr. Hill to emancipate his slaves, it seems the trio while in California *thought* sooner or later they would be released. And, if he had arranged with Hill to free them, Charles upon further reflection, had changed his mind.) In the words of an antebellum Southerner, "Is it not that by his [the slave's] labor he, the master, may accumulate wealth?"[69]

In the long run, Charles had won the legal battle. Yet, on the other hand, assuming the slaves had indeed made their escape, he had lost the financial war, having nothing to show for his expensive legal undertaking. (However, he had gained substantial profits from the labor of his three slaves during his eighteen months in the goldfields.)

And, if the slaves had escaped while in Harden Scales' custody, it will be left for the reader to imagine what transpired in any ensuing face-to-face conversation between Charles and his unfortunate Tennessee cousin once Charles had learned that his three slaves would not be returning to the Mound Plantation.

After the Supreme Court's ruling in the Perkins matter upholding the constitutionality of the state's Fugitive Slave Law, other blacks in California felt the law's persistent sting almost immediately. Two black stewards working on the *Golden Gate* were returned to bondage under the terms of the law.[70] Just over three weeks after the Supreme Court's decision, a San Francisco newspaper reported the apprehension of a female slave brought to California prior to its admission. In a sequence eerily familiar to the second arrest of the Perkins slaves, she was taken into custody on board a ship just before its scheduled morning departure from San Francisco. Subsequently, a magistrate remanded her to the custody of her owner. A local newspaper noted, "This is the third

[69]Stampp, *Peculiar Institution*, 5.
[70]*Thirteenth Annual Report of the American and Foreign Anti-Slavery Society*, 42.

case that has been brought before Justice Shepherd since the decision of the Supreme Court upon the constitutionality of the State fugitive slave law."[71] These three cases heard before the same judge in San Francisco in a three-week span do not take into consideration, of course, other such slave arrests in other California jurisdictions where the cases were heard before different magistrates. Furthermore, no accurate count exists of the total number of California's *unreported* black victims arrested under the terms of its fugitive slave law. Charles Perkins may never have recovered his slaves, but other slaveholders in California certainly did. At the same time, California's black and white antislavery activists remained determined to prevent or reverse such outcomes.[72]

---

[71]*Daily Alta California*, September 22, 1852, 2.
[72]The California legislature allowed the state's fugitive slave law to expire on April 15, 1855, exactly three years after its inception.

VIII

Antebellum Bolivar County

*This morning after breakfast Venn dressed the children & took
them down to the daguerreian boat to have their likenesses taken.*

Mary Bateman Diary entry
Tuesday April 1, 1856[1]

  In the early 1850s, the Bolivar County plantations along
the Mississippi River thrived. But, at the same time, large tracts of
still uninhabited wilderness stretched for miles inland and eastward to the Sunflower River, so residents saw evidence of the
county's continued backwoods character everywhere. In 1854,
seven years after the Perkins family had settled there and eighteen
years after Bolivar had become a county, there were still no merchants. Local plantation owners obtained food and supplies in
New Orleans, generally during an annual visit or purchased
needed items from supply boats that stopped at various landings
during their river runs. In 1855 the Bolivar County Board of Police
had authorized a bounty of five dollars for each wolf killed within
the county. One year later Mary Bateman, at the Campbell's Argyle Plantation (Map 3, above) south of the Perkins plantation,
reported the shooting of a panther near her home.

  However, signs of 'civil progress' gradually began to appear in the area. In approximately 1856 a "wagon track cut
through the towering cane along the bank of the Mississippi
River," and also through a portion of the Perkins' cornfield, extended from the Mound Plantation south, into Washington County

---

[1]"Mary E. Bateman Diary, 1856-1856," *University of North Carolina Southern
Historical Collection*, accessed February 25, 2011,
http://dc.lib.unc.edu/cdm/search/collection/ead/searchterm/folder_2!00047-
z/field/contri!descri/mode/exact!exact/conn/and!and/order/relatid/ad/asc/cosuppr
ess/0. Bateman lived at the riverfront plantation of the deceased William R.
Campbell Sr. near Greenville in Washington County, with her cousin Margaret
Tiedeman Campbell and others including Campbell's daughter Caroline. The
diary contains entries on plantation life along the Mississippi and several references to the Perkins family.

and then on to the city of Greenville (Map 3).[2] Just wide enough
for one carriage, it covered a total distance of approximately seventeen miles. The road, laboriously scratched out by slaves, also
provided a convenient link between several of the riverfront plantations. Yet, during the rainy season, it "was very muddy and
seemingly almost impassable for people to travel."[3]

Bateman mentioned various families traveling by carriage
or horseback on the road - in good weather, presumably. The widowed Mrs. Jane Perkins called on the Campbells in June 1856 using the thoroughfare while Daniel Perkins and his sister Jane were
able to take carriage trips from the Mound Plantation into Greenville.

One cloudy and cold morning in late March 1856, Daniel
Perkins and a neighbor made a shopping trip south to Greenville
successfully navigating the new road. Passing the Indian mounds
in the distance on the carriage ride down, Perkins returned by four
o'clock in time to enjoy a meal with the Campbells at their Argyle
Plantation. He arrived home at the Mound Plantation later that
same day, perhaps reflecting on the novelty of his journey and
contrasting it to a decade earlier when, before the road had been
constructed, such a trip would have been impossible.

Residents soon learned, though, that not everything always went as planned on these excursions. On a visit from Washington County to Bolivar County, Bateman witnessed a buggy
driven by Caroline Campbell experience a broken axle in the middle of Mrs. Perkins' cornfield while using the passageway.[4]

As time passed other positive and conspicuous signs of
progress in this land of cotton and magnolias had also begun to
emerge. Both a post office and a Methodist Church established at
the small community of Glencoe, very close to the Perkins plantation, served the few local residents in that area. Moreover, Bateman described how supply boats sailing up the Mississippi from
Greenville now *delivered* previously-ordered groceries to the
Campbell plantation and to Mrs. Jane Perkins at Mound Landing.

---

[2]Sillers, *History of Bolivar County*, 102-103.
[3]Westfall Diary, January 6, 1861.
[4]Bateman Diary, June 25, 1856.

Over time Mound Landing became one of the vicinity's preferred landings for the increasing number of steamboats, flatboats, and blacksmith boats working the river. It could also have served as one of the river's principal fueling points. By 1850 seven local wood merchants were supplying the essential cords of wood laboriously cut from the county's dense forests to fire the steam engines of the paddle wheelers navigating the river. As the number of steamboats on the river rose during the decade, their insatiable demand for the county's wood also increased, as did the number of wood merchants.

Soon, smaller roads were cut from the inland, cultivated plantations to also allow those planters, with their wagonloads of cotton, access to Mound Landing or other anchorage points.[5] At the same time, passenger steamers arrived at the various landings with news and newspapers from New Orleans or Memphis. In addition, 'daguerreian' boats called at different points along the river offering to 'make likenesses' for those willing to pay the going rate.[6]

Finally, by 1860 at least two stores in the county had opened (to the delight of the locals), one in the city of Bolivar and the other near the Perkins plantation at Glencoe. Mrs. Perkins could now pick up groceries at her convenience from the local merchant, William Harrison.

Later, and somewhat in contrast to the road leading south to Greenville, another 'road' emerged. Cut through the backwoods and leading eastward through the county's interior toward the Bogue Phalia River, it proved to be even more rudimentary and far less reliable than the first road. As late as 1861, one traveler described both it and eastern Bolivar County as "a rather hard looking country, almost a perfect wilderness & the worst road that I ever saw." On another occasion, he recalled nearly having to swim with his horse in order to follow the same road.[7] The same traveler also reported that in 1861 the six-mile journey from the Perkins

---

[5]Sillers, *History of Bolivar County*, 103. Steamers also called at nearby Stop Landing but only when flagged (to stop).

[6]Bateman Diary, April 1 and April 7, 1856. Daguerreian boats were floating photographic (daguerreotype) studios that regularly plied the Mississippi River.

[7]Westfall Diary, February 19 and March 19, 1861.

plantation to Lake Bolivar took two hours by horseback. Proceeding north from the lake, he had to cross a swamp to reach his lodging at the John Burrus Plantation.[8]

The essentially rural nature of Bolivar County had not prevented the Perkins family and other planters from continuing to realize tremendous profits from their cotton plantations. All continued to be inextricably linked (more so each year) to the financial web spun by the cotton industry – the South depended on cotton and cotton depended on slavery. Together, cotton and slavery with landownership, the third major component of the Southern cotton culture, lifted the standard of living and social stature of these already affluent planters to even loftier levels as the decade progressed.

This is not to say that every planter in the region enjoyed success in the antebellum era. On the contrary, some were guilty of overindulgent personal spending, overinvestment, or simply mismanagement of their plantations, resulting in financial problems.[9]

Antebellum Bolivar County's rising land values reflected the region's growing prosperity and contributed to the overall wealth of its planters. Since William's first land purchases in Bolivar County in 1842, the worth of the family's acreage by 1854 had appreciated considerably. The county's tax assessment records for 1846, 1850, and 1854 illustrate the changing values of seven sections of the Perkins family's land (Table 1).

The table shows that by 1854 the total value of Perkins' seven sections had increased more than three times, exceeding $53,000. (Other landowners across the county experienced similar such gains.) Noteworthy are William's section three lands that fronted the Mississippi River and understandably proved to be his most valuable parcel. (Omitted from the chart, however, is a 480-acre tract in section 29 owned by the gold mining Charles Perkins and valued at $2,400 in 1850. In the ensuing land valuation document for 1854, it is described as 'vacant' and not valued even though Charles had returned from California by then.) Overall, the

---

[8]Ibid., January 13, 1861.

[9]Stampp, *Peculiar Institution*, 391.

per-acre value of *some* of William's parcels had increased from $3-5 in 1846 to as much as $20-25 for prime acreage by 1854.[10]

Table 1 - Values for William P. Perkins' land 1846, 1850, 1854[11]

Section	Value-1846	Value-1850	Value-1854
3	$4,014	$3,345	$13,380
4	$471	$393	$1,572
10	$277	$231	$925
17	$3,511	$2,526	$11,708
21	$1,920	$1,200	$6,400
22	$3,840	$3,200	$12,800
23	$1,914	$1,595	$6,380
Totals	$15,947	$12,490	$53,165

[10]The *decreased* value for the same sections in 1850 possibly can be explained by a "market adjustment" or a different method of valuation used by the local assessor.

[11]Sections are located in Bolivar County, Range 20 North, 9 West. Mississippi, State Archives, Various Records, 1820-1951, Bolivar County Tax Rolls 1846-1858, Box 3455, *1846*, images 20-24, Box 9845, (Bolivar County Land Roll), *1850*, images 30, 31, and *1854*, images 77, 78, accessed October 31, 2011, *Family Search*, https://www.familysearch.org/search/image/index#uri=https%3A//api.familysearch.org/records/collection/1919687/waypoints. Figures are rounded to the nearest dollar. Perkins owned section sixteen, unassessed school land, not included here. Also omitted is Perkins' shared acreage in section 1 that had not been purchased until after1846 and had apparently been sold by 1854.

In both the antebellum and postwar years, land in Bolivar County, particularly in the alluvial riverside areas, continued to be highly prized. Looking to the future, the Perkins family could depend on these valuable sections to provide not only a significant source of wealth from the crops they yielded (in most years) but also a potential cash source should the family ever want or need to sell. William Perkins' wise investment in buying up this Mound Plantation acreage typified that of other planters in the burgeoning Delta region.

Even though many of the county's planters enjoyed great success, some still sought ways to generate even more income. Possibly not typical of Bolivar County's planters at the time, but certainly existent nonetheless, was the system used by some enterprising owners to gain additional earnings by hiring out their slaves. Normally, a master might hire out one, two, or several slaves for a specified length of time and for a specified 'salary' paid by the new employer to the original master, of course. One Bolivar County planter, Isaac Hudson, hired out two Negro males for four years, 1857-1860, receiving $1,320 for their labor over that time, or about $165 per slave per year. In another instance Bolivar County estate commissioners (managers) hired out thirteen slaves in 1861, including a mother with an eleven month old, for a total of $1,575 per year. Males, aged seventeen to sixty-one, brought $150 income each for the estate, hired females $100 or $125, except for Ellen, age fifty, and Becky age ten. They generated only twenty-five dollars each, most likely due to Ellen's advanced age and Becky's youth. The infant, Mary Francis, was only included in the group so as to avoid a separation from her mother.[12] Because of the size of the Mound Plantation and its constant demand for maximum labor, it is doubtful that the family hired out any of its slaves, although the potential for such an arrangement always existed.

---

[12]Mississippi Probate Records1781-1930, Bolivar Wills and Inventories 1861-1924, Volume C-D, images 10 and 26, accessed September 4, 2012, at *Family Search*, https://familysearch.org/pal:/MM9.3.1/TH-1942-30970-20663-68?cc=2036959&wc=MMY2-QH3:743804828.

As the mid-1800s progressed, the profits these wealthy planters achieved, because of the world's demand for King Cotton, allowed them to indulge in a lifestyle accessible to only a privileged elite in the slaveholding South. Spacious, finely furnished plantation homes, children educated in prestigious eastern colleges, and lavish dinner parties all became a typical part of their lives in Bolivar County. A resident recalled, "Every lady [of the planter aristocracy] had her carriage, a pair of fine horses, and coachman at her command; this meant much visiting, many picnics, fish frys, dinner parties, and balls."[13]

Planter families also spent the days involved in a variety of other activities. Planters like William Perkins conducted business transactions and saw to the operation of their plantations, while other family members exchanged notes, played backgammon or draughts (checkers), joined each other for river outings, and jaunts to the Indian Mounds (those on the Perkins plantation or at present-day Winterville in Washington County). Ladies put up preserves, read recent books, and fished. Jane Perkins (the daughter) gained attention for her ribbon rosette creations.[14] Mary Bateman also mentions a group of local gentlemen attempting to serenade the residents of her Argyle Plantation.[15]

The wealthy Bolivar County slavocracy also spent time away from their plantations. Many prosperous planters and their families journeyed North during Mississippi's oppressively hot summer months (". . . warm days, almost warm enough to make us all sick in this country" wrote one resident) seeking relief in cool mountain or seaside resorts while leaving their plantations in the hands of reliable overseers.[16] In the fall when they returned,

---

[13]Walter Sillers in James Cobb, *The Most Southern Place on Earth*, (New York: Oxford University Press, 1992), 16-17.

[14]Jane (Perkins Moore) later received an honorable mention for her ribbon rosettes at a St. Louis Fair in 1870. John Tracy, ed., *Tenth Annual Report of the Saint Louis Agricultural and Mechanical Association*, (St. Louis: Democrat Book and Job Printing House, 1871), 80.

[15]Bateman Diary, April 10, 1856. The singers were unaware that the Argyle residents were not home.

[16]Westfall Diary, June 15, 1861.

parties and dinners with neighbors were commonplace.[17] For these extraordinarily prosperous Bolivar County planter families - it was the best of times.

While residing in this atmosphere of prosperity, Bolivar County's whites nonetheless understood that in their midst a great disparity existed between their small numbers and the large black population. As in both Madison and Wilkinson Counties, the persistent fear of a slave insurrection existed on every plantation up and down the river creating a necessary vigilance. No recorded slave uprisings occurred in Bolivar County, but one contemporary noted in 1857:

> I am told that in Bolivar County – containing 5 to 10,000 blacks & 171 voters [white polls] - there is great apprehension of insurrection. Judge [unnamed] made several speeches on the importance of strict discipline on every plantation and abolitionists are suspected to be amongst them in the disguise of teachers.[18]

Of note, as much as the author's mention of insurrection, is her reference to disguised abolitionists in their midst. Her allusion (illusion?) revealed the South's long-standing fear of abolitionists and simultaneously its ongoing protectionist attitude regarding slavery - a sign that Northern antislavery rhetoric had made an undeniable impact on the Southern slaveholding psyche.[19]

Within the county two deadly *individual* acts of black resistance did occur in 1857, fueling white anxiety and reinforcing the need for watchfulness. In the first instance, a female slave of the Lafayette Jones family, the owners of the Rosedale plantation, allegedly poisoned her owners with tainted tea, causing the death of Jones' daughter while rendering other family members violently

---

[17]Samuel Worthington, a member of a large and affluent slaveholding family in Washington County just south of Bolivar County, in Cobb, *The Most Southern Place*, 16.

[18]Lizinka Brown letter in Paul D. Casdorph, *Confederate General R.S. Ewell: Robert E. Lee's Hesitant Commander*, (Lexington: University Press of Kentucky, 2004), 82.

[19]Not all antislavery proponents were abolitionists, but all abolitionists were antislavery. Abraham Lincoln, early on, fit into the first category.

ill. Locals hoped, though, that this was an isolated incident of personal revenge after they learned that Jones' repeated sexual assaults on this slave might have provoked her.[20] In a second occurrence, three runaway slaves in northern Bolivar County at Carson's Landing murdered an overseer, a Mr. Bradley, as he attempted to arrest them.[21]

* * * * *

        Following his father's death and on his return from the goldfields in mid 1851, Charles Perkins, the Princeton graduate and landed heir to the eighteenth century Southern aristocracy of his grandfathers, had emerged as the head of the Perkins family. Thrust into this dynamic world of the county's booming cotton culture, he assumed the duties of plantation caretaker and resumed his privileged lifestyle while bringing a new generational quality to the family plantation. Whether Charles was actually prepared to manage his sprawling estate is unknown. His attendance at Princeton for four years during part of the 1840s, combined with his approximately two-year stay in California may have more or less placed him in a position as a 'planter in training'. Given Charles' success in the goldfields and his apparent high level of intelligence, perhaps his transition from student and gold rush miner to planter was not all that difficult.[22]

        Locally, Bolivar County was producing more than 4,000 bales of ginned cotton yearly, and that number was projected to increase as the decade progressed and as more acres came under cultivation. Despite signs of expansion throughout the county, Charles did not seek to acquire additional land nor (apparently) slaves. Instead, he appeared content to maintain the status quo in those two areas even though expansion had become the statewide

---

[20]Jones had raped this particular female slave, Josephine, on several occasions and reportedly had fathered mulatto children with other female slaves on his plantation. Josephine's ultimate fate remains unknown.

[21]*Memphis Daily Appeal*, April 28, 1857, 2, 1.

[22]It is uncertain what Charles did during the year between his graduation and his 1849 departure for California. A document dated January 17, 1849, indicates that Charles Perkins resided not on the Mound Plantation then, but in Madison County. *Bolivar County Deed Book C*, FHL, microfilm roll 886086, 544.

mantra of many other planters. (Charles, while in the goldfields, probably remained unaware of the fact that the number of planters statewide had risen to 5,343 by 1850, while the number of overseers reached 2,324.[23])

As Charles began adjusting to his new role, he also encountered in this antebellum era a changing world that required a degree of adaptability. While slavery had become more firmly entrenched than ever in Mississippi and Bolivar County during his nearly two-year absence, the institution itself and the slaveholders who benefited from it endured a constant battering by some Northerners who demanded its abolition and emancipation for its victims. "They [slaveholders] found themselves increasingly isolated, increasingly on the defensive, increasingly compelled to improvise, as the code by which their fathers had justified the holding of slaves became less and less intelligible."[24] In such a hostile atmosphere, how long could slavery, the very foundation of the Perkins family's livelihood, even survive? In the family's history spanning nearly two centuries in America none of Charles' slaveholding ancestors ever had to seriously consider such a daunting question.

Meanwhile, as the decade of the 1850s progressed, and despite the abolitionist's unsettling antislavery rhetoric, plantation life for the Perkins clan continued with a degree of normalcy - William Perkins' heirs matured, married, and cotton, of course, thrived.

In New Orleans on December 14, 1851, oldest daughter Jane Perkins married a tall, blonde-haired, South Carolina native, Stephen B. (S. B.) Curry.[25] The union of the eligible Jane - who one observer later described as an "excellent, pleasant, agreeable, [and] quite lively" lady to this prosperous thirty-four-year old

---

[23]Seventh Census, 1850 Agriculture, Bolivar County, Mississippi, Table X, *Professions, Occupations, and Trades of Male Population*, 455, and for cotton figures 458.
[24]Stampp, *Peculiar Institution*, 19.
[25]*New Orleans Daily Picayune*, December 17, 1851, 2, column 4. In *Biographical and Historical Memoirs of Mississippi*, 586, the author errs in stating that Jane Perkins Curry married in 1853 or 1854. On July 4, 1852, Ann Hardeman wrote that the recently married Currys (Stephen B. and Jane) joined her for a wedding at her home near Jackson, O'Brien, *An Evening*, 242.

planter proved mutually beneficial.[26] Jane had gained a financially astute, upwardly mobile husband while Curry, at once, became part of the most affluent family in Bolivar County. Of course, he would be expected to maintain Jane's already advantaged life style with profits from his plantation and a partnership in a New Orleans business.

Curry regarded himself as primarily a planter according to the census of 1850. He claimed thirty slaves on his plantation, valued at $24,000, in East Carroll Parish, Louisiana, on the Mississippi River. (By 1860 he would claim ninety-one slaves in Bolivar County.)[27] Later, Jane and Stephen Curry resided not on his plantation but in New Orleans, the flourishing commercial city of fever and fortune, where Curry could be closer to his other livelihood.[28]

In New Orleans Curry partnered with businessman J. J. Person, an acquaintance of several years. Both Curry and Person had resided in Claiborne County, Mississippi, in the 1840s where Curry alone had recorded merchandise sales of between $8,000 and $15,000 from 1841 to 1847. Sometime after 1847 the men formed Curry, Person, and Company, cotton and sugar factors or agents, and conducted their transactions first in an upstairs office at 29 Commercial Place, then at 48 Carondelet St. in New Orleans.[29] Using his business expertise, Curry also gradually eased into the role of aiding Perkins family members in a variety of dealings.

In April 1850 Curry had facilitated the successful final payoff arrangements for his then future father-in-law, William Perkins, involving Perkins' $12,400 loan from Charles Henry Fisher of Philadelphia.[30] Between 1853 and 1857 Curry, in his ca-

[26]Westfall Diary, March 7, 9, 1861.
[27]Eighth Census, 1860, Bolivar County, Mississippi, Slave Schedules, s. v. " S. B. Cuny," 43-44, accessed September 21, 2011, *Ancestry.com*. Due to the census taker's handwriting Curry's name appears as S. B. "Cuny" in the 1860 Mississippi Slave Schedules.
[28]Ann Hardeman diary entry, July 4, 1852, in O'Brien, *An Evening*, 242.
[29]*New Orleans Commercial Bulletin*, July 2, 1852, 4, column 1. In 1861 Person still operated the business but without Curry who, by then, had resided on the Mound Plantation since approximately 1856.
[30]*Bolivar County Deed Book C*, FHL, microfilm roll 886086, 441-442. Charles Henry Fisher (1814-1862) was a leading Philadelphia businessman in the decade 1840-1850. He accumulated a huge fortune in property management, money

pacity as a cotton and sugar factor, personally conducted business with the influential and respected Wilkinson County planter James Alexander Ventress, his mother-in-law's (Jane Stewart Perkins) cousin.[31] Later, in transactions involving the estate of William Perkins, Curry acted as an agent for Louisa Ann Perkins Pugh, his sister-in-law, then living in Louisiana.[32] Curry later would utilize both this business knowledge and his experience as a cotton planter to great effect on the Mound Plantation.

In 1853 the oldest two Perkins brothers Charles, approximately twenty-seven, and Daniel, now twenty, became involved in Bolivar County government. That year the Board of Police voted to pay Daniel Perkins and others for their work as election officers or clerks. Charles later assumed the role of county coroner, while Daniel held another post as county ranger, the person in charge of overseeing the securing and return of the county's stray domestic animals. Whether these were elected or appointed positions is unclear. Questionable are Charles' qualifications for his coroner's position. Nothing in his college course work would have prepared him for such a job. Near the end of the year, Charles, perhaps one of the county's more eligible young bachelors, assumed an entirely new responsibility unrelated to his Bolivar County civic duties.

On December 22, 1853, Charles Perkins married Emeline Mobrey Adams, twenty-three, in Hinds County, Mississippi.[33] Born on September 13, 1830, in Frankfort, Kentucky, Emeline

---

lending, and as a corporate agent. Much of his wealth was lost due to several shady transactions in 1859. How William in Mississippi managed to secure this loan from Fisher in Philadelphia is unknown, but the transaction further demonstrates the link between Northern capital and Southern planters.

[31]James Alexander Ventress (1805-1867) was a college educated (in Europe) lawyer, a highly respected Mississippi politician (state representative and senator, and Speaker of the Mississippi House of Representatives), a driving force in the founding of the University of Mississippi (Ole Miss), and a member of its Board of Trustees from the time it was founded until he passed away. A true Renaissance man, he also owned a cotton plantation in Wilkinson County and other land in Texas and Louisiana. Ventress's mother, Elizabeth Stewart Ventress, was the sister of Charles Stewart, Jane Stewart Perkins' father.

[32]*Bolivar County Deed Book F*, FHL, microfilm roll 886087, 220.

[33]"Mississippi Marriages, Hinds County, 1776-1935," s.v. "C. S. Perkins," accessed June 15, 2011, *Ancestry.com*.

Advertisement for Curry & Person, cotton factors, in the *New Orleans Commercial Bulletin,* July 2, 1852.

and her parents had arrived in Mississippi prior to 1844, residing in or near Jackson. Little is known of her family other than the fact that her father had died when she was fourteen. By 1850 her widowed mother, Anna Mobrey Adams, claimed a modest plantation worth $5,000 and possessed fourteen slaves. Emeline's marriage into the wealthy Perkins family immediately improved her social position, thrusting her into the world of Mississippi's affluent planter class as well as necessitating her move to the Mound Plantation.

After their wedding the couple lived on the Mound Plantation for approximately three years, all the while enjoying life and the benefits associated with the planter aristocracy.[34] Their marriage produced no children. Charles managed the family plantation, but he still owned independently 480 acres in section twenty-nine which he had purchased from his parents in January 1849.[35] Though Charles (and his brother Daniel Perkins) only claimed five slaves each, by October 1855 the estate of William Perkins, administered by Mrs. Perkins, claimed 125 slaves.[36] Combined, these 135 servants and field hands remained under Charles' control as the plantation's manager.

After the death of her father in 1850 and before the return of her brother from the goldfields, William's daughter Louisa Ann Perkins Pugh and her husband Dr. J. J. Pugh had temporarily moved from Madison County, Mississippi, to the Mound Plantation. Remaining there for several months, the Pughs had consoled Ann's mother while assisting in the operation of the plantation. By 1855 the Pughs had long since returned to Madison County, though Dr. Pugh still practiced medicine at the lucrative Cooper's Well spa in nearby Hinds County.[37]

In late August of that year, tragedy struck the Perkins family with Dr. Pugh's unexpected death from yellow fever at age forty-eight. He left behind his widow, Ann, and the six children. Pugh's death proved to be the harbinger of a serious outbreak of the disease "which broke with the force of a thunderbolt" accord-

[34]In contrast to the notoriety Perkins had gained as a result of his California fugitive slave case, few historical references to Charles exist after his return from California. However, on September 12, 1853, just months prior to his wedding C. S. Perkins, age twenty-seven, a "planter", arrived in New Orleans from Vera Cruz, Mexico, aboard the steamship *Texas*. "New Orleans Passenger Lists, 1820-1945," s. v. "C. S. Perkins", *Ancestry.com*. His reason for journeying to Mexico remains unknown. One year later in a September 3 or 4, 1854, diary entry, Ann Hardeman recorded that Cousin C. (presumably Charles) Perkins and his wife visited her home near Jackson, Mississippi. O'Brien, *An Evening*, 256.
[35]*Bolivar County Deed Book C*, FHL, microfilm roll 886086, 544-545. Part of the Mound Plantation, this acreage was valued at $4,800 in 1856, twice the price he had paid seven years earlier..
[36]Mississippi State, Archives, Various Records, 1820-1951, Bolivar County tax rolls 1846-1858, Box 9845, images 126 and 134, accessed October 29, 2011, *Family Search,* https://www.familysearch.org/search/image/index#uri=https%3A//api.familysearch.org/records/collection/1919687/waypoints.
[37]O'Brien, *An Evening*, 425.

ing to Ann Hardeman, first at Cooper's Well where over forty
cases were reported by September 18. Later, yellow fever deaths
occurred throughout central and southwestern Mississippi, particularly along the river.[38] According to one account, his family had
remained unaware that Pugh actually suffered from the disease
until a doctor's diagnosis, just before Pugh's death. Jane Curry,
who may have joined her sister Ann at Pugh's bedside, became
quite ill also, but it is doubtful that she suffered from the fever.[39]
Lamenting Pugh's loss, Ann Hardeman recorded that he was buried at 6 a.m. the morning after his death presumably near his home
in Madison County.[40]

Mosquito borne diseases had now claimed the lives of
Ann Perkins Pugh's father and her husband in a span of just five
years. For decades dengue and yellow fever had been the scourges
of Natchez, New Orleans, and other locations where swampy conditions allowed mosquitoes to proliferate, leading to massive, seasonal outbreaks of these killers. Neither were newcomers to North
America by any means.

The genus (*Aedes aegypti*) of the mosquito that transmit-
ted the diseases that killed William and his son-in-law along with
thousands of others in North America over the centuries had arrived here aboard slave ships from Africa. Yellow fever had origi-
nated there and then spread to the New World beginning in the
1500s at the onset of the trans Atlantic slave trade. The same mosquito genus that carried the yellow fever virus also transported the
virus causing dengue fever, outbreaks of which first occurred in
the Americas during the 1780s. Ironically, these slave ships which
had transported the ancestors of the slaves that William Perkins,
Dr. Pugh, and other white slaveholders worked on their plantations, also unknowingly carried the original mosquito vectors
whose offspring eventually led to the two slaveholders' own
deaths centuries afterwards. The slave ships had not only transported the source of Perkins' and Pugh's wealth, but also the seeds
of their destruction.

---

[38]Jefferson Davis, Lynda Lasswell Crist (ed.), *The Papers of Jefferson Davis*,
(Baton Rouge: Louisiana State University Press, 1985), 5: 134, fn 2.
[39]O"Brien, *An Evening*, 264.
[40]Ibid. In Bolivar County as late as 1880, yellow fever still raged intermittently.

As the family attempted to cope with Dr. Pugh's death in
August, Charles Stewart Perkins also died, just months later in late
1855 or in January 1856 of unspecified causes.[41] As the family's
oldest son, but still a young man at twenty-eight, Charles had been
destined to direct the family's interests into the 1860s and beyond.
But, now he had joined his deceased father on the family burial
mound near Williams Bayou.

The surprising deaths of Dr. Pugh and then Charles in
rapid succession must have caused great consternation in the Perkins and Pugh families. Both men seemed poised to make an impact - Dr. Pugh in medicine at Cooper's Well and a matured Charles, as the head of the Perkins family and a planter aristocrat in a
thriving cotton economy.

Following Charles' death, his widow Emeline initiated a
series of events, that if considered individually might not merit
any comment. However, taken collectively and with some speculation, they might indicate that a rift existed between Emeline and
her Perkins inlaws.

First, Emeline chose not to remain in Bolivar County with
the extended Perkins family. Instead, she returned to the city of
Jackson in Hinds County, possibly to live with her family. Then,
approximately one year later, on January 31, 1857, Emeline, while
still residing in Hinds County, managed to purchase from the heirs
of the William Perkins estate administered by her mother-in-law
Jane Perkins several tracts of Mound Plantation land, "heretofore
of the plantation known and designated as Southland" [the name
given for that portion of the Mound Plantation reserved for William Perkins' heirs]; specifically those in *parts* of sections twenty-
one to twenty-three and section twenty-nine totaling 1,040 acres.[42]

---

[41]Legal documents found in the Bolivar County records in the Mormon Genealogical Library in Salt Lake City provided the clue as to the date of Charles'
death. Commissioners assigned to administer certain parts of the deceased William Perkins' will mentioned in their report dated January 26, 1856, Charles'
estate, meaning Charles had passed away before then. *Bolivar County Deed Book
F,* FHL, microfilm roll 886087, 220.

[42]Ibid., 219-220. Section twenty-nine had belonged to Charles Perkins since
1849, so it is unknown why it had not become part of Emeline's inheritance. In
turn, Mrs. Perkins divided the proceeds from the $12,500 sale between her chil-
dren, Noland S. and James W. Perkins, the Currys (S. B. and Jane), Daniel Per-

Subsequently, Emeline sold either all or a portion of this recent purchase to Lewis Galloway, undoubtedly understanding the negative impact the sale would have on the Perkins family. Though Galloway was a neighbor owning acreage adjacent to the Perkins' plantation, his acquisition of this land meant that for the *first* time since the Perkins family's arrival in Bolivar County part of the vast acreage of the Mound and Southland Plantations now rested in the hands of non-family members.[43] Furthermore, this acreage, part of which straddled Williams Bayou, lay at the very heart of the Perkins family property. (Galloway later sold the same acreage to his brother-in-law Thomas B. Lenoir.) Apparently, Emeline had completed this purchase intending to quickly sell it, because that is exactly what occurred. Could her intent have been to spite the Perkins family for some perceived wrong? While we will never know Emeline's true motive, the fact remains that due to her choices the Perkins plantation by mid 1857 had been reduced in size by approximately one third.

With Charles' death the operation of the Mound Plantation passed first to Jane Perkins. Soon, she enlisted both Daniel, now her oldest son, and later her son-in-law Stephen Curry to assist in managing the estate. In order to be nearer to Mrs. Perkins, the Currys had moved to Bolivar County in 1856, perhaps just after Charles' death. A later reference made by Stephen B. Curry himself in 1858 or 1859 as part of his testimonial promoting a plow seems to substantiate that by then the plantation had come under his stewardship.[44] He wrote to the manufacturer:

---

kins, and the widowed Louisa (Ann) Pugh. Since Mrs. Perkins made no provisions to include her eighteen-year old son William S. in the distribution, he may have been deceased by then.

[43] In January 1860 the widowed Emeline married Dr. P. T. Bailey (or Baily) of Hinds County, the son of a mayor of Jackson, Mississippi. Together they raised six children. Neither of their two boys was named Charles. The couple resided in Jackson, Mississippi, for decades. Coincidentally, living next to the Baileys in Jackson in 1860 was William Yerger. It was Judge Yerger who had provided a young Charles Perkins with the necessary power of attorney document eight years earlier during Charles' efforts to recover his three slaves. Perhaps at some point, neighbors Yerger and Emeline discussed memories of the late Charles. Emeline died in Jackson on July 24, 1884, at age fifty-four.

[44] In a June 25, 1856, diary entry Mary Bateman hints that the Currys in fact resided at the Mound Plantation by then. She wrote that "after supper Mr and Mrs

I tried your double plough and scraper on my plantation
in Bolivar County, Miss. last spring [1857 or 1858] and
found its performance fully equal to your representation
of it. As a labor saving machine, it supplies a want long
felt in the cultivation of cotton and corn.

                              Respectfully yours,
                              SB Curry[45]

The operative word in Curry's note is his use of the pos-
sessive "my" with plantation. Had Charles been alive or had Daniel still resided there (he had left by then to manage his own plantation), the Mound property would of course have been under their
guidance. Thus, most likely with Jane Perkins' blessing, her son-
in-law, the business-wise slaveholder Stephen Curry, assumed the
operation of the entire Mound Plantation for the next several
years. However, as the family's oldest son and now the head of the
Perkins clan, the youthful Daniel most likely would have still participated in any management matters that arose. The Currys soon
combined their 103 slaves with the sixty-eight slaves Mrs. Perkins

---

Curry, & Mr Dan Perkins came to see us; when they left we all went over with
them & spent about half an hour with Mrs [Jane] Perkins; . . . Mr Curry, Mr
[probably Calhoun] Haile & Mr Perkins came back to Vane's with us and when
Mr Curry and Mr Perkins went *home* they took Mr Haile with them to spend the
night" (italics and underlining mine).
[45]Curry addressed his note to Oscar J. E. Stuart of Holmesville, Pike County,
Mississippi. Stuart, who was married to a Hardeman family member, attempted
to patent the "double cotton scraper in front of which is attached two ploughs."
Supposedly, it would reduce the labor involved, enabling one man and two horses
to do the work of four men and four horses. Stuart's problem in seeking his patent was that a *slave*, Ned, had invented the device. Because slaves were not citizens, neither Stuart nor Ned could patent the invention. With the onset of the
Civil War, the issue became lost in other important matters. Nonetheless, an unusual situation emerged in which the law worked against a slave while at the
same time benefiting him; denying Ned's master legal right to an invention that
was not his. Rayvon Fouche, *Black Inventors in the Age of Segregation: Granville T. Woods, Lewis H. Latimer & Shelby J. Davidson*, (Baltimore: Johns Hopkins University Press, 2003), 11.

had ceded to her minor sons to form a work force *larger* than William Perkins had claimed in 1850.[46]

In 1857 not long after the deaths of Dr. Pugh and Charles Perkins, Daniel Perkins, now twenty-four, married eighteen-year old Caroline Campbell, the daughter of the late William R. Campbell. He had met Caroline (Carrie) due to the proximity of the Campbell and Perkins plantations and because of the long-standing and close relationship between their two families.

In 1856 as he began courting young Caroline, Daniel had paid several visits to the Campbells. Mary Bateman, then residing with the Campbells, mentioned a number of these calls (during the seven months in 1856 in which she kept her diary) but writes of no flirtations between Daniel and Caroline. Typical of Bateman's entries was, "Mr. [Daniel] Perkins called on us this morning [continuing his apparently secretive courtship of Caroline] and staid [sic] about two hours. He left before dinner [lunch]."[47] This encounter was the young couple's second in two days, as Caroline, escorted by Mary Bateman and others, had visited the Perkins' plantation the day before. As the months passed, the couple's relationship grew, culminating in their marriage in February of the following year.

On February 3, 1857, at the Campbell's Argyle Plantation in Washington County the Methodist Reverend William Wadsworth presided over Daniel and Caroline's wedding.[48] Wadsworth conducted the ceremony in an area which gives an insight into the opulent scope of plantation 'homelife' - the spacious main hall, nearly sixty feet long and twenty feet wide, one of the many re-

---

[46]Mississippi, State Archives, Various Records, 1820-1951, Bolivar County tax rolls 1846-1858, Box 9845, images 146, 154, accessed October 29, 2011, *Family Search*, https://www.familysearch.org/search/image/index#uri=https%3A//api.familysearch.org/records/collection/1919687/waypoints. The records indicate these slave numbers represented only those slaves under sixty. Therefore, the family would have counted additional slaves if the total of the sixty-and-over slaves had been included. Some of the Currys' 103 slaves may have been those Jane Curry had inherited from her father's estate, thus reducing the number of slaves her mother Jane Perkins owned.

[47]Bateman, *Diary*, Thursday, June 26, 1856.

[48]Wiltshire, *Marriages*, 4: 227. The wedding announcement had appeared in the *Vicksburg Weekly Whig* on February 11, 1857.

markable features of the Campbell's two and one-half story colonial style riverside home complete with a gated entrance.[49] (Given the Perkins' comparable wealth, their Mound residence may have been at least as opulent.) The wedding ceremony and reception must have been one of the county's great social events. Guests would have arrived on horseback, by carriage, or by boat using the Campbell's landing on the Mississippi. A void existed in the celebration, however, as both the bride and groom's distinguished and respected fathers, the patriarchs of their respective families, had both passed away earlier in the decade.

The newlyweds shared many family similarities. Both were of partly Scottish decent, Caroline from her deceased father's family and Daniel from his mother's Stewart line. Both, too, had been raised in lives of privilege in the homes of two of the area's richest planter families. The Campbell's great wealth had also allowed them over the years to purchase various tracts of land in Bolivar County; some even near Williams Bayou and the Perkins plantation. Like the Perkins family, the Campbells also claimed a parent with a college degree. Caroline's mother, Margaret Tiedeman Campbell, held the distinction of being not only beautiful but also intelligent, as she had graduated from Clinton, Mississippi's first college, now Mississippi College (an exceedingly rare achievement for a woman in rural mid-century America).[50]

Following their marriage, the newlyweds resided at Daniel's inland plantation, Mecca, (expanded to 1,400 acres by 1865) approximately nineteen miles north of Mound Landing, on Laban's Bayou near Beulah.[51] Located next to County Sheriff Dick-

---

[49]William McCain, *Memoirs of Henry Tillinghast Ireys: Papers of the Washington County Historical Society, 1910-1915*, (Jackson: Mississippi Dept. of Archives and History and Mississippi Historical Society, 1954), 167. This reference is found in "Reminiscences of Argyle, the Home of William R. and Margaret Campbell" by Mrs. Hugh Miller from a paper delivered before the Washington County, Mississippi, Historical Association on March 3, 1913. Religious services were often conducted in this same great hall during the year.

[50]Ibid., 166. In 1831 Mississippi College became the first coeducational college in the United States to grant a degree to a woman.

[51] Sillers, *History of Bolivar County*, 567. Specifically, the location was in Township 22 North, Range 7 West, sections 10-12. The size of the plantation is based on information in Daniel Perkins' Amnesty Petition filed in July 1865. These petitions provide a wealth of information for the researcher. Completed by former

inson Bell's riverfront Belle Isle Plantation (Map 3 above), Mecca also was situated near an Indian mound.[52] Daniel initially claimed forty slaves, but this total had soon increased to sixty-nine. His forty-three males and twenty-six female slaves allowed Perkins to prosper over the next several years in his dual role as a full owner of his plantation and a shared owner of the Mound Plantation.[53] Though Mecca probably did not equal the grandeur of the Mound and Argyle Plantations, by June 1860 Perkins cultivated 500 of his 960 acres while claiming 175 bales of cotton on hand. He esti-

Confederate citizens like Daniel who did not fall under President Andrew Johnson's general amnesty, the petitions were evaluated on a case-by-case basis. (Perkins had claimed more than $20,000 worth of taxable property at war's end, thus triggering the need for his petition.) Amnesty Petitions are found online (payment required in some cases) at "Case Files of Applications from Former Confederates for Presidential Pardons 1865-1867," (Amnesty Papers), *Fold3* (formerly *Footnote.com*), publication number M1003, Roll 0034, Record group 94, p. 3, s.v. "Perkins, Daniel P. or Curry, Jane Perkins," accessed September 20, 2011, http://www.fold3.com/search.php?f_ancestor_id=hCLUo81Ws&df_ancestor_id= Within%3AConfederate+Amnesty+Papers&query=daniel+p.+perkins&submit=S earch. Complete copies of Daniel Perkins and Jane Perkins Curry's applications are in the author's possession. The name of Daniel Perkins' plantation is found in the papers of his estate in Mississippi Probate Records 1781-1930, Bolivar Wills and Inventories 1861-1924, Volume C-D, image 243, accessed September 4, 2012, at *Family Search*, https://familysearch.org/pal:/MM9.3.1/TH-1961-30970- 22228-76?cc=2036959&wc=MMY2-QH3:743804828.

[52]Dickinson Bell was the nephew of John Bell the former Speaker of the House of Representatives and in 1860 the Presidential candidate of the Constitutional Union Party who ran against Lincoln. The strong possibility exists that Daniel's father William knew John Bell. Both men were about the same age and grew up in or near Franklin, Tennessee. Bell had attended Cumberland College but had graduated a few years earlier than Perkins. In 1816 at age twenty, John Bell began practicing law in Franklin at the same time a twenty-one year old William Perkins resided there.

[53]Eighth Census, 1860, Bolivar County, Mississippi, Slave Schedules, s.v. "D. P. Perkins," 18,19, accessed September 28, 2011, *Ancestry.com*. Perkins' slaves shared fourteen slave cabins on his plantation. The number of slave houses per slaveholder appears for the first (and last) time in the 1860 census's slave schedules. Some slaveholders' names, however, appear minus any "number of slave houses." Daniel and his sister Jane are enumerated in the 1860 Slave Schedules and also the Agricultural Census, but they are not recorded in the 1860 population census as would be expected. Because the 1860 Bolivar County census tabulation occurred in July, it is quite possible that the absence on the census rolls of Daniel and Caroline Perkins along with Jane Curry was due to the fact that they had all journeyed North to escape the heat.

mated mated the plantation's worth at $38,400 with an additional
$4,650 invested in farm implements and livestock.[54]

* * * * *

For the Perkins family, the joy of Daniel's wedding was
eclipsed by several events during the closing years of the decade.
In the span of just two years between 1858 and 1860, multiple
misfortunes struck the family. First, the small city of Bolivar, just
north of Mound Landing, suffered an "inundation" almost entirely
destroying the crops there.[55] The flood may also have affected the
crops on the Mound Plantation and others situated southward
along the river. Next, only weeks later, on August 5, 1858, young
Noland Perkins died at his brother Daniel's plantation.[56] Following
that tragedy, Jane's husband, Stephen Curry, passed away some
twenty months afterward on April 18, 1860, while in Memphis,
Tennessee.[57] Presumably both he and Noland were buried at the
Perkins' Mound Cemetery near William and Charles Perkins.

At approximately the time of Curry's death or just before,
Jane Perkins may have ceded the remainder of her plantation's
slaves and land to her daughter Jane. Both the 1860 Agricultural
Census and the Slave Schedules show the land and slaves owned
by "Jane P. Perkins," Jane Curry's maiden name. With Stephen
Curry's death, the operation of the plantation had passed to the
only remaining adults residing there, the widows Jane Curry and
her mother. The younger Jane possibly assumed the more active
management role while, in all probability, she continued to receive
assistance from her brother Daniel. Noteworthy was her unique
standing as a female planter/manager in a traditionally male-
dominated occupation.

---

[54]The Agricultural and Manufacturing Census for Mississippi, 1860, Bolivar
County, reel 178, 9. Daniel claimed 4 horses, 16 mules, 10 milk cows, 12 working oxen, 41 cattle, 50 swine, and 800 bushels of Indian corn.
[55]*New York Times*, July 21, 1858.
[56]Wiltshire, *Marriages*, 4: 251. Reported in the *Vicksburg Weekly Whig*, September 8, 1858.
[57]*New Orleans Daily Crescent*, April 20, 1860, 4, column 4, "DIED: At Memphis, Tenn., on the 18.h inst., S. B. Curry, formerly of this city."

By June 1860, two months after her husband's death, Jane Curry reported cultivating just 430 acres, while the value of the livestock and farm equipment totaled $4,300. She inventoried 450 bales of ginned cotton, valued at estimated $30,000,[58] The 1860 Census Slave Schedules show she claimed the forty-three slaves previously owned by her mother and also the ninety-one slaves she and Stephen Curry owned just before his death.[59] With 134 slaves (living in thirty slave cabins), a beautiful home, and at least 1,430 acres of prime Delta property, Jane Curry continued the family tradition, emerging as one of the richest planters in the county. Though the size of Daniel's share of the Mound/Southland Plantation is unknown, for nearly the next ten years he and his widowed sister Jane would co-manage it while Daniel still resided on his Mecca Plantation.

Early in 1861, as Jane Curry continued to adjust to the loss of her husband and her enlarged management responsibilities on the plantation, her mother became critically ill. On a rainy Sunday, January 13, an itinerant, young, unmarried Methodist minister, Milton Westfall, visited the Mound Plantation, arriving by horseback. Then residing with the family of local planter, slaveholder, and judge, John C. Burrus Sr., at Burrus' nearly completed two-story home on his inland Hollywood Plantation, Westfall made the trip in part to console the ailing Jane Perkins.

This visit would be the first of many Westfall would make in 1861 to the Mound Plantation in his capacity as a minister. He often ate dinner with Jane Curry, her family, and other guests. He also preached to both Jane and her Negroes on the plantation, or at the nearby Methodist Church in Glencoe (for whites only). Occasionally, Westfall described holding religious "class meetings" with Mrs. Curry's servants. On numerous visits he spent the night, before traveling to another plantation the following day.

As the rain continued outside, inside the Perkins' home Westfall talked and prayed with "sister" Perkins in her room. He

---

[58]The Agricultural and Manufacturing Census for Mississippi, 1860, Bolivar County, reel 178, 1. Jane also counted 1 horse, 20 mules, 10 milk cows, 6 oxen, 60 other cattle, 60 swine, and 2,000 bushels of Indian corn.
[59]Eighth Census, 1860, Bolivar County, Mississippi, Slave Schedules, s. v. "Jane P. Perkins," 65 and 43-44 for the Stephen Curry (shown as 'Cuny' in the census) slaves, accessed September 28, 2011, *Ancestry.com*.

recorded in his diary, "think she will die eer [sic] many days."[60]
Lending emphasis to the seriousness of Jane Perkins' illness was
the arrival from Louisiana of her other daughter, Ann Perkins
Pugh, and granddaughter, twenty-year old Florence Pugh. Presumably, soon after Westfall's visit, Jane Perkins did indeed pass
away of an undisclosed illness at age sixty-one.

Buried next to her husband William on the Indian
mound's summit near her home of fourteen years, the elder Jane
joined her two deceased sons and her son-in-law Stephen Curry
also interred in the cemetery there. Living in a Southern patriar-
chal society since birth, Jane had enjoyed a privileged life, first as
a child, then later as a wife and mother, in two prominent slaveholding families. She must also have been a strong woman, to
withstand the challenges of living in early, undeveloped Madison
and Bolivar Counties, combined with the fact that she had delivered her last two sons late in life, the last when she was forty-
eight. Jane's final few years must have been filled with sadness, as
she lost a succession of male family members, several at young
ages. Her husband William had died in his fifty-fifth year, and in
the five-year span from 1855 to 1860 four others had joined him:
Dr. Pugh had died at age forty-eight, son Charles at twenty-eight,
Noland just seventeen, and most recently son-in-law Stephen
Curry at age forty-three. In the aftermath of each these deaths and
further accentuating the losses she had suffered, Jane Perkins had
witnessed the control of the plantation pass from William to Dr.
Pugh, then to Charles, later to Stephen Curry, and most recently to
her children Jane and Daniel in less than a decade.

Following her mother's death Jane, the only remaining
Perkins adult in the house, resided there with her younger brother,
"little Jimmie [James Perkins]" and Mr. Cating, an overly talkative

---

[60]Westfall Diary, January 12, 13, 1861. Milton S. Westfall (December 1831 - ?)
was a twenty-nine year old graduate of Allegheny College in Pennsylvania, an
institution affiliated with the United Methodist Church. A native of Carroll
County, Ohio (a free state), Westfall had arrived in Bolivar County just days into
the new year beginning a two-year posting there as an itinerant Methodist
preacher. He refers to his fellow Methodists as "brother" or "sister" throughout
his diary. Because Jane Curry was a Presbyterian, he referred to her as Mrs.
Curry. In none of his diary entries does he offer an opinion on the institution of
slavery, though he often bemoans the tragedy of the Civil War.

Englishman who served as Jimmie's tutor.[61] At the same time, Jane often welcomed visitors, some from out of state, into her home. Reverend Westfall mentioned Jane's warm hospitality, despite the recent deaths in her family. On one occasion he wrote, "... spent the evening very pleasantly in her [Mrs. Curry's] company ... feel perfectly at home." On another visit to the Mound Plantation several months later, Westfall stated, "The place is quite a pleasant & agreeable one. I feel perfectly at home here. She [Jane] is an excellent lady."[62] Considering Westfall had visited and lodged with many of Bolivar County's most prominent citizens – the Burrus, Wilkerson, Newman, Childers, Fields, and Lobdell families to name a few – his comments regarding his time at the Curry home constitute high praise.

* * * * *

On the eve of the Civil War, Mississippi's slave-based cotton economy had undergone a momentous expansion in the decade of the 1850s. In 1860 the state counted 30,943 slaveholders, approximately nine percent of its white population of 354,674. This nine percent claimed 436,631 slaves, an increase of more than 126,000 since 1850. The number of Mississippi's overseers had risen also to 3,941, a gain of more than 1,600 in ten years.[63] Not surprisingly, Mississippi, with its Delta counties at the forefront, produced over one million bales of cotton in 1859 (reported in the 1860 census), making it the nation's leading cotton producing state.

Locally, Bolivar County's development during the decade showed impressive growth. Its number of slaveholders had increased from sixty-eight in 1850 to 297.[64] By 1860 of its 10,471 residents, 9,078 were slaves compared to 1850 when it had counted 2,180 blacks out of its 2,577 inhabitants. The more than

---

[61]Ibid., March 29 and April 13, 1861.

[62]Westfall Diary, June 8, and September 7, 1861.

[63]Eighth Census, 1860, Mississippi, Population of the United States, *Occupations*, 670.

[64]Eighth Census, Agriculture of the United States, 1860, Mississippi, *Slaveholder and Slaves*, 232. Note, this is a different document than the Agricultural and Manufacturing Census.

fourfold gain in Bolivar County's slave numbers during the decade meant that it still remained an overwhelmingly slave-populated county. The percentage of slaves in the county's total population reflected an increase also, from 84.5 percent in 1850 to 86.6 percent in 1860. (The percentage of blacks in the population remained in the low to mid eighty percent ranges from 1860 onward, reaching a high, however, of eighty-nine percent in 1890.)[65]

Further evidence of Bolivar's increased wealth is seen in the amount of land tilled during the decade and the resulting increase in cotton production; the 16,973 tilled acres in 1850 had expanded to 85,188 acres in 1860. Consequently, the cotton yield soared during the same period - 4,723 bales by 1850, 16,027 in 1857, and 33,452 bales by 1860 (more than a seven fold increase in ten years).[66] (At 400 pounds per bale, the 1860 cotton crop totaled 13,380,800 pounds!) In Memphis, "A gentleman just up from Bolivar County" boasted that plantations there were enjoying a yield of a bale to an acre by October 1860.[67]

Moreover, coinciding with these significant population and production gains, Bolivar County farm values had reached dramatic levels, increasing from $739,211 in 1850 to $8,759,270 by 1860.[68] In fact, four Delta counties, Bolivar, Coahoma, Issaquena, and Tunica, were "listed in the 1860 census among the thirty-six wealthiest in the United States," based more on the value of the slave property held by Delta planters there than any other

---

[65]John Moore, *The Emergence of the Cotton Kingdom in the Old Southwest: Mississippi, 1770-1860*, (Baton Rouge: Louisiana State University Press, 1988), 128-129. Robert Lowry and William McCardle in their *History of Mississippi*, (Jackson: R.H. Henry & Company, 1891), 447, cite the 1890 census in stating that Bolivar County's population numbered 26,734 blacks and just 3,220 whites.
[66]The figure for 1857 is taken from the Bolivar County Tax Rolls 1846-1858, Box 9845, image 158.
[67]*Memphis Daily Appeal*, October 31, 1860, 1,1.
[68]Moore, *The Emergence of the Cotton Kingdom*, 128 and John Otto, *The Final Frontiers, 1880-1930: Settling of the Southern Bottomlands*, (Westport, Connecticut: Greenwood Press, 1999), 3. Also, Seventh Census, 1850 Agriculture, Bolivar County, Mississippi, Table XI, *Agriculture-Farms and Implements Stock, Products*, 456, and Eighth Census, Agriculture of the United States 1860, Bolivar County, Mississippi, *Agriculture Produced*, 84. Statewide, Bolivar County's "cash value of farms" figure was second only to Yazoo County.

factor.[69] By the end of the decade, these impressive numbers reflected a degree of growth and prosperity later viewed as Bolivar County's golden era.

Given Bolivar County's accelerated growth in its slave and slaveholder populations during the decade of the 1850s, it would be logical to assume that a similar increase in the county's number of overseers would also have occurred as it had statewide. On the contrary, in the Bolivar County Population Schedules and in the separate Slave Schedules of the 1860 Federal Census not a single overseer is designated. Though in 1850 Bolivar County tallied twenty-five overseers, ten years later the census enumerator 'failed' to identify any men in that occupation. That is not to say, however, that overseers had disappeared from the county, an impossibility given its more than 9,000 slaves and 297 slaveholders. Though we have no way of knowing exactly how many overseers Bolivar County claimed, they do 'appear' in the population lists of the 1860 census, but under the occupation of farmer or with no occupation shown.

For example, in a sampling of seven wealthy Bolivar County planters whose real and personal property ranged from $27,000 to $205,000 we find their names and census data followed *immediately* by the name of a usually young, single, male 'farmer', apparently unrelated to the planter, who either lived in the next dwelling or at the *same dwelling* as the slaveholder.[70] These, then, were undoubtedly some of the county's unspecified overseers. (In neighboring Coahoma County, the census enumerator referred to such individuals as 'managers' while in Madison County they were still recorded as overseers.) Inasmuch as George Poindexter, the county's census enumerator in 1860 and later a local judge, must have been a Bolivar County resident (though his name does not appear in the census records for any Mississippi

[69]James Bell, *The Evolution of the Mississippi Delta From Exploited Labor and Mules to Mechanization and Agribusiness*, (Bloomington, Indiana: iUniverse, 2008), 38.
[70]Eighth Census, 1860, Bolivar County, on pages 9, 20-22, 27, 29, and 31 see wealthy planters F.P. Wood, Sidna Deeson, D.S. Cameron, F.G. Gamble, D. C. Herndon, R. O. Starke, and Jefferson Wilkerson, followed by these men whom the author believes are their respective overseers: John Griffin, M. J. Tidwell, S. B. Stafford, J. L. Martin, Theodore Wood, L. B. Scruggs, and William Davidson.

county that year), and thereby familiar with many of the county's citizens, it seems his failure to designate any overseers in his count was due to his personal preference. Conceivably, Poindexter in his tallies sought to 'remove' the term from the record, maybe due to the stigma attached to the job. Perhaps, too, Poindexter had read Stowe's *Uncle Tom's Cabin*, and his recollection of that most villainous overseer in fiction, Simon Legree, compelled him to omit such undesirable references, thus 'cleansing' the public record. Whatever Poindexter's motive, his failure to include those Bolivar County men he knew to be overseers rendered the state's total of overseers in the 1860 Federal Census inaccurate.[71]

But, whatever the reason for this census anomaly, it foreshadowed the monumental changes about to descend on the South and Bolivar County. Within three months of Jane Perkins' death in January 1861, the prosperous Perkins clan would experience the beginning of the most serious challenge ever imaginable to both its economic stability and survival. The days of prosperity, along with the terms "slave" and slave "overseer" in not just Bolivar County, Mississippi, but across the entire slave-holding South, would become little more than memories and relics of a bygone era.

---

[71]Of the sixty-eight slaveholders in Bolivar County in 1850, twenty-five employed overseers, or about 37%. If we use this 1850 percentage, then 110 of the county's 297 slaveholders would have employed overseers in 1860.

IX

Civil War

"I have lately written articles, urging a separation of the union as our only salvation, for nothing short of it will give the south [sic] peace . . . as the tide of Abolition is fast overflooding the entire North, they will soon attempt the liberation of our slaves by legal enactment, when a civil war must ensue."

> John Munn, a native of Vermont then
> living in Canton, Mississippi, in a letter
> to his sister, July 8, 1836

Sir: I send by steamer New National two prisoners, residents of Mississippi, by the names of D. P. Perkins and Isaac Hudson.

> Union Lieutenant Commander Jas. M.
> Prichett, December 27, 1863

In April 1820 Thomas Jefferson, while discussing slavery as it related to the Missouri question stated, "But, as it is, we have the wolf by the ear, and we can neither hold him, nor safely let him go. Justice is in one scale, and self-preservation in the other." In the ensuing forty years following Jefferson's observation, little had been done in America to solve the growing and ultimately white hot slavery issue. In Congress mutual appeasement regarding Missouri (the Missouri Compromise)[1] and then later California (the Compromise of 1850) by increasingly antagonistic Northern and Southern politicos had kept secession and possibly war at bay. More recently, the publication of Harriet Beecher Stowe's strident antislavery novel *Uncle Tom's Cabin* (1852) had inflamed Southerners as much as the Supreme Court's ruling in the Dred Scott case (1857) had infuriated Northerners with its ruling ending the prohibition of slavery in federal territories and prohibiting Con-

---

[1]Congress passed the Missouri Compromise in 1820 trying to preserve the balance of power between slave and free states in Congress. Missouri thus entered the Union as a slave state and Maine was admitted as a free state. With the exception of Missouri, slavery was outlawed in the Louisiana Territory north of the 36° 30′ line.

gress from regulating slavery anywhere. In 1859 abolitionist John Brown's failed raid on the Federal Arsenal at Harper's Ferry – an effort to seize weapons there and incite a slave rebellion – and his subsequent execution made a him a martyr in the North, a pariah in the South, and served to polarize the nation even further.

In Bolivar County local planter and owner of the Beulah Plantation Frank A. Montgomery, who would later become a captain in the Confederate Army, recalled that before Brown's raid he had been a staunch unionist, but afterward he had supported secession. As Montgomery later explained, the raid itself had not been the catalyst for his change in position, but instead,

> the manner in which his [Brown's] death [execution] was received in the north, for he was looked upon as a martyr to the cause of freedom and was almost deified by many, convinced me as it did thousands of other union men in the state, that if our liberties were to be preserved and the rights of the states held sacred, we must endeavor to defend them out of and not in the union.[2]

As the schism, impossible to mend, between the North and South widened in the months leading up to the 1860 Presidential election, war clouds began to form over an anxious America. Northern abolitionists' sentiments continued to be challenged vehemently by an increasingly hostile and suspicious South that, while trumpeting both state's rights and independence doctrines, denied independence and freedom to its nearly four million slaves. Locally, evidence of such hostility can be found in an incident that occurred at Friar's Point in Coahoma County, just north of Bolivar County. An abolitionist there was barreled up and rolled over the bluff into the Mississippi River.[3]

Lincoln's victory in the Presidential election in the fall of 1860 (he had promised to allow slavery to remain where it existed but vowed to stop its expansion into the territories - content instead to have it eventually suffocate from within) set in motion the

---

[2]Montgomery, *Reminiscences*, 35-36.
[3]*Athens Post* (Tennessee) reporting a story in the *Memphis Enquirer*, December 14, 1860, 2, column 6.

secession of the Southern states beginning that December with the hotbed of secessionism, South Carolina, taking the lead. On January 9, 1861, Mississippi became the second state to secede. In a letter to the President of the Alabama Secession Convention, Hon. William S. Barry, President of the Mississippi Convention, wrote:

> I am instructed by the Mississippi State convention to inform you that the State of Mississippi, by vote of her convention approaching unanimity, has seceded unconditionally from the Union, and desires on the basis of the old Constitution, a new union with the seceded states.[4]

Soon, other Southern states followed suit, and the Confederate States of America proclaimed itself a new country. One Bolivar observer noted at the time, ". . .unless something of a compromise turns up very soon there will be civil war."[5]

Approximately three months later, on April 12, 1861, Civil War did indeed erupt, in Charleston Harbor, South Carolina, with a resounding Confederate cannonade. The consequences of those fateful shots lobbed on the Union's Ft. Sumter impacted all Americans during the next four years and resulted in the most destructive war in American history.

In the years prior to the Ft. Sumter attack - during the late 1840s and on into the 1850s - in Bolivar and other counties, events relating to the all-absorbing slavery question would have remained at the core of conversations between local planters, friends, and neighbors. Initially, the Perkins family may have remained passive in response to the sectional and political crisis beginning with the failed Wilmot Proviso (Chapter VI) in 1846. With William Perkins' death in 1850, the succession of the family's plantation managers – Dr. Pugh, Charles Perkins, S. B. Curry, Jane Perkins, Jane Perkins Curry, and Daniel Perkins – almost certainly struggled with the ensuing, well-publicized, controversial, and divisive is-

---

[4]Robert N. Scott, *The War of the Rebellion: A Compilation of the Official Records of the Union and Confederate Armies*, Series I, Volume LII, Part II, Confederate Correspondence, Etc. (Washington: Government Printing Office, 1898), 4.
[5]Westfall Diary, January 17, 1861.

sues as they occurred, wondering if and how they would impact a slave labor based plantation economy at a personal, local, and a national level.

Gradually, the Perkins family's stance may have evolved from restrained to hardline as reports and rumors reached Bolivar County of other national slavery-related events that occurred amidst increasing threats from the North.[6] The inevitable discussion(s) at the Perkins dinner table of the Compromise of 1850 and *Uncle Tom's Cabin*, with its negative portrayal of slavery, must have been very compelling. In the Perkins household, the Dred Scott decision was sure to have elicited strong opinions as well as kudos to the United States Supreme Court, given the similarities in circumstances and language between it and the 1852 Perkins slave case in California.

While it is impossible to say with certainty, the most recent events, John Brown's Raid and Lincoln's victory in the 1860 Presidential election, may have, on the one hand, finally and irrevocably solidified the Perkins' attitudes regarding the North's intentions and the slavery question to the point where they believed secession was the South's only remaining option. Thus, it is not difficult to imagine the Perkins family adopting at this time a secessionist stance similar to Frank A. Montgomery's and the "thousands of other [former] Union men" in Mississippi.

On the other hand, "as the momentum for secession gained strength, many of the Mississippi Delta leaders were philosophically against the argument for leaving the Union."[7] The area "was home to a large number of planters whose families had been well established in the planting class [like the Perkinses] before they moved into the Delta." These conservative planters, unlike their younger, upwardly mobile counterparts who were the most likely advocates of secession in Mississippi, had benefited from the status quo. "And for many of them the best hope for maintaining their wealth and status seemed to lie in remaining within the Union and, perhaps, seeking further constitutional guar-

---

[6]Charles Robinson, *Forsaking All Others: A True Story of Interracial Sex and Revenge in the 1880s South*, (Knoxville: University of Tennessee Press, 2010), 9.
[7]Bell, *The Evolution of the Mississippi Delta*, 39 and Cobb, *The Most Southern Place*, 31.

antees to preserve slavery."[8] (With their connections to the Southern cotton economy, northern bankers, merchants, textile mill owners, and shippers also desired a stable Union.) However, the fact that Mississippi had been the second state to secede indicated that many more of her citizens embraced the secessionist cause. And, despite the voiced reservations heard in the Delta, when the time came for a vote on secession, of the Delta counties' delegates only the Washington County representative voted against secession. (Miles McGehee, the prominent planter and slaveholder representing Bolivar County at the Mississippi Secession Convention, had voted in favor of seceding.) Whether or not the Perkins family uniformly supported the secessionist movement is unknown (perhaps they were internally divided), but once the war came its collective fate was tied to the success or failure of the Confederacy.

Upon hearing the news of the attack on Ft. Sumter on April 12, 1861, (via telegraph) from South Carolina, Reverend Westfall, in Bolivar County, recorded: "War is upon us now & we must fight – or be overwhelmed at once, if the war has commenced it will not terminate soon."[9] The following day Westfall visited the Mound Plantation where he "spent a very pleasant evening" with Mrs. Curry and the tutor, Mr. Cating. At some point the evening's conversation must have turned to the ongoing Confederate attack on Ft. Sumter and its implications, though Westfall and Mrs. Curry may have had a difficult time getting a word in – "He [Cating] is a very talkative person & seems to use more words in describing an idea than any person I know."[10]

During the first year of hostilities Bolivar County, more safely situated in the Deep South, remained untouched by the fighting though a great number of its men trained and then eventually went off to war. For different reasons no Perkins family men participated in the war. Only sons William S. Perkins, age twenty-two in 1861, and Daniel, twenty-eight, would have been age eligi-

---

[8]Ibid., Cobb.

[9]Westfall Diary, April 12, 1861. The first Confederate salvo fired on Ft. Sumter occurred at 4:30 a.m. Later, that same morning *in Mississippi*, Westfall read the news of the attack, attesting to the rapidity with which telegraphic dispatches traveled, even to remote Bolivar County.

[10]Westfall Diary, April 13, 1861.

ble to join the Confederate Army. But, William S. may have been deceased by then, and Daniel's undisclosed disability prevented him from serving. However, several of the Perkins' neighbors took up arms for the Confederacy. William Campbell Jr. (Daniel Perkins' brother-in-law), planters Dickinson Bell, Frank and William Montgomery, John Burrus Jr., his brother Edward, (Generals) Peter B. Starke and Charles Clark (Mississippi's wartime governor after he was wounded), Lt. Lafayette Jones, and a former overseer, Milford Coe, all served in various units during the war. In addition to these men, Thomas B. Lenoir, ironically a graduate of a northern school, Bowdoin College in Maine and the recent purchaser of a portion of the Perkins' Southland Plantation, served as a Bolivar County guerilla fighter. In a letter home, he implored his sister to teach his young son to hate Yankees and traitors.[11]

In May 1861 just weeks after the Ft. Sumter attack, the Glencoe and Bolivar home guard met and drilled amid great excitement from the local population.[12] Later that same month in a patriotic ceremony, a general presented a flag to the Bolivar Troop (a cavalry unit), made by the "Ladies of Bolivar County." Local officers, Bolivar Troop commander Captain F. A. Montgomery and General Starke, along with a dignitary from Vicksburg, addressed the onlookers, many of whom were their neighbors.[13] In the midst of this patriotic fervor, Reverend Westfall observed that, "war news seemed to linger in the minds of the people," and then he prophesized that "there will be thousands of lives lost before it [the war] terminates."[14]

Soon, Bolivar County volunteers were posted to local infantry or cavalry units, and later saw action in different states during the war. The recently organized Bolivar Troop, nearly 100 strong, received its orders to leave on June 12. One observer later predicted that, "I look for nearly all that are able to fight to be

---

[11](Washington D. C.), *Daily National Republican*, October 17, 1863, 4, column 2.
[12]Westfall Diary, May 11, 25, 1861.
[13]Ibid., May 29, 1861.
[14]Ibid., May 31, 1861.

called out and . . . very soon."[15] Eventually, nearly 300 Bolivar men served during the course of the war.[16]

As their fighting men departed, locals began to assume a war footing during the early months of the conflict. Planters faced the twin threat of a reduced cotton crop and a suddenly deteriorating economy. Perhaps echoing what he had heard from locals, Reverend Westfall wrote during this period, "the cotton crop will fall short at least fifty per cent on account of so much bad weather [excessive rain]." To make matters even worse, Westfall noted locals seemed to avoid making some purchases given the uncertainty of the time: "The business of any kind seems very dull. I never saw such hard times in all my life before." And two days later, barely five months into the war, he added, "I never knew of money being so scarse [sic] in all my life before – it seems almost impossible for the planters to get any at all."[17] On the horizon, though Westfall and other locals couldn't have predicted it, was an unprecedented inflationary cycle.

Initially, for the non-combatants living in counties along the river (like Bolivar), the Mississippi River continued to fulfill its usual role as a means of transportation and a lifeline. But, as the war continued, the river would assume an unexpected function, as a Yankee invasion route into the heart of the Delta. An early hint of the Union's grand strategy to control the Mississippi River from New Orleans north to Memphis appeared in a brief entry in Westfall's diary in October 1861. Unaware of its eventual impact on the war in Mississippi, the Reverend reported casually that three or four Federal steamers had been engaged at the mouth of the Mississippi River with one taken as a prize of war.[18]

---

[15]Ibid., June 10, September 9, 1861.
[16]Mississippi, State Archives, Various Records, 1820-1951, Bolivar, Civil War Records, 1936-1939, (Box 11053), images 4-9, accessed August 31, 2012, at https://familysearch.org/pal:/MM9.3.1/TH-1942-20636-13615-71?cc=1919687&wc=13644675.
[17]Westfall Diary, August 29, September 9, 11, 1861.
[18]Ibid., October 14, 1861. On October 12, 1861, Westfall penned the first of two very unusual (for him) and inexplicable diary entries regarding the small community of Glencoe where the Perkins family and other planters resided and where he had always been well received: "I do not feel like putting forth much of an effort here in the Glencoe community meeting with but very little encouragement." On

Seven months later, beginning just after the Union Navy's arrival below Vicksburg on May 18, 1862, Bolivar County citizens in the next three years saw the war at their doorsteps. In a letter written on May 27, 1862, Brigadier General Charles Clark, Bolivar County resident and Commander of the First Division in the Army of Mississippi, requested a company of cavalry to help protect the county from the impending arrival of small Union raiding parties. In requesting this support, Clark also provided a situation report of sorts on Bolivar County at the beginning of the war's second year:

HEADQUARTERS FIRST DIVISION, FIRST CORPS,
Corinth, [Mississippi] May 27, 1862
Maj. George Williamson, Assistant Adjutant-General:

> Major: There are but few persons left capable of bearing arms in the county of Bolivar and the adjoining counties on the Mississippi River. Those counties contain a very large negro population. Some of the citizens have removed their cotton but two or three miles from the river, and if the enemy takes possession of the country they will easily find it through information derived from the slaves. One company of cavalry would be of great service in protecting from the small parties that would be sent out by the enemy. The company of Captain [probably F. A.] Montgomery (Lindsay's regiment), raised in Bolivar County, knowing the county well, would be best qualified for this service, and I respectfully suggest, for the consideration of the commanding general, the propriety of sending that company or some other on this duty.
>
> I am, very respectfully, &c.,
>
> > > > Chas. Clark, Brig. Gen., Comdg. 1st
> > > > Div., 1st Corps, Army of the Mississippi[19]

November 17, 1861, Westfall preached again at Glencoe "with some few white people present."
[19]Scott, *The War of the Rebellion*, Series I, Volume LII, Part II, Confederate Correspondence, 319.

As it turned out, Montgomery's company operated both in and out of Bolivar County, while another led by Major (later Colonel) W. E. Montgomery proved very effective in harassing Union forces locally during the war. It functioned as a partisan band, and because they dispersed at night and slept in theirs or other people's homes, they were referred to as "feather-beds." Often, by necessity, Major Montgomery's guerillas established temporary camps in the swampy bayous and canebrakes of Bolivar County's remote, eastern section away from the threat of Federal forces that tended to operate in areas near the Mississippi River. As a result, his men and others who periodically joined them suffered severely from 'swamp fever' (malaria).

While the Union threat continued up the Mississippi River toward Vicksburg, Federal forces were systematically advancing through *northern* Mississippi southward in hope of eventually slicing the Confederacy in two. Fighting near Tunica and Coahoma Counties, both situated on the river north of Bolivar County and protected only by a small contingent of Confederate cavalry (the Bolivar Troop), resulted in locals fleeing their homes while the Yankees seized their cotton and slaves. The *Memphis Daily Appeal* lamented on August 9, 1862, that the Yankees were pretty much having it their own way in these counties, closing with the provocative question: "Cannot our military authorities furnish the people on the river some assistance?"[20] As the Yankees continued their southward advance, they soon reached the next county along the Mississippi, Bolivar.

On September 17, 1862, near dusk, billowing plumes of smoke arose from the direction of Prentiss, the Bolivar County seat, not far from Daniel Perkins' Mecca Plantation near Beulah. Because Rebel forces on the Mississippi River's shoreline had fired on a passing Union gunboat killing three and wounding seven, a Union raiding party had torched the town in retaliation. Later, approximately one-quarter mile above Prentiss, the same force burned the abandoned home of the widowed Mrs. Coffee, a long time resident of Bolivar County.[21] Other county residents closer to the Mound Plantation also experienced the war first hand.

---

[20]*Memphis Daily Appeal,* August 9, 1862, 2, column 2.
[21]Ibid., October 3, 1862, 2, column 4, reporting events of September 17, 1862.

At the beginning of the war, the Perkins' neighbors in the Glencoe area, the Lobdells, owned some ninety-two slaves on their Egypt Plantation, valued their real estate at $70,000, and claimed personal property worth $60,000, making them one of the county's most prosperous planter families. The widowed Minerva Lee (Coffee) Lobdell later recalled her experiences beginning in 1862 at the onset of the Yankee presence in the county during the war's second year. Apparently dictated to a local official in 1868 as part of her estate's yearly accounting (she served as its administratrix), Mrs. Lobdell's recollections (she referred to them as 'Remarks') provide a dispassionate account of the war's effects on the family's once highly successful plantation. Oozing wealth and viewed as symbols of a corrupt lifestyle in Union eyes, these palatial Southern estates with their vast cultivated acreages and large slave populations continued to be prime targets for invading Federal armies as the war progressed:

> Remarks – The administratrix offers the following remarks as to the matters touching her administration. . . . 250 bales was burnt by the soldiers of the Confederate states under orders as she is informed of Governor John Pettus, Gov. of Miss. The corn crop of that year amounted to about seven thousand bushels, was destroyed by soldiers of the Confederate states Army or by other means unavoidable by any powers in [of] this admin.[istratrix] who in order to try and save other property more valuable, abandoned her home only a few miles from the Miss River which at the time was filled with Federal gunboats & other vessels of war. The 22 mules . . . were all taken away from admin. by Federal and Confederate soldiers, except . . . five. The five horses mentioned in the inventory have died. The 36 head of cattle except 4 cows & calves now on the place were destroyed during the war, under circumstances beyond power of the admin. to prevent, except a few that were sold for beef to [the] Confederate Army for Confederate money. The hogs were either destroyed during the war or used for meat in home consumption of the hands [slaves] of the estate. The wagons were taken by [the] Federal Army without compensation. The slaves

were emancipated before the date of emancipation [1863,
by Lincoln's Executive Order, in the Emancipation Proc-
lamation], by reason of the war. Admin. managed the
property of the estate by hiring out the slaves aforesaid as
far as she could secure hire of them, and the benefits of
their labor, as well as the hiring of mules until taken from
her by soldiers of the armies barely enabled admin. to pay
expenses of their [the slaves] support and maintenance.
She paid taxes on the lands of the estate during the war,
but was unable to rent it out or turn it to any advantage for
the taxes and support of the slaves up to the date of
emancipation.[22]

To escape such destructive Union raids, the shelling from
Federal gunboats along the river, and/or to limit as much as possible surrendering their slaves, harvested crops, and valuables, some
Bolivar County riverside planters and others who resided inland
like Mrs. Lobdell, evacuated themselves, their slaves, and whatever else they could transport inland or to other Confederate states.
Locals referred to this relocation, particularly by the county's riverside plantation families, as 'refugeeing'.[23]

In some cases refugeeing was accomplished preemptively,
but at other times it came after the first Yankee incursion. Bolivar
County planter Christopher Field, the owner of the Content Place
Plantation near the Perkins' land, relocated all of his at least thirty-
two slaves to Texas in the extreme western portion of the Confederacy for the duration of the war. Similarly, the wife of General
Clark attempted to move their approximately 121 slaves from Bolivar County inland to Fayette in Jefferson County, just north of
Natchez. Union troops, however, intercepted them enroute, separated the male slaves from the females, and then enlisted some of

[22]Mississippi Probate Records, 1781-1930, Bolivar, Wills and Inventories, 1861-
1924, vol. C-D, image 149, accessed September 4, 2012,
familysearch.org/pal:/MM9.3.1/TH-1961-30970-21974-
27?cc=2036959&wc=MMY2-QH3:743804828.
[23]Sillers, History of Bolivar County, 567.

the males into the United States Army.[24] In another instance in October 1862, an established planter transported his slaves to Virginia, abandoning his plantation and crop in Bolivar County.[25] Jefferson Wilkerson, owner of the Choctaw Bend Plantation adjacent to the Perkins land, likewise refugeed to Texas, but in 1864. He conveyed only a portion of his slaves, while leaving some behind in Bolivar County with a foreman.[26]

Most likely cognizant of what had befallen the Lobdell estate, the widowed and childless (but still the guardian of her younger brother James) Jane Curry left, but did not abandon, her Mound Plantation in 1862 or 1863. Moving in with her brother Daniel and sister-in-law Caroline on their inland plantation, she escaped the progressively more frequent Union naval bombardments near her home. In refugeeing Jane probably also relocated her slaves to her brother's plantation, an outcome that many blacks detested because of the hardships (separation from family and the crowded and inadequate living arrangements) involved. However, Jane may have refugeed with her brother only temporarily, possibly when the danger of Union shelling was greatest, because later she declared she had resided on "her plantation during all the late unfortunate war."[27]

During February 1863 Union naval forces and Confederate cavalry/infantry engaged in intermittent skirmishes up and down the Mississippi River from the city of Greenville to Cypress Bend just above Mound Landing. From the excellent concealment

---

[24]Noralee Frankel, *Freedom's Women: Black Women and Families in Civil War Era Mississippi (Blacks in the Diaspora)*, (Bloomington: Indiana University Press, 1999), 15.

[25]*Memphis Daily Appeal*, October 22, 1862, 1, column 5.

[26]G. E. Harris and G. H. Simrall, (reporters), *Report of Cases in the Supreme Court for the State of Mississippi*, (Chicago: Callaghan and Company, 1876), 51: 132-134.

[27]"Case Files of Applications from Former Confederates for Presidential Pardons 1865-1867," (Amnesty Papers), *Fold3*, s.v. "Curry, Jane P.," accessed September 20, 2011, (payment required), http://www.fold3.com/search.php?f_ancestor_id=hCLUo81Ws&df_ancestor_id=Within%3AConfederate+Amnesty+Papers&submit=Search&nav=0&query%5B0%5D=jane+p.+curry. It appears Jane Curry signed the application, but an attorney had penned the document using facts supplied by Jane. Copies of the petitions of Jane Curry and Daniel Perkins are in the author's possession.

afforded by the dense cane and timber in certain places along the riverbank, the Confederates directed harassing fire at passing Union gunboats and troop ships. Moreover, Bolivar County's levees afforded an ideal breastwork for concealed Confederate sharpshooters and artillery, while the many bends in the Mississippi served as perfect positions from which to launch additional ambush attacks.[28] On February 14 Union naval forces reported receiving artillery fire from five cannons positioned by Confederate guerillas at the river bend at Bolivar Landing.[29] These rebel hit and run tactics soon resulted in further Union retaliatory and preventative incursions into the areas along the river.

Some three weeks later, on March 12, 1863, probably in response to this recent attack near Bolivar Landing, United States forces landed near the Manly and Topp plantations, just north of the Mound Plantation and south of General Vick's estate. Assisted by a group of contrabands (slaves who escaped or were brought to Union lines) armed with all the picks and shovels available, this force proceeded to cut a fifty-foot gap in the levee at Bolivar Landing. The Union Navy's Lt. Commander Selfridge reported, "The water is pouring out very rapidly," and then added his intention to "drown out Mrs. Monley [Manley] and old (Robertson) Topp."[30]

At one point later that month, a Union commander had prepared to offload troops at Perkins' Landing (Mound Landing) in an effort to cut off a Confederate retreat by using the road that ran along the river south to Greenville and beyond. He lamented that inclement weather thwarted his plans, and remarked that there were no "road improvements in the country", meaning in the countryside away from the river.[31]

[28]Scott, *War of the Rebellion*, Series I, Volume XXIV, Pt III, Confederate Correspondence, March 10, 1863, 660.
[29]*Official Records of the Union and Confederate Navies in the War of the Rebellion*, (Washington, D. C: United States Government Printing Office, 1911), Series 1, Volume XXIV, 696.
[30]Ibid., 467, 468, 472.
[31]Ibid., 363.

The Union gunboat Ft. Hindman, on the Mississippi River
As the war progressed, gunboats similar to the Ft. Hindman appeared on the river from Memphis to New Orleans bringing the
war to the doorsteps of Southerners living along the Mississippi.
Library of Congress photo

Near the end of March, Union plans to take possession of
the village of Greenville in Washington County were underway.
As part of the correspondence involving this strategy, Union Rear
Admiral Porter wrote, "Rebel cotton . . . is a good prize; take it
when you can find it. . . ."[32]

At last, though, in April 1863, Union forces, intent on
halting these nagging Confederate attacks, launched another punitive expedition against the local rebels while simultaneously raiding plantations along the river. Union troops aboard gunboats arrived at Jefferson Wilkerson's Choctaw Bend Plantation (probably
that April and before his move in 1864 to Texas) and the Mound
Plantation. At Wilkerson's (near section six), Federals promptly

---

[32]Ibid., March 26, 1863, 513.

seized as much of his livestock and corn and as many of his *slaves* as they could transport.[33] Meanwhile, this same Union raiding party spared the Perkins' house, perhaps because of Jane's status as a widow without adult males in the home or serving in the Confederate Army. However, they did confiscate among other things the greater part of her livestock and sixty bales of cotton valued at $12,000.

In contrast, it appears that at least in the early stages of the Union's presence in Bolivar County Daniel Perkins' plantation may have been spared. Though Union forces had raided the Mound Plantation in April 1863, his Mecca Plantation situated miles from the river did not feel the sting of a Union incursion until late December of that year. As a result, one year later, in a county tax assessment for 1864, Jane (and Daniel Perkins) claimed just two carriage horses or mules each (with one carriage) and a total of ninety cattle, thirty on the Mound Plantation and sixty on Daniel's plantation. Among the animals seized, Jane's forty-six mules were an especially difficult loss to bear because of their vital role in plowing/cotton production. Though it is not documented, this Union force might have been the first to seize some of Jane's slaves as they had done at the Wilkerson plantation. If not, additional opportunities would arise later that year. Apparently, Daniel never filed any postwar reimbursement claims against the Union Army so the extent of the losses he incurred is unknown. On the other hand, decades later Jane Curry, as part of a reimbursement claim, itemized her losses attributable to Union confiscation:

---

[33]Harris and Simrall, *Report of Cases in the Supreme Court for the State of Mississippi*, 131.

4 horses at $150	$600
46 mules at $180	$8,280
35 cattle at $30	$1,050
10 oxen at $40	$400
125 sheep at $5	$625
1,000 lbs. bacon at .15	$150
100 bushels meal at .50	$50
100 bushels corn at .50	$50
6 wagons at $40	$240
1 lot house linen	$25
60 bales cotton at $200	$12,000
Total	**$23,470**

Items confiscated by Union forces during the Civil War from Jane Perkins Curry's (later Moore) plantation and their estimated value.[34]

Based on her omission of any personal household articles in her claim, perhaps Jane had the foresight to bury any family silver, money, or other valuables prior to the arrival of Union troops. Fortunately for Jane Union forces remained unaware that she had previously rendered aid and comfort to individual Confederate soldiers (as she acknowledged in a postwar statement). Had the Federal raiders learned of this offense, their actions at her plantation most likely would have been far harsher.

Nor were Union soldiers the only ones causing havoc on the Mound Plantation. Jane Curry later recalled in a postwar affidavit the destruction wreaked by her own Confederate Army:

> previous to this last occurrence [Union troops' confiscation of her cotton, livestock, etc.] the Confederate forces had burned seven hundred bales of her cotton – barely

---

[34]"Jane P. Moore v The United States," *United States Congressional Series Set*, (Washington, D. C.: Government Printing Office, 64th Congress, 1st Session), 6954: Document 165, 1-2, March 21, 1910. By the time Jane submitted her claim she had remarried.

allowing her time to remove the same from her gin
& mill house to save that from destruction.[35]

Per their common practice (see Mrs. Lobdell's account
above), local Confederate troops had burned Jane's cotton to prevent it from falling into Union hands. According to another Bolivar County source, Confederate forces, acting on military orders,
had destroyed his cotton crop but earlier, in 1861 or 1862.[36] The
overall effect of the order (by 1863) resulted in the burning of tens
of thousands of bales belonging to those Mississippi planters residing along the river.[37] Like the Union raids they endured, locals
were obliged to tolerate these often equally destructive and unavoidable Confederate actions on their plantations – meant also to
deny Union forces any other crops they might plunder - no matter
how painful the results might be. Combining these cotton and
crop losses with those caused by Union forces, planters, caught in
the middle, faced a devastating and virtually unavoidable shortage
of their primary cash crop and thus a substantial loss of income.
        Even though fluctuating cotton prices often reached highs
of between forty-one to forty-four dollars a bale after Lincoln's
election in the fall of 1860, Jane's $200 valuation of an 1863 bale
in her statement of losses above appears to be accurate.[38] At that
rate the Confederate action at her Mound Plantation had inflicted a
catastrophic $140,000 loss. Both the burning and confiscation

---

[35]Confederate Amnesty Papers, Jane Curry. It seems the Confederate forces had
failed to burn Jane's sixty bales during their action at her plantation. Perhaps
they had overlooked it, or Jane may have hidden the cotton away on a remote part
of the plantation.

[36]Robert Desty, *The Supreme Court Reporter*, (St. Paul: West Publishing Company, 1891), 11: 420.

[37]Michael Wayne, *The Reshaping of Plantation Society: The Natchez District,
1860-80*, (Urbana: University of Illinois Press, 1990), 33. The Confederate government directed planters along the Mississippi to burn their own cotton, but
many ignored the order.

[38]In November 1863 another Bolivar County resident, Miles McGehee, filed a
claim following a Union raid in February 1863 (*two months* before the Union
action at the Perkins plantation) in which he valued his eight bales of cotton at
$3000, or $375 per bale. *Official Records of the Union and Confederate Navies*,
Series I, XXV: 728. McGehee had hidden several hundred bales in the cane to
avoid its confiscation by Union troops or Confederation destruction.

brought about by the two warring armies cost Jane approximately $152,000 in cotton revenue alone. Her other itemized losses totaled more than $11,000.

The fact that Jane had stored by the early spring of 1863 more than 700 bales of cotton meant this, the 1862 crop picked in late summer and fall of that year, had not yet been conveyed to market. (The Union Navy's presence on the Mississippi even as early as 1862 would have prevented most planters from successfully transporting their baled cotton to New Orleans or Memphis.) Like other local planters, she simply suffered the loss without hope of reimbursement from the financially challenged Confederate government. Perhaps, though, she found some solace in the fact that her cotton gin and mill had been spared destruction.

Daniel Perkins' widowed mother-in-law, Margaret Campbell, at her Argyle Plantation fared far worse than Jane Curry in her encounter with Union soldiers. Following their incursion at the Perkins' plantation, Federal forces focused on eliminating other Confederate gun emplacements, especially those harassing Union ships along the river *south* of Mound Landing between Greenville and Argyle in Washington County. On April 24 and May 9, 1863, they launched punitive expeditions against light opposition, this time directed at Chicot Island and Argyle Landing. As a result, a "dozen houses, cotton gins, a large barn containing 5,000 bushels of corn, Negro [slave] quarters, outbuildings and stables were 'scorched'."[39] Watching from her plantation house window (on April 24), Mrs. Campbell witnessed the Yankees loading her cotton onto their transports and driving off her nine horses and fifty-five mules. Later, their gunboats shelled the slave quarters and her home, rendering it unsafe for the family to remain there. Finally, the Yankees burned the gin and house, the same house where Daniel, just a few years earlier in a different world then, had celebrated his marriage to Campbell's daughter Caroline.[40] The Union troops

---

[39]Myron J. Smith, *Tinclads in the Civil War: Union Light-draught Gunboat Operations on Western Waters, 1862-1865*, (Jefferson, North Carolina: McFarland and Company, 2010), 125.

[40]Mrs. Hugh Miller in McCain, *Memoirs of Henry Tillinghast Ireys*, 169. Following the war Margaret Campbell submitted a $9,600 reimbursement claim for her horses and mules. The Federal government denied her request. Just upriver from the Campbell and Perkins plantations, Union forces had likewise burned the

may have been more strongly motivated in their raid and destruction of the Campbell plantation because they were aware that Margaret Campbell's son, William Campbell Jr., was serving as an officer in the Confederate Army. As a result of the raid, the Campbells were forced to refugee with another local family.

With the fall of Vicksburg to Union forces in July 1863, the Mississippi River fell under Union control, dividing the Confederacy in two. As a result, northern gunboats expanded their areas of operation, and continued to patrol, shell, and harass Confederate land forces. Eventually they occupied other towns upriver *north* of Vicksburg in the direction of Bolivar County. The Union Army's increasingly successful and repeated raids (working in concert with the Union Navy) extended gradually up the Mississippi River as well and resulted in the additional confiscation of any cotton it encountered.

At about this same time, an incident occurred which probably could not been imagined in April 1861, when spirited Bolivar men had willingly answered the call for volunteers. The officers of a Confederate company of Bolivar County's state troops under the command of a Captain Henderson refused to obey an order by a colonel to leave Bolivar County to guard a steamboat in another sector. The colonel, James R. Chalmers, reported their insubordination and prepared to prefer charges against the officers in question. He attributed their defiance and lack of discipline to the "style of command and position of things in this district, where the men have been permitted to do just what they pleased. . . ."[41] He added, "that men will not make good soldiers near home." Whether this was an isolated incident or indicative of a larger, ongoing problem (the beginnings of decline in local discipline and morale?) among the state troops is unknown. Nonetheless, refusing to obey a direct order in wartime is a serious offense.

Later, throughout November and December 1863, Union forces continued operations along the Mississippi shoreline in the vicinity of both Perkins' plantations. On November 8, 1863, Union

---

venerable Vick plantation, a Bolivar landmark since the early 1840s. Federals also destroyed the home of Confederate General Peter B. Starke.

[41]Scott, *War of the Rebellion*, Series I, Volume XXIV, Pt III, Confederate Correspondence, June 27, 1863, 981.

cavalry under the command of Capt. O. F. Brown landed at Glencoe (adjacent to the Mound Plantation), but apparently they accomplished little in their foray into the interior. Two days later a
separate contingent struck farther north, near Beulah, at the plantation of Union nemesis and local Confederate guerilla leader Colonel W. E. Montgomery. (Not to be confused with Capt. F. A.
Montgomery of the Bolivar Troop, W.E. Montgomery now commanded a local, unattached cavalry unit consisting of men of extreme youth, or advanced age, and previously wounded soldiers
unfit for regular army duty.) From his Mecca Plantation, Daniel
Perkins may have observed smoke in the distance, the result of this
Union raiding party's burning of Montgomery's home and his cotton gin (but not the slave quarters) in retaliation for the sinking of
a Union steamer by Montgomery's men. The proximity of this
most recent reprisal raid to his plantation, combined with the previous attack at Prentiss in September 1862 may have given Daniel
Perkins special cause to worry.

Subsequently, in December 1863, Union forces arrived at
Mecca. This time Daniel himself ran afoul of Federal troops. Prevented from serving in the army due to his disability, he opened
his home to Confederate soldiers on leave. On Christmas Day Perkins hosted a huge party and dance for local irregulars and his
neighbors. Suddenly, in the midst of the celebrating, someone
shouted, "Yankees!" Forces under the command of Union Captain
Brown, acting on a tip from a Union spy, swooped in unexpectedly, surrounding the revelers before they realized the danger.
Some startled Confederates managed to escape into the countryside, hastily fording bayous in their efforts, while others were
made prisoners. Brown's men confiscated all the horses and mules
from the guests' carriages and took Dan Perkins prisoner along
with Isaac Hudson, a former Bolivar County Board of Police
member and state representative. The Union force apparently
spared Perkins' plantation house. Later, the commander of a gunboat involved in the action reported:

U.S. Gunboat Tyler,
Mouth of White River, December 27, 1863

Sir: I send by steamer *New National* two prisoners, residents of
Mississippi, by the names of D. P. Perkins and Isaac Hudson. The
charges against them are for harboring and feeding guerrillas. The
guerrillas were found in their houses by Captain Brown [probably
the same Union cavalry commander who had landed at Glencoe in
November], of the *Queen City*. Perkins was giving a Christmas
party to a company of guerillas, commanded by Captain Montgomery and to some Bolivar troops.

Very respectfully, your obedient servant,
Jas. M. Prichett, Lieutenant Commander.

[To]: Rear-Admiral D. D. Porter, Commanding Mississippi Squad-
ron[42]

Whether his Union captors imposed any sort of punishment on Perkins remains unknown. Nor do we know the length of
time he remained in Union captivity. Perkins, though, survived the
experience, and by war's end or before he had returned safely to
Bolivar County.

As the war continued, Bolivar County residents saw all
facets of the their cotton-based economy – marketing, labor, and
production – adversely affected because of the continuous Union
raids and presence. Powerless, planters had to endure and adapt as
best they could.

Marketing - Beginning in April 1862, with New Orleans
and the lower Mississippi in Union hands, conveying any remaining cotton to market had become impossible for Bolivar County
and other Mississippi planters. Desperate for money, some of Bolivar's citizens had resorted to what would have been considered
unthinkable less than two years earlier. In February 1863 a report
by a local Confederate commander described how a "whole community" in upper Bolivar County had been engaged in trading cotton with the enemy. Making matters even more disconcerting was
the fact that these same citizens had *warned* the Union trading

---

[42]Sillers, *History of Bolivar County,* 567-568. See also, *Official Records of the
Union and Confederate Navies,* Series 1, XXV, 664.

boats of the approach of a Confederate force allowing the Yankees to escape.[43]

By 1864 with their plantations under total Union control, local planters hoping to legally transport their cotton to market encountered several obstacles. First, they had to obtain approval of the United States Special Treasury agent in Issaquena County, Mississippi. Second, any shipped cotton could only be cleared if planters paid a one-cent per pound tax and proved to Union authorities that only free labor produced it. Furthermore, by May 1864 planters also needed to submit applications for United States government permission to use *freedmen* as laborers on their plantations. Of course, Jane Curry and Daniel Perkins would have been compelled to comply with these same regulations if they desired to ship any of their remaining cotton.[44]

Labor and Production - Beginning with the more frequent Union attacks and later with the firm Union presence in occupied Bolivar County by 1864, Delta slaveholding planters experienced the novelty of a dramatic *decrease* in their slave populations. This reduction occurred due to an increasing number of runaways who took advantage of the opportunity to escape and also because of the Union Army's emancipation of the thousands of slaves they encountered as they advanced through the countryside. Combining this reduced number of slaves with the new Union regulations regarding the employment of freedmen, the lack of necessary labor and the resulting decline in production emerged as acute and vexing problems for the already economically challenged planters during the remainder of the war.

As Federal forces invaded the South, among the first civilians to be impacted were the slaves. Though most were illiterate, slaves had not lived in an information vacuum during the war. Since the outbreak of hostilities, slaves had remained alert, listening for war news, often overheard from the conversations of

---

[43]Scott, *War of the Rebellion*, Series I, Volume XXIV, Pt III, Confederate Correspondence, 631.

[44]The applications were part of a system established by the United States government in occupied Southern lands and were set forth in a document entitled, Rules and Regulations for Leasing Abandoned Plantations and Employing Freedmen.

whites. Later, the eavesdroppers shared the information with other slaves. As witnesses to some of the fighting, especially in those Delta Counties along the river, slaves (who had not been refugeed) were fully aware of Union forays and their successes or failures.

At some point during the war many slaves faced choices about their fate. Some chose to escape the plantations. Those thousands who did so invariably sought refuge in Union camps established for runaways along the river. In contrast, some slaves, uncertain or fearful of what change might bring, elected to stay on the plantations, the only homes they had ever known. (In one instance in Bolivar County, an old Negro man and a boy "positively refused" Union soldiers' orders to board an evacuation boat and were eventually allowed to remain on a burned plantation as its only residents.)[45] Still other slaves stayed out of loyalty to their masters or because of a desire to maintain the unity of their families. A smaller group was deprived of any such choices, because some masters who had previously resisted refugeeing now removed their slaves to secluded parts of the state.

During the war's final two years, the Perkins' slave population gradually decreased with additional runaways and because of continued forced emancipation by Federal troops. Unknown is whether Jane Curry or Daniel Perkins, bowing to the inevitable, willingly freed any of their remaining slaves. Common sense says probably not.

As time passed slaves certainly had become aware from the slave grapevine or invading Union soldiers of Lincoln's Emancipation Proclamation of January 1863 (freeing only slaves in the states in rebellion, i.e. the slave states, where masters were not subject to Union law). Thus emboldened by both Union activity in Bolivar County and the Proclamation, many more slaves (Perkins' slaves included) crossed over to Union lines. While there was no uniform emancipation experience, black males, more than females, appeared most likely to flee. Though many females did escape, consideration for their children often dictated the best path to follow.

---

[45]*Memphis Daily Appeal*, October 3, 1862, 2, column 4. Their mistress, Mrs. Coffee, had abandoned the plantation prior to the soldiers' arrival.

The Perkins clan felt the financial effects of a dwindling
slave population as much as any family. In 1860 Jane Curry and
Daniel Perkins had counted on their respective plantations a combined total of 203 slaves. Four years later in the fall of 1864, due
to Union emancipation and runaways, Jane, James, and Daniel saw
their collective slave populations decline to only ninety-one slaves
(in the fiscal year ending June 1), just *forty-five percent* of their
total prewar labor force on the Mecca and Mound Plantations (Table 2).

Slave Age Groups	Year	Owner	Owner	Owner
	1860	Jane Curry	Daniel Perkins	
Under 15		**43**	**20**	
Male 15-under 45		32	33	
Female 15-under 45		**31**	**10**	
M & F 45-60		23	3	
Greater than 60		**5**	**3**	
Total of slaves		134	69	
	1864	Jane Curry	Daniel Perkins	James Perkins
Under 15		**0**	**26**	**18**
Male 15-under 45		2	6	8
Female 15-under 45		**0**	**15**	**7**
M & F 45-60		0	3	6
Greater than 60		**0**	**0**	**0**
Total of slaves		2	50	39

Table 2 The Perkins and Curry Slaves - 1860 and fall 1864 [46]

[46]Eighth Census, 1860, Bolivar County, Mississippi, Slave Schedules, s. v. "S. B.
Cuny," 43-44, "Jane Perkins," 65, and "D. P. Perkins," 18, 19, accessed September 21, 2011, *Ancestry.com.* Mississippi, State Archives, Various Records, 1820-

A comparison of the family's slaveholdings in 1864 and 1860 offers an estimate of the dollar value in lost slave property the Perkins family incurred. In 1864 the Bolivar County tax assessor divided slaves into four groups based on age and sex and assigned a dollar value to each group. The following groupings and their worth appeared on the tax rolls:

1864 Bolivar County Tax Rolls - Slave Valuation[47]

Age of Slave	Value
Under 15	$250
Male 15-under 45	$1,000
Female 15-under 45	$700
45-60	$250

On the Mound Plantation that same year, Jane Perkins Curry claimed two males slaves (15-under 45) valued at $2,000, while her seventeen year old brother James held the remaining thirty-nine slaves (of various sexes and ages) worth $18,900 (Table 2). Using the same valuation basis for the fifty slaves on Daniel Perkins' plantation, their worth equaled $23,750. Thus, the combined value of the Perkins family's *ninety-one slaves* in 1864 amounted to $44,650 (Table 2).

Using the 1864 sex and age groupings and their associated values for ease of comparison, we can approximate the value of the slaves owned by Jane Curry and Daniel Perkins on their separate plantations in 1860. Totaled, their *203 slaves* represented a

---

1951, Bolivar County tax rolls *1864,* Box 3191, images 6 and 13, accessed October 29, 2011, *Family Search.*

[47]Ibid., tax rolls, image 4 (heading). Jane's tax liability in 1864 for personal property and slaves amounted to $10 while her brothers James and Daniel owed $55.70 and $55.80 respectively.

prewar worth of approximately $115,950.[48] The difference between the Perkins' 1860 slave count and the diminished 1864 number reveals a total wartime slave property *loss* to the Perkins family of $71,300, or sixty-one percent of prewar worth.

Though the specific numbers in this example apply to just one slaveholding family claiming 203 slaves (prewar), they are representative of the calamitous monetary losses in slave property and therefore production incurred by slaveholders across the county and the South as more and more Confederate territory came under Union control. Of course, there soon would be no market for slaves at all.

The percentage of slaves that remained on all other Bolivar County plantations in late 1864 proved to be similar to the Perkins' forty-five percent. In 1860 Bolivar County counted 9,078 slaves. By the fall of 1864, planters claimed only 3,624 slaves, just forty percent of their prewar total. Most all of the 'missing' 5,454 slaves had, of course, been freed by advancing Union forces or had fled to Union lines.[49]

Due to various factors, members of the Perkins family during the Civil War thus experienced a gradually escalating series of financial challenges for the first time in their heretofore advantaged lives. The Union confiscation of their livestock, their initial inability and later the difficulty in producing and marketing cotton (and the loss of Jane's 760 bales), a steady reduction in their number of slaves, combined with a transition to wage labor spelled financial hardship even for the most affluent of planter families. Surely, the Perkins family by this time must have understood that with a Confederate defeat looming, the monetary value of any

---

[48]Eighth Census, 1860, Bolivar County, Mississippi, Slave Schedules, s. v. "S. B. Cuny," 43-44, "Jane Perkins," 65, and "D. P. Perkins," 18, 19, accessed September 21, 2011, *Ancestry.com*.

[49]Mississippi, State Archives, Various Records, 1820-1951, Bolivar County tax rolls *1864*, Box 3191, image 18, accessed October 29, 2011, *Family Search*. The Federal Census of 1860 counted all slaves regardless of age, while slaves over sixty years old were not counted or *taxed* in local 1864 county rolls. These figures do not account for any increases or deaths in Bolivar County's slave population between the years 1860-1864.

slaves remaining on the plantation would soon become an inevitable loss as well.

Yet, the Perkins' situation may have been eased slightly by the fact that James Perkins (on the Mound Plantation) reported $8,000 in cash on hand in 1864, while Daniel Perkins claimed $1,600.[50] However, if the two Perkins men were holding Confederate currency (graybacks), Mississippi or Confederate States Treasury notes, 'cotton' money of the state of Mississippi, or any of the numerous other Confederate states' individual wartime currencies (Alabama or South Carolina money for example), it would all have been worthless at the time of the surrender.

Another factor seriously affecting Bolivar County planters and others along the Mississippi in the so called Department of the Gulf - an area extending from New Orleans north to Helena, Arkansas, approximately eighty-five miles north of Mound Landing - was that by Union decree they must *compensate* the laborers (the freedmen) they now employed on their plantations. On February 3, 1864, Union General Nathaniel Banks, Commander of the Department of the Gulf, issued a proclamation regulating the free labor system in his department.

Item XII in Banks' decree specified the *salary* for employed wage laborers (former slaves):[51]

First class hands	$8.00 monthly

Second class hands	$6.00 monthly

Third class hands	$5.00 monthly

Of course, General Banks' decree would only be as effective as the Union authorities' desire and ability to enforce its provisions. Nonetheless, this work-for-pay edict became a part of the emerging 'new' plantation economy.

Related to this ongoing social and legal transformation being played out before them, Bolivar County planters also began

---

[50]Mississippi State Archives, Bolivar County Tax Roll, Box 3191, image 13.
[51]Knox, *Camp-fire and Cotton-Field*, 365, 366.

to feel the first overt signs of slave defiance. Beginning as early as January 1862, sixteen slaves on the plantation of the absent General Charles Clark rebelled against the overseer and quit.[52] On the Burrus plantation, the Negro stockman cooperated with the Yankees and rounded up his master's cattle for confiscation.[53] Such acts would become even more prevalent in the coming months.

For whites and for those slaves who remained on the plantations, Bolivar County took on a decidedly different appearance during the war's last two years. Conscription of white male adults into the Confederate army and refugeeing had reduced the white population considerably. Only *eighty-one* white polls (those not actively serving in the Confederate Army) of all ages remained in Bolivar country by 1864. (Unfortunately, no record for the entire Bolivar County population for that year has been found. Given this reduced amount of white polls, the county population of other white men, women, and children may have only approached only 400-500.)

Accordingly, Bolivar County's whites couldn't help but notice the change in blacks' attitudes. As a Bolivar County citizen observed in June 1863, "the county is left almost alone and the negroes are going whare [sic] they please."[54] A Confederate commander that same June directed a company of soldiers to remain in Bolivar County, "to get out supplies and keep the negroes in subjection...."[55] In August 1864, eight months before the war ended, another Bolivar resident wrote, "[the] recent withdrawal of the military patrol from the [Bolivar County] vicinity had been followed by manifestations of *insubordination and rebellion* among the Negroes" [italics mine].[56] Clearly, where white control was lacking, disturbances by blacks were becoming common.

Ironically, it seems that for a few months during the war Bolivar County whites had as much to fear from one of their own

---

[52]Cobb, *The Most Southern Place,* 39.
[53]Ibid. The Burrus house was reportedly spared destruction because of Burrus' previous acquaintance in college with the invading Union commander.
[54]Bell Irvin Wiley, *Southern Negroes,* (New Haven: Yale University Press, 1938), 38.
[55]Scott, *War of the Rebellion,* Series I, Volume XXIV, Pt III, Confederate Correspondence, 981.
[56]Wiley, *Southern Negroes,* 67.

as they did from invading Union forces or disobedient slaves. In 1863 Milford Coe, a thirty-three old former Confederate soldier and Bolivar County overseer, established a camp on Island 76 in the Mississippi River opposite the early site of the town of Bolivar (near the Vick plantation) and just a short distance upriver from the Mound Plantation. There, his band of approximately fifty runaway slaves (males, females, and some children) along with renegade whites engaged in treasonous activity. They provided information to the Yankees, sold wood to passing Yankee steamboats, and occasionally conducted raids on Bolivar County plantations near the river, accumulating mules, cattle, and fugitive slaves. There is no record of Coe pillaging the Perkins property situated on the river with its convenient (for Coe's raiders) landing, perhaps because the area's residents may have remained especially vigilant during this time. Though Coe's band apparently did not commit any murders, they had become a persistent threat to the county's citizens. Accordingly, in early 1864 a small band of Confederate soldiers raided Coe's island camp, captured him and several others in his band. Later, they executed Coe, one white, and one Negro. The remaining runaway slaves were released to return to their plantations.[57] Despite the elimination of Coe's gang, matters soon worsened for local residents.

A local Confederate scout in the Bolivar County area reported on July 27, 1864, ". . . a Federal force about 500 strong have established themselves in Bolivar County, Miss., opposite the mouth of White River, and it is supposed for the purpose of organizing a garrisoned post at that point."[58]

Two months later in late September, Union cavalry commander Colonel E. D. Osband filed an after action report summarizing the results of Union forays into Bolivar County and the surrounding area. In a particularly significant one-sentence observation, the Colonel noted that war weariness had taken root in Boli-

---

[57]J. C. Burrus Jr. in Curt Lamar (ed), *History of Rosedale, Mississippi*, (Spartanburg, South Carolina: Reprint Company, 1976), 105, 106. William Sullivan authored this Coe episode.

[58]Confederate Captain Perry Evans, commanding scout, to Major P. Ellis, Assistant Adjutant General, in Scott, *The War of the Rebellion*, Series I, Volume XXXIX, Pt. 2, Confederate Correspondence, 730.

var County and the Delta: "I found the inhabitants anxious for peace and willing to accept it under Federal rule."[59]

Consequently, in the closing months of 1864, while observing Yankees in their midst, witnessing the breakdown of the plantation system, experiencing the previously unheard of demonstrations of black independence, and with news of a steadily increasing number of Confederate battlefield defeats, informed, but mentally and economically defeated Bolivar County whites reached an unmistakable conclusion: These collective circumstances foretold the demise of those halcyon days of the Old South, its peculiar institution, and the entire Confederacy.

In April 1865 the bloodiest conflict in United States history ended with the Confederate surrender. With peace had come change, none greater than the elimination of slave labor - an entrenched institution many in the South had believed was divinely ordained - by both decree and later in 1865 with the adoption of the Thirteenth Amendment. With the Confederate surrender and the resulting emancipation of *all* slaves, planters' slave property losses equaled 100 percent of their 1860 value, resulting in a collective deficit of hundreds of millions of dollars.

Slaveholders, non-slaveholders, and freedmen suffered together. Swept away in the currents of the Civil War were farms, homes, confiscated or destroyed livestock, and ravaged crops. In Bolivar County cotton sold for eighty-five dollars a bale in May 1865 but raising it proved to be another problem altogether.[60] Also, the tens of thousands of killed and wounded Confederate soldiers, when combined with the property losses, equaled a level of disaster unseen in the South since the country's formation. Half of Mississippi's surviving soldiers returned with a lasting disability (mis-sing arms or legs) of the war, while as many as 26,000 had died. For the entire South, and specifically for the once elite, privileged Perkins slaveholding family, a period of readjustment became a certainty in an otherwise uncertain postwar setting.

---

[59]Ibid., (1892), Series I, Volume XXXIX, Pt. 1: Reports, 572.
[60]Mississippi Probate Records, 1781-1930, Bolivar, Wills and Inventories, 1861-1924, vol. C-D, image 32, accessed September 4, 2012, https://familysearch.org/pal:/MM9.3.1/TH-1942-30970-20524-86?cc=2036959&wc=MMY2-QH3:743804828.

X

Aftermath

She [Jane Perkins Curry] makes this application praying your
Excellency [President Andrew Johnson] to grant her a pardon,
relieving her from the finalities of the confiscation laws of the
United States . . . and restoring her to all the rights and immuni-
ties to which she was entitled before the late war.

Amnesty application, Jane Perkins
Curry, October 1865

In the aftermath of the South's surrender, former Confederate General Joseph E. Johnston declared in August 1865, "We of
the South [in 1861] referred the question at issue [states' rights]
between us and the United States to the arbitrament of the sword.
The decision has been made and it is against us."[1] Though many
in the South reluctantly recognized their defeat and its implications, it would take decades for an equal number of their fellow
citizens to accept both. Some never did.

Four months after the Confederate surrender, a Mississippi
convention met on August 17, 1865, and declared the ordinance of
secession null and void. Before the war, no state's interests were
more deeply aligned with the slave system than Mississippi's. Its
slave population had ranked third among all slave states, but with
the Confederate defeat in 1865, Mississippi and the South sought
now to adjust, as did a free black population numbering nearly
4,000,000 nationwide. Concurrent with the demise of slavery
came the end of plantation life, a consequence not even the Perkins family could avoid. And, in their case, this meant the collapse
of a generations-old lifestyle dating back to colonial Virginia in
the 1600s.

The South's capitulation had ended more than two decades of remarkable material progress for Bolivar County and its
planter families. Wartime Yankee raids, beginning in 1862, had

---

[1]"Monthly Record of Current Events," *Harper's New Monthly Magazine*, Volume XXXI: (June - November 1865), 665.

brought extensive physical destruction and disarray to the prosperous riverside Delta counties and altered the lifestyle of a previously ordered, resolute, and defiant populace resulting in an economically challenged region. Just after Robert E. Lee's surrender,
one resident recalled the scene in Bolivar County,

> In the early spring of 1865, the levee near Prentiss
> caved into the river, and all the country east and south
> of the break was deluged. Soldiers, ragged and war-
> torn, who came straggling back, worked their way
> through the overflow in dugouts and other crude water
> craft as best they could to the high lands on the river
> front. Levees to the north were broken also, and the Mis-
> sissippi poured its waters over the county, and the counties
> to the south, making the country practically a wilderness
> and a waste.[2]

Given this daunting set of circumstances in the months
leading up to and following the surrender, an important and en-
compassing question emerged, and then lingered in the minds of
Bolivar County's blacks and whites, *What would tomorrow bring?*
Like most Southerners in the months immediately following the war, the Perkins family likely had no obvious or immediate
answer to this profound and confounding query. But, undoubtedly
they realized massive change and a consequent need for readjustment loomed - which is not to suggest they would remain passive
to their future and fate. Ironically, uncertainty also existed as to
what legal freedom would actually mean for the thousands of
black Mississippians who were once the property of white owners.
As it turned out, their (both former masters and former slaves)
immediate futures would remain bound in numerous and significant ways.
However, some changes did come surprisingly swiftly.
With military posts established and marital law initiated, all of
Bolivar County's white males were notified to take the oath of

---

[2]Walter Sillers in Sillers, *History of Bolivar County*, 156.

allegiance to the United States. According to one local, every man in his neighborhood did so.[3]

In July 1865, three months after the Confederate surrender, Daniel Perkins took several steps toward repatriation offered by the United States government to former Confederate citizens. He submitted the required loyalty oath, promising to "faithfully support, protect and defend the Constitution of the United States," while at the same time swearing to "abide by and faithfully support all laws and proclamations which have been made during the existing rebellion with reference to the emancipation of slaves." Perkins also filed an amnesty petition addressed, as instructed, to President Andrew Johnson.

In his appeal, Daniel described himself as a thirty-two year old married man with an adopted son (the 1866 census shows the boy was ten years old or under). Perkins then followed with a description of his somewhat bleak postwar circumstances. He claimed 1,400 acres of farmland at his Mecca plantation, while owning taxable property, which no longer included slaves, valued at more than $20,000. Mindful of the recent April 1865 levee collapse that had rendered much of Bolivar County's farmland useless, Perkins explained his land remained unprotected from flooding due to the wartime destruction of the nearby levee by Union troops. (Daniel and other Delta planters faced the burden of paying for the repairs. Levee taxes would reach $4.15 per acre by 1874.)[4] Referring to his plantation's farm animals, he noted that few remained - just several mules and meat cattle. Perkins added that his "stock horses being very limited and [were] entirely inadequate to cultivate the plantation."[5] Daniel failed to declare his number of cultivated acres, but with his lack of labor due to the slaves' recent emancipation and the loss of his work animals and equipment, he may have found it difficult to exceed the 500 acres he had planted in 1860. Perkins, in closing, stated that while he never served in the Confederate Army (due to his disability), nor held any sort of

---

[3]John C. Burrus, Jr. in the *Bolivar County Democrat*, February 23, 1923. John was the son of Judge Burrus and a member of the Bolivar County family who had housed the Reverend Westfall in 1861-2.

[4]Cobb, *The Most Southern Place*, 64.

[5]Confederate Amnesty Papers, D. P. Perkins.

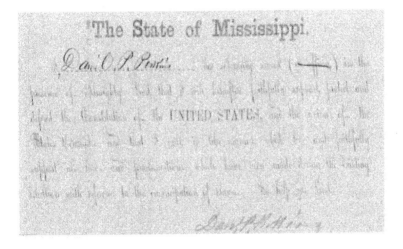

Loyalty oath signed and submitted by Daniel P. Perkins July 17,
1865, three months after the war ended.
Copy courtesy of *Fold3*.

office in the Confederate government, he had paid the required
taxes/tithes to the officers of the Confederate States. He also
vowed to "remain hereafter a loyal and law abiding, orderly, and
peaceful citizen of the United States." Lastly, Perkins requested a
full amnesty and pardon.[6]

Daniel's sister Jane Curry likewise filed for amnesty but
not until October 1865. In her lengthy statement, Jane echoed
many of the same details as her brother; much of her livestock had
been confiscated by Union forces in April 1863, leaving her with
only "a few mules, meat cattle, and hogs and her household furni-
ture" on a 1,420 acre plantation (her number of acres under cultivation is unknown).[7] She also declared, "she now has no cotton on
hand except that of the present years growth [since March-April
1865] unmatured and maturing and having no income other than
what is provided from stated property."[8] Jane swore that she
played no active part in the late rebellion, but out of sympathy for

---

[6]Ibid. Daniel had no real reason to mention his arrest at the hands of Federal
troops in 1863.
[7]Ibid., Amnesty Papers of Jane Curry.
[8]Ibid.

their plight she had rendered aid and comfort to individual Confederate soldiers. Witnessing the document were Jane's brother Daniel Perkins, along with Daniel's friend Dickinson Bell, and two others. Hedging slightly by not mentioning their sibling relationship, Daniel declared he "had known Miss Jane Curry for many years past."

Despite these dire summaries reported by both Jane and Daniel Perkins in their amnesty petitions, somehow a portion of the Perkins family's wealth remained. Intact it seems were their homes, while their respective plantations had also apparently escaped major destruction.[9] (Daniel's home had been spared perhaps because of its inland location, out of the range of shelling by Union gunboats.) And possibly, as some Southern families had done prior to the war, the Perkins clan had even placed currency (greenbacks) in England, or Texas, given the family's wartime connections to the latter, as a hedge against a Confederate defeat, though no documentation exists to support such a supposition. Overall, the Perkins family may have felt fortunate about their postwar situation, especially so when they considered the devastated plantations of local families, the Coffees, Campbells, both Montgomerys, Lobdells, Vicks, Starkes, and others.

Postwar life meant struggle and adjustment on many fronts (see below), but the Perkins family may have been able to adapt better than most. Though the war and nearly two years of crop failure had brought at least half of Mississippi's population "to want," by the end of 1866, both Jane and Daniel were able to pay thousands of dollars in cotton taxes despite their admittedly reduced cotton yields.[10] By 1870 Jane would declare the value of her property at $50,000. Her sister in Louisiana had, perhaps, suffered more hardship both during the conflict and afterwards.

Before the war William Perkins' other daughter, the widowed Louisa 'Ann' Perkins Pugh, resided in Madison Parish, Louisiana. She lived with her five children next to her Pugh inlaws in

---

[9]Confederate Amnesty Papers, D. P. Perkins and Jane Curry. This statement is based on information provided by the two in their postwar amnesty applications. Each described her/his wartime losses to a degree, but neither mentioned the loss of a home.

[10]Elizabeth Thompson, *The Reconstruction of Southern Debtors: Bankruptcy After the Civil War*, (Atlanta: University of Georgia Press, 2004), 9.

relative comfort following the death of her husband Dr. Pugh in 1855. Ann, in 1860, had claimed ten dwellings, $3,500 in livestock, fifty-two slaves, $90,000 in real estate value, $20,000 in personal estate value, and 1,000 acres of land on her plantation.[11] Like many Confederate civilians, though, the Pughs experienced ever-increasing hardships once the war began.

Early in the fighting, Ann had lost her oldest son, the only known casualty of the extended Perkins family during the conflict. J. J. Pugh Jr., an eighteen-year old sergeant in the Second Arkansas Cavalry, died in action near Denmark, Madison County, Tennessee, on September 1, 1862, not long after his enlistment. He was the six-year old J. J. to whom a dieing grandpa William Perkins in 1850 had gifted the slave Grandville.[12] Strangely, J. J. was born in Madison County, Mississippi, spent part of his life in Madison Parish, and died in Madison County, Tennessee. Other evidence indicates that while the war had claimed Ann's son, the Pughs also suffered financially.

According to a friend and neighbor, Kate Stone, the Pughs, due to the increased Yankee presence in nearby Vicksburg and on the Mississippi River, left their plantation in early May 1863 and refugeed in Texas. Stone wrote on May 5, 1863,

> "We went yesterday to see Florence Pugh [Louisa Ann Pugh's twenty-one year old daughter] (now Mrs. Morrison), an old schoolmate. The family are near here now on their way to Texas. She is a dear, sweet girl but looks dreadful. How marrying does change a body for the worse. She was a pretty girl a year ago, fresh and dainty. Now she is married and almost ugly.[13]

---

[11]Eighth Census, 1860, Madison Parish, Louisiana, s.v. "L. A. Pugh," 307, line 15 accessed online through author's library account, June 10, 2011, *Heritage Quest* and Joseph Karl Mann, *The Large Slaveholders of Louisiana: 1860*, (New Orleans: Pelican Publishing Company, 1998), 285.

[12]On March 6 in the year of his eighteenth birthday, 1862, young J. J. had enlisted at Delhi, Louisiana, near his Madison Parish, Louisiana, home. He transferred to Company C, 2nd Arkansas Cavalry, on May 15, 1862, and seventeen days later he received a promotion to fifth sergeant.

[13]Kate Stone, *Brokenburn, The Journal of Kate Stone, 1861-1868*, (Baton Rouge: Louisiana State University Press, 1955), 206. Brokenburn was the name of the Stone family's plantation in Madison Parish.

Stone's judgment of Florence's appearance perhaps was unfounded. The change may have had more to do with the harsh realities of the war and its effects on individuals than with Florence's recent marriage. Quite possibly the wartime loss of her brother J. J. some eight months earlier, combined with the family's decision to leave its Louisiana home for an uncertain future in Texas may have taken a toll on Florence.

At the end of the hostilities, Ann Pugh, then in her mid forties, had returned to the family plantation in Madison Parish. Valued later at just $49,000, or about fifty-four percent of its pre-war worth, the plantation was the postwar home for Ann and just two of her children.[14] Due in large part to the effects of war, her personal wealth had dwindled to a mere $250. By 1880 Ann Pugh may have passed away, having never remarried. She is not shown in the census that year, and three of her children, William Perkins' grandchildren, had returned to Texas, living in Robertson County.

* * * * *

On January 2, 1866, just a few months after completing her amnesty application, Jane P. Curry married former Confederate Colonel Matthew H. Moore, a Missourian. Soon after the war, Moore had relocated to Aberdeen, Mississippi, and then became acquainted with the widowed Jane Curry. Their wedding ceremony, like Jane's first, occurred in New Orleans.

In keeping with the Perkins family's propensity for associating with the important and powerful, Reverend Dr. Benjamin Palmer of New Orleans' First Presbyterian Church performed the ceremony. Palmer, a proslavery secessionist before the war, was one of the most influential men in New Orleans. Following their wedding and honeymoon, the Moores returned to Bolivar County and settled on Jane's plantation.

A lawyer by profession, the tall and portly Moore had a fair complexion, blue eyes, and dark hair. "He was an energetic

---

[14]Ninth Census, 1870, Madison Parish, Louisiana, 173, s. v. "Ann Pugh," accessed online through author's library account, July 15, 2010, *Heritage Quest*.

A page from Jane Perkins Curry's amnesty application addressed
to President Andrew Johnson, dated October 1865. Copy courtesy
of *Fold3*

public spirited citizen and although he did not practice law he often advised the negroes [pre and postwar] for their good."[15] On
one occasion in 1857 while living in Cape Girardeau, Missouri, at
the request of a group of seven slaves, Moore had helped these

---

[15]*Biographical and Historical Memoirs of Mississippi*, 586.

several "minor persons of color" sue for their freedom after their mistress had died.[16]

Prior to the war, Moore had resided with his first wife Julia in Cape Girardeau, where since 1859 he had been an associate editor of the local newspaper, the *Eagle*. In the 1860 presidential election, Moore had strongly supported John Bell, the moderate Constitutional Union Party's candidate who ran against Lincoln. As a Missouri delegate, Moore had attended the party's Baltimore nominating convention in 1860, which had delivered the nomination to Bell. (Bell's nephew, Dickinson Bell, lived in Bolivar County near Daniel Perkins and the Moores.)

Following Lincoln's victory the *Eagle*, under Moore's guidance, had evolved rapidly from a sheet condemning South Carolina's secession in December 1860 into an ardent secessionist publication. In a prewar editorial, Moore wrote, "Unless the Northern States make the necessary concessions and guarantees for the securing of the Constitutional rights of the people of the Slave States, there should be a dissolution of the Union."[17] Later, in a response to a Lincoln statement regarding the South, Moore warned, "Should this insane policy of this political madman [Lincoln] be attempted to be enacted, then will our worst fears be realized, and civil war be upon us; but woe! to the administration."[18] Moore's tenure at the *Eagle's* helm soon proved to be short-lived.

With the outbreak of the war, Missouri, a border slave state, sided with the Union. Moore, however, cast his lot with those Missourians who joined the Confederacy. Assigned to the Quartermaster Corps of the Confederate Missouri State Guard on June 1, 1861, Moore, who had very poor eyesight, was thus prevented from serving at the front lines. Union troops soon occupied Cape Girardeau, forcing Colonel Moore and his family to flee. Following the Union occupation of their house and confiscation of their property, Moore's wife died 'of a broken heart'.

In postwar Mississippi Moore's service as a former officer in the Confederate Army caused him difficulties. Under the terms

---

[16]*Digital Library on American Slavery*, s.v. "Matthew Moore," Missouri, Petitions 21185804 and 21185707.
[17]Karen Grace, "Let the Eagle Screame [sic]," *Ozarks Watch*, (summer, 1993): 30.
[18]Ibid., 31.

of the recently enacted (1868) Fourteenth Amendment (specifically section three) Moore temporarily lost his voting right. Furthermore, he was disqualified from holding state or Federal elective office. While these restrictions undoubtedly troubled the opin-
ionated Colonel, he faced other, more formidable problems that
affected his and Jane's livelihood.

Moore, an experienced cotton planter, realized that managing a profitable cotton plantation would be a difficult task in
postwar Mississippi. A combination of flooding, fluctuating and
generally descending cotton prices, cotton worms, lack of capital,
a new Federal cotton tax, local higher property and levee taxes, a
shortage of mules and equipment, and an absence of protecting
levies (as Daniel Perkins described in his amnesty application)
conspired against even the most experienced planters. Moreover,
the Colonel faced other unavoidable postwar problems, perhaps a
novelty to him, but nonetheless certain of diminishing profits even
further.

The recently discharged Colonel Moore probably had
never experienced paying salary or compensation to blacks, while
for Jane and other plantation owners, black labor costs had been a
part of the cotton business for the last several years during the Union occupation. After the fall of Vicksburg, when Union forces
took charge of Mississippi's cotton belt, many blacks had worked
for individual planters under contracts supervised by the Union
Army. Since around the time Union forces had arrived in Bolivar
County in 1863, Jane had witnessed the beginning of the end of
slave labor on her plantation, a first in the Perkins' family history
dating to Constantine Perkins in mid 1700s Virginia. Now, in
1866, it fell to Colonel Moore and other planters to undertake the
task of turning a profit on their plantations while employing labor
that was no longer free.

In the broader spectrum, with the abolition of slavery in
1865, came the disintegration of the established Southern plantation agricultural system and a change in some blacks' attitudes.
Delta landowners faced a suddenly free black labor force eager to
exercise its recently acquired rights. A Federal official reporting
from Bolivar County in July of that year wrote, "Their [the former
slaves] idea of freedom is that they are under no control; can work

when they please, and go where they wish."[19]

By January 1866 this attitude among the freedmen had resulted in a labor shortage in Bolivar County forcing some local planters (perhaps Moore) "to send to Georgia and Alabama for [additional] hands."[20] At the same time a local noted that, "We pay our best hands [freedmen] twelve dollars per month, the larger amount of it due at the end of the year. [Some planters offered even higher wages to lure additional workers.] We allow them one-half of every other Saturday [off], and a garden patch to each family."[21] The observer added, "So far they have worked very well and are pleased with their situation."

Despite the labor shortage and the uncertainties associated with cotton production, planters who survived the disastrous 1865 season continued their efforts to turn a profit. Another observer noted,

> The hopes of the Southern people are suspended, so to speak, upon a fair cotton crop. As the prospect for this grows bright or gloomy, so will the hearts of the tillers of the soil swell with exultation or sink into something akin to despair.[22]

Records show that in the first complete growing season following the Civil War, the myriad of problems facing planters (mentioned above) guaranteed a reduced cotton production level that could never approach Bolivar's 1860 figure. For the year December 1865 to December 1866, Bolivar County planters produced just 5,997 bales of cotton, whereas in 1860 they had produced 33,452 bales. This devastating *eighty-two percent decline* in cotton production hit at the very core of the county's primary and

---

[19]Leon Litwack, *Been in the Storm So Long*, (New York: Alfred A Knopf, 1980), 341.
[20]From a letter by a Bolivar County resident to a friend in Nashville printed in *The Daily Phoenix* (Columbia, South Carolina), January 31, 1866, 1.
[21]Ibid.
[22]*The Charleston Daily News* (South Carolina), July 29, 1867, 1. This correspondent for the *Louisville Journal* summarized the planters' efforts at cotton production and the plight of the freedmen based on his observations during a trip down the Mississippi to New Orleans that summer.

traditional cash crop and the population's livelihood.[23] As late as 1870, *Mississippi's* cotton production still had not improved. It continued at reduced levels, just approximately fifty percent of its 1860 total.[24]

Cotton yield data for individual Bolivar County planters exists from 1865 to 1866. It provides insight into the war's impact on these planters and particularly the combined Curry-Perkins duo, two of the county's foremost prewar cotton producers. These records reveal how reduced cotton yields and taxes, especially the new federal cotton tax, greatly impacted not only the Moore (Curry) and Perkins families, but also other planters countywide.

In November 1866, nineteen months after the war ended, M. H. "Moor" (Matthew Moore and wife Jane) claimed land parcels, at Mound "Place" and a smaller one at Carson's Landing. Simultaneously, Daniel Perkins cultivated both his share of the Mound Plantation and his Mecca (Beulah) acreage. That year the Moores produced on their portion of the Mound Plantation 131 bales of cotton, while Daniel's share there yielded forty bales (Table 3).[25] The combined 171 bales represented just *thirty-eight percent* of the Mound Plantation's 1860 crop of at least 450 known bales. Table 3 shows Daniel Perkins fared better (in terms of percentage harvested) at his Mecca plantation, where in 1866 he claimed 132 bales of cotton from October to December 1, *seventy-five percent* of his prewar total of 175 bales.[26] Significantly, 1866 cotton production levels at *both* the Moore's and Perkins' plantations, while reduced, *exceeded* by far the countywide average of eighteen percent of the 1860 crop.

---

[23]United States IRS Tax Assessments List, 1862-1918, Mississippi, District 3 Annual Monthly and Special Lists, December 1865-December 1866 (Bolivar County)," images 148-150, 191-193, and 256-261, accessed March 10, 2011, *Ancestry.com.*

[24]James Wilford Garner, *Reconstruction in Mississippi*, (New York: Macmillan Co., 1901), 125.

[25]"United States IRS Tax Assessments List, 1862-1918, December 1865-December 1866 (Bolivar County)," s. v. variously under "M. H. Moor, M. Moor, M. H. Moore, Daniel P. Perkins, Dan P. Perkins, and D. P. Perkins," accessed March 10, 2011, *Ancestry.com.* A planter's name may appear more than once on a tax sheet for a particular month. Not included in the Moore's 131 Mound Place bales is the lone bale produced on Colonel Moore's Carson Landing property.

[26]Ibid.

Both families may have also earned a diminished level of profit due to any wage payments they incurred, their smaller crop sizes compared to 1860, and the sale price of their cotton in a fluctuating 1866 market. On the other hand, selling at any random higher cotton price they chanced upon compared to 1860 helped offset a loss of profits from these other factors.

A Bolivar County resident, trying to remain optimistic, wrote at the time: "There will not be more than an average old [prewar] crop made down here, and the planters thinking such will be the case throughout the South are confident that cotton will rule [sell] higher twelve months from now [1867] than at present."[27] No matter what price planters received, though, a new Federal tax was sure to contribute to their financial woes.

In 1866 the assessment of the much-despised (by planters) three cents per pound Federal cotton tax amounted to a further burden for cotton growers. For the Moores it equated to an additional outlay of $1,900 and for Daniel Perkins $563.10 on their respective Mound Plantation crops (also Table 3). Daniel paid additional taxes totaling $1,973.70 for his crop at Mecca, which increased the combined tax bill for both of his plantations to $2,536.80.[28]

Additional taxes, but on property, also raised concern but impacted small farmers more than large planters. Before the war the tax on personal property, derived mainly from the levy on a planter's slaves, had been a major source of tax revenue. After the war and with the elimination of slavery, this tax shifted to real property. Though planters were affected by this land tax, the bothersome slave tax had been eliminated. Yet, Daniel still paid property taxes on the Mecca plantation totaling $540 for the three-year period 1867-1869 (about $180 yearly). Taxes on his share of the Mound/Southland Plantation totaled $339.50 under the new system.[29]

---

[27]*The Daily Phoenix*, January 31, 1866, 1. Talk of harvesting even an average prewar-size crop was especially optimistic in 1866.

[28]Ibid. The Federal tax on cotton ended in 1868. Unfortunately, no such IRS Bolivar County cotton tax records are available for 1867.

[29]Mississippi Probate Records, 1781-1930, Bolivar, Wills and Inventories, 1861-1924, vol. C-D, image 243, accessed September 4, 2012, *Family Search,* https://familysearch.org/pal:/MM9.3.1/TH-1961-30970-22228-

Table 3
1866 Bolivar County Cotton Production and Tax Assessment for
Jane and Matthew Moore and Daniel P. Perkins[30]

DATE	LOCATION	BALES	Cotton- lbs.	TAX
Moore				
8-Oct	Mound Place	33	15,275	$458.25
	Mound Place	2	927	$27.81
18-Oct	Mound Place	36	17,640	$529.20
3-Nov	Mound Place	6	2,962	$88.86
3-Nov	Mound Place	42	20,365	$610.89
17-Nov	Carson's Lndg	1	406	$12.18
7-Dec	Mound Place	12	5,763	$172.89
	Totals	**132**	**63,388**	**$1900.08**
Daniel Perkins				
8-Oct	Mound Place	20	9,429	$282.87
19-Oct	(Mecca) Beulah	30	14,880	$446.40
19-Oct	Mound Place	15	7,128	$213.84
2-Nov	Mound Place	5	2,213	$66.39
?	Beulah	38	21,072	$632.16
24-Nov	Beulah	63	29,348	$880.44
1-Dec	Beulah	1	490	$14.70
	Totals	**172**	**84,560**	**$2536.80**

Despite the tax(es) and the countywide decline in cotton production, Bolivar's planters in 1866 hoped that their yields that year could exceed the calamitous 1865 season. (*Hope* proved to be a recurring word in the postwar South.) Also, offering some encouragement was at one point in 1866 cotton sold unusually high, at between thirty-two and fifty-two cents per pound, or $128-208 per bale in the New York market compared to a mid forty-dollar

---

76?cc=2036959&wc=MMY2-QH3:743804828. The records do not indicate whether Daniel's tax bill for the Mound Plantation represented one, two, or three years, but given the amount it probably represented a two-year tax bill.
[30]"United States IRS Tax Assessments List, Mississippi, District 3 Annual Monthly and Special Lists, December 1865-December 1866 (Bolivar County)."

prewar price.[31] But, this increase soon proved to be an anomaly. And, of course, any discussion of postwar cotton prices and their effect on cotton producers' bottom lines has to be tempered by the fact that labor was no longer free.

Generally, waning cotton values continued for decades following a Civil War that had brought abnormally high prices. Due to competition from Brazilian, Egyptian, and Indian cotton and a general lower demand, New York cotton prices showed a yearly downward trend from an 1866 temporary high of $208 a bale to a little more than twelve cents per pound (forty-eight dollars per bale) in 1878.[32]

In September 1867 the *Memphis Daily Appeal* valued a sample of Bolivar County low middling cotton at twenty-three cents a pound or ninety-two dollars per 400-pound bale, disturbingly *less* than in 1866.[33] As it turned out, according to another observer in July 1867, even with favorable weather that season only *half* the amount of Mississippi's 1860 crop was expected.[34] The same writer *hoped* that because of the 1867 cotton prices (though they were declining) even this smaller crop would bring as much money to planters as the whole prewar crop.

More specifically, one year later Daniel Perkins, offering his cotton in the New Orleans market, experienced the fluctuating prices common during this time of economic uncertainty. He sold his cotton there for approximately eighty dollars per 400-pound bale in December 1868, while one month later he received eighty-nine dollars per bale. By August 1869, however, as cotton remained scarce, Daniel sold bales at $109 each.[35] However, by then, under the terms of a recent bargain he had struck, he was

---

[31]Wayne, *Reshaping of Plantation Society*, 64 and Charles M. Goodsell and Henry E. Wallace (eds.), *The Manual of Statistics*, Volume 12, (New York: Investors Publishing Company, 1890), 291.

[32]Goodsell, *The Manual of Statistics*, 291.

[33]*Memphis Daily Appeal*, September 8, 1867, 3, column 3.

[34]*The Charleston Daily News*, July 29, 1867, 1.

[35]These cotton prices are derived from Daniel Perkins' estate papers showing the price *he* received for his cotton sales for the dates indicated above and are found at, Mississippi Probate Records, 1781-1930, Bolivar, Wills and Inventories, 1861-1924, vol. C-D, image 243, accessed September 4, 2012, *Family Search*, https://familysearch.org/pal:/MM9.3.1/TH-1961-30970-22228-76?cc=2036959&wc=MMY2-QH3:743804828.

compelled to share *half* the proceeds of the sales with his freedmen (see below).

Though they sought to regain even a semblance of their
prewar yields, many planters in the Reconstruction Era found the
struggle hopeless. In Bolivar County much of the land remained
uncultivated, with certain parts resembling its undeveloped look of
the early 1840s due to wartime neglect or destruction. Some planters simply gave up, and began to sell their plantations for far less
than their prewar value. They simply couldn't afford to keep land
that was producing less than the taxes owed on it. By 1871 residents in seven Delta counties had forfeited 1.4 million acres of
land.[36]

Planters eventually sensed a time of adjustment was at
hand. Beset by a litany of nagging negative factors - reduced production and prices, a new, previously inconceivable, and mind
boggling social and labor structure, increased cotton, land, and
levee taxes, and/or a loss of land, and all the while unable to afford
or unwilling to pay wages to workers (for the Perkins and Moore
families probably more of the latter) - many former slaveholders
began instituting a system/solution later synonymous with the
postwar South. It proved to be the salvation of many.

As he observed two plantations while passing through
Mississippi in July 1867, a reporter provided the following concise
explanation of a novel planter-freedmen work relationship: ". . .
the freedmen have half the crop, the employers furnishing the supplies [tools, seed, etc.] at a slight advance upon the original cost.
This appears to be the rule generally adopted."[37] Without using the
word, the writer had just described in a nutshell the innovative
concept of sharecropping, which contrasted sharply with the
wages-for-labor system employed just eighteen months earlier.
Sharecropping, then, became the final stage in the transformation
of the generations-old plantation agriculture system.

In the postwar era, blacks learned that adjusting to freedom proved to be no easy matter, especially in an economically
challenged and racially tense Mississippi. Despite its recently
achieved freedom, the black population found that independence

---

[36]Cobb, *The Most Southern Place*, 64.
[37]*The Charleston Daily News*, July 29, 1867, 1.

came with a price. Acquiring many of the day-to-day necessities, food, clothing, medical care, and shelter, all previously provided by their masters, now became the responsibility of the landless black freedmen. Thus, black wage earners likewise embraced sharecropping, which on the surface, appeared to be a panacea for some of their economic woes as well. As time passed, planters and freedmen were agreeing to such 'sharing' bargains all across the South.

Under sharecropping, planters divided their lands and rented out each plot, or share, to a black family. Blacks farmed their own crops on these rented plots (sometimes residing there and abandoning their old slave quarters in the process) in exchange for a percentage of the yield. Sharing in crop production offered blacks a financial incentive to generate maximum output on these twenty-five to forty acre shares, a concept beneficial to owners as well. Landowners, like the Moores and Daniel Perkins, paid no wages and reaped the benefits of a wageless system, no longer having to part with cash. Replacing both slave and wage labor, the system proved to be a compromise for whites, as it allowed them to retain their prewar social power (elite status) while creating a low-cost workforce tied to rented plots and also indebted to white land-owners for tools and credit.

Ironically, then, the system had developed on the basis of mutual need; whites required inexpensive or no cost black labor on their plantations, and penniless blacks, unable to afford land of their own, 'gained' the land they needed to raise crops in the form of rented acreage. While sharecropping couldn't solve the planters' problem of declining cotton prices, it ameliorated the issues of labor and wages. For blacks sharecropping provided independence in their daily work routine and social lives, and liberated them from the traditional gang-labor method representative of the slavery era.

Opportunities for abuse ran rampant within the system. White planters maintained the books for their illiterate black workers. Furthermore, some landlords (the Moores included) also owned the plantation stores where they sold blacks their seed, tools, and food products, often with high interest cash advances. Consequently, such 'loans' often increased black indebtedness to and dependence on white owners.

As a result, economic prospects for sharecropping blacks were usually poor. In many cases former masters sharecropped with some of their same poor and landless former slaves who again worked the same fields in which they had labored for years before emancipation. Many blacks even lived in the same ramshackle slave cabins they had occupied before the war. (On the Mecca plantation new cabins went up and old ones were repaired in 1869.)[38]

Other freedmen, succumbing to the desire to leave the plantations and intent on severing all ties with their former masters, chose to work for different landowners in different settings, but as sharecroppers still. In some reality, perhaps, sharecropping differed little from slavery - blacks had just exchanged masters for bosses. Furthermore, many white Mississippians still harbored the idea that despite emancipation, blacks still belonged to whites.

* * * * *

The war and the black exodus from Bolivar County's plantations had not lessened the county's overwhelming black majority. Mississippi's first postwar state census certified in Bolivar County on August 31, 1866, showed the customary racial disparity remained firmly in place, though the percentage of blacks in the population had decreased. Among the county's 7,490 people were 1,334 whites (only fifty-nine less than in 1860) and 6,156 blacks.[39] Blacks totaled eighty-two percent of Bolivar County's total population, less than their eighty-four percent and eighty-six percent shares documented in the 1850 and 1860 Federal Censuses. Even though more than 2,500 blacks had returned to the county since the 1864 counting, the 1866 black population figure was approxi-

---

[38]Mississippi Probate Records, Bolivar County Minutes 1865-1870, image 167, accessed September 4, 2012, *Family Search,* https://familysearch.org/pal:/MM9.3.1/TH-1961-30968-2581-33?cc=2036959&wc=MMY2-QHM:1888823323.

[39]Mississippi, State Archives, Various Records, 1820-1951, Bolivar County, State Census Returns, 1866, image 13, accessed October 21, 2011, *Family Search,* https://www.familysearch.org/search/image/index#uri=https%3A//api.familysearch.org/records/collection/1919687/waypoints. Nearly 1,800 of the 6,156 blacks were children ten years and under.

mately 2,900 less than in the Federal Census of 1860 (Appendix F).

Mississippi state census takers in 1866 did not record the names of the county's blacks (though they were now free). Instead, retaining the prewar method of rendering Negroes anonymously, the enumerators tallied them under the heading *Freedmen* (this also included women), *Free Negroes, and Mulattoes.* The number in the appropriate age column represented the total of freedmen in that category. On the other hand, named whites appeared on the lists and in such a manner as to give the impression they still owned the blacks.

Based on these 1866 records, under the sharecropping system, more than 240 freedmen and their families would have occupied land owned by the Moores and Daniel Perkins on their two plantations. The Moores reported eighty-four freedmen of various ages and sexes on the Mound Plantation, while Daniel Perkins counted eighty-two blacks there (coincidentally, this total of 166 freedmen on the Mound Plantation amounted to the exact number of slaves William owned in 1850). Additionally, Daniel counted another seventy-five freedmen on his Mecca plantation.[40]

Many in an agitated, postwar white populace viewed the freedmen as living reminders (in their midst) of the changes wrought by the war and sought to subjugate them by any means possible. While the census tabulation method only *hinted* at a sense of white superiority while reinforcing black anonymity (again), Mississippi's implementation of the infamous and prejudicial Black Codes at nearly the same time took white attempts at racial domination to a new level, all allusions aside. Designed to restrict and control blacks' lives (and to replicate slavery as much as possible), the Codes buttressed the legal foundation for discrimination and resulted in *actual* inequity and an accompanying second-class citizenship status for former slaves. These regulations, which were most severe in Mississippi and South Carolina, prevented blacks from owning firearms, preaching without a license, marrying whites, quitting their jobs before their contracts had expired, selling liquor, making seditious speeches, or demon-

---

[40]Ibid., images 5,6.

strating insulting gestures, language, or acts. For blacks in this postwar world of quasi freedom, the Black Codes and planters' practices (including the implementation of sharecropping) formed the basis for a reversion to the days of slavery. The shackles still existed; they were just invisible.

As an example a Freedmen's Bureau agent reported in September 1866, "it is the practice of planters in Coahoma and Bolivar Counties, Miss. to systematically tie up and whip the hands [freedmen] employed by them for any, and all causes. . . . Numbers of them have reported that they are worse off now than when they were slaves."[41] The determination of many Southern whites to maintain their prewar status quo of racial superiority would become a precept of Southern life well into the twentieth century regardless of any emancipatory rulings or postwar Constitutional amendments to the contrary. This unwavering effort to suppress the freedmen resulted in the founding of a clandestine organization destined to strike fear into blacks all over the South.

In summarizing what many whites believed in the postwar era, one Bolivar County resident stated, "Only those who lived through those dark days [Reconstruction] can know the horror of having one's slaves become his rulers."[42] Additionally, poor whites who, because of their freedom and whiteness, had previously regarded themselves as above blacks on the Southern social ladder now blamed emancipation for removing a distinct difference between themselves and the former slaves. Now that blacks were free, only skin color separated these two groups. In their threatened personal world, these whites, and others, soon issued calls for white supremacy.

A prominent Bolivar County citizen, Civil War veteran, and later a justice of the peace and a state representative, John C. Burrus Jr., recalled in 1923, "Then a great and inspired man caught the vision of an invisible empire, which was realized in a surprisingly short time by the organization of the Ku Klux Klan, to which every true Confederate soldier and every white man of the

---

[41]Capt. H. Sweeney to Maj. Gen Thomas Wood, September 3, 1866, in Bell, *The Evolution of the Mississippi Delta*, 61.
[42]W. B. Roberts in Sillers, *History of Bolivar County*, 161.

South, loyal to his race, belonged."[43] During the early years after the war, the racist and violent Ku Klux Klan, desirous of returning Bolivar and other Southern counties to white-dominated ante-bellum rule, first appeared in Mississippi and the South. The Klansmen were working in fertile soil. Until its decline several years later, these hooded terrorists intimidated blacks and denied them their recently won civil rights.

Former Confederate cavalry officer and lawyer Frank Montgomery organized the first Ku Klux Klan in Bolivar County but failed to make any reference to it in his published reminiscences cited earlier.[44] He did mention, though, his long acquaintance with Nathan Bedford Forrest, his former Civil War commander, and later the Klan's first Grand Wizard.[45]

The extent of the Klan's repression in postwar Bolivar County is unclear, but it is safe to say that wherever the Klan existed blacks lived in fear. (None of the sources examined by the author indicate any involvement by Daniel Perkins or Colonel Moore in the organization.) One supporter, a Mississippi state senator, later wrote, "There can be little doubt that there would have been many more outrages upon our [white] people in those dark days had it not been for the restraining influence of the clansmen [sic] upon the newly enfranchised blacks. . . ."[46] "Restraining influence" included intimidation and murder. Ironically, the work of a former slave helped ameliorate, to a degree, the tense racial situation over the years in Bolivar County.

In his memoirs Frank A. Montgomery, the Bolivar County lawyer and Klansman, and local planter and lawyer Walter Sillers Sr., who had studied law in Montgomery's office and was by no means a black advocate, both praised an influential, well-respected former slave, the politically moderate Blanche K. Bruce. While the tactful Bruce later held several elective offices in Bolivar County and became a United States Senator from Mississippi, Montgomery recalled Bruce's early efforts at "keeping down hostility on the part of the negroes" which helped Bolivar escape "the riots and

---

[43]Sillers, *History of Bolivar County*, 109.

[44]James B. Lloyd, ed., *Lives of Mississippi Authors, 1817-1967*, (Jackson: University Press of Mississippi, 2009), 337.

[45]Montgomery, *Reminiscences*, 225.

[46]W. B. Roberts in Sillers, *History of Bolivar County*, 161.

disorders which vexed others counties in the state" during the postwar era. Sillers wrote that, "Bruce was tactful and very deferential to the old slave-holding class and courteous to all white men."[47] Despite Bruce's efforts the black population continued to encounter groups of whites bent on restricting their freedoms as much as possible.

During the Reconstruction era, the struggle by Bolivar County's blacks to exercise their voting rights guaranteed by the Fifteenth Amendment in 1870 was fraught with difficulties. Prominent Bolivar County lawyers Walter Sillers Sr. and state senator W. B. Roberts later wrote openly and unashamedly of the efforts of organized whites to alter the election process.

Sillers was instrumental in organizing a "Democratic Club" in Bolivar County which was actually a front for a militant, armed group of whites clad in red shirts, many of whom were former Confederate soldiers. Intent on restoring Democratic power to the Republican-dominated county, they sought to repress Negro voting rights through fear and intimidation. Sillers described the tactics and "outcome" of one election in 1876:

> When the election came off in the fall, the Negroes . . . marched to the polls in companies with fife and drum. The ticket handler gave the man at the head of the column a ticket, who voted and took his place at the foot of the column, and so on until all had voted. It was of no avail; all the boxes went overwhelmingly Democratic. There were 20 white men registered at Beulah and 400 Negroes. When the "smoke" of the ballots had blown away, 400 Democrats had voted and only 20 Negroes. It [the bogus ballot count] stuck, however. *The white man was armed, dressed in red, and looked dangerous* [italics mine].[48]

Senator Roberts of Bolivar County recalled a meeting that laid the foundation for several later incidents of election fraud:

---

[47]Montgomery, *Reminiscences*, 279, and Sillers, *History of Bolivar County*, 157. The author, Florence Sillers, was the wife of Walter Sillers Sr.
[48]Sillers, *History of Bolivar County*, 159.

... in 1882 and 1883 the older men called me into
conference with them and in deep earnestness explained to
me that to retain even a show of white supremacy, which
they regarded as necessary, it was my duty as a young
lawyer and citizen to use my brains and skill to devise
ways of preventing negro control by any means in my
power. And so all of us worked toward that end.[49]

Roberts then described specifically the ploys used to subvert the
black voting process:

On one occasion Congress had passed a law providing that
the Federal judge should appoint two inspectors at each
[ballot] box to guarantee a fair election of Congressmen.
Two inspectors at one of our large boxes were appointed,
and at the close of the election, when a box had been
prepared with which to change the result of the election,
the two negro inspectors positively refused to leave the
room even for supper. Under this stress, one of the white
managers, who was a doctor, told them this was one time
when the colored and white folks would eat together; and
he went out and returned presently with a number of boxes
of sardines and crackers. He had, with a hypodermic nee-
dle, injected croton oil, or some other violent drug, into
the two boxes handed the Negroes. In a very few minutes
the Negroes were sick and had to leave hurriedly, and the
box showed at the count a big majority for the Democrats.

At the box at Bolivar where I lived at the time, there were
five hundred negro voters and only about twenty-five
white voters. One can imagine the difficulty of making
that box show a Democratic majority. One favorite
scheme was to mix bills of lading at the river and ship by
mistake a ballot box to St. Louis while a coil of rope or
bale of cotton was sent to the county site to be counted; or
the ballot box might, accidentally, be dropped out of the

---

[49]Ibid., 162.

window of a train; in fact, any trick might be employed that seemed to promise a chance of success.[50]

Thus, it appears that some whites at the highest levels of post bellum Bolivar County society, even those working in the legal profession, proved to be instrumental in instigating voter fraud through a variety of means.

The first postwar Federal Census illustrated the changing nature of Bolivar County society and for that matter Southern society in general. Bolivar County's blacks still far outnumbered whites in 1870, but Federal Census records finally included the *names* of these former slaves, commingled on the lists with whites.[51] Moreover, despite resistance from the Ku Klux Klan and some former masters who viewed freed black's educational efforts as a threat to establishing a subservient black labor pool, many former slaves attended school by 1870. Both amazing and immensely rewarding to black parents was the fact that their children also could now attend school. The appearance of black children's names on the census pages with an accompanying note of "at school" signifies a heretofore unheard of milestone in America's slaveholding counties where educating blacks had been illegal for centuries.

Most of these schools in the postwar South and in Bolivar County were established as a result of the efforts of the Freedmen's Bureau. Initiated by Congress in 1865, the Bureau organized schools (one of its many tasks designed to help struggling freedmen) for thousands of blacks during the late 1860s. Though segregated, these places of instruction provided blacks with their first real opportunity to achieve an education despite the fact that

---

[50]Ibid., 162-163.
[51]Blacks totaled 7,816 and whites 1,900. Ninth Census, 1870, United States Population by Counties 1790-1870, Table II, Mississippi, 42. The 1870 Mississippi *state* census for Bolivar County certified on December 17 of that year reveals 527 fewer people than the number reported in the Federal Census: Mississippi, State Archives, Various Records, 1820-1951, Bolivar County, State Census Returns, 1870, image 305, accessed October 21, 2011, *Family Search*, https://www.familysearch.org/search/image/index#uri=https%3A//api.familysearch.org/records/collection/1919687/waypoints. See Appendix F for the two sets of figures.

white resistance in Mississippi to the Bureau's Northern white instructors (who initially staffed many of the schools) was greater than in any other state.[52]

Another feature found in the 1870 Bolivar County Federal Census pages concerns the proximity of white and black inhabitants. The Moores (and other whites across the county) are listed alongside their black neighbors indicating they lived near each other. On the census pages immediately preceding and following the Moores, 120 people are named. All but eight of the 120 are blacks with a few mulattoes included. Though masters and slaves had always lived in proximity to one another before the war, the possibility existed that once emancipation came the freedmen might not remain in place. In certain cases this proved correct. However, in other instances, such a scenario could not have been farther from the truth. In counties all over the South, some former masters and their former slaves often lived close to each other as before, due in large part to sharecropping. Some of the blacks residing (and sharecropping) near the Moores were previously Perkins family slaves who had worked for Jane's father William decades earlier. One such example is that of Sandy Jones' descendants.

Nearly two decades after Sandy Jones, along with Carter and Robert Perkins, had disappeared from the written record, Sandy Jones' grandson, Sandy II, age thirty-six and a former slave to first William Perkins, then Charles and later Jane Curry, appears in the Bolivar County 1870 census. He lived with his wife and four children next to his mother Matilda in the Beulah/Bolivar Landing post office district.[53] Shown as census family number 1105, the Jones family is listed just below Jane and Matthew Moore, family number 1092, thirteen dwellings away but still a

[52]Christopher Span, *From Cotton Field to Schoolhouse: African American Education in Mississippi, 1862-1875*, (Chapel Hill: University of North Carolina Press, 2009), 118.
[53]Ninth Census, 1870, Bolivar County, Mississippi, s. v. "Sandy Jones," p. 129, line 39, accessed online through author's library account, July 18, 2010, *Heritage Quest*. Matilda had been married to Wake Jones, the son of Sandy I. Family number 1089 reveals the name of a seventy-seven year old black, Henry Ford. Most likely this was William Perkins' slave mentioned above in (prewar) *Bolivar County Deed Book C*, microfilm roll 886086, 441.

world apart. A farm laborer, the illiterate Sandy II sharecropped on the Moore's land, laboring in the same fields and performing the same tasks just as he, his father, and his grandfather Sandy had done as slaves in the decades before the war. Now, however, he was a *free* man, working and eking out a living by receiving a share of the crop (while unwittingly becoming ensnared in the life of a sharecropper), a simultaneously gratifying, yet baffling experience, for a man who had spent thirty-one of his thirty-six years in bondage. He would continue sharecropping with the Moores until at least 1883.

A sampling of an original 1870 Bolivar County Federal Census sheet showing M. H. Moore and Jane (Perkins-Curry) Moore (top). Note Jane's property valued at $50,000. For the first time in the nation's history, Southern black children are shown attending school (George, 14, and Bettie, 12, at the bottom). The "b" in the sixth (race) column denotes black. Lest we forget, blacks' access to education and the right to work freely did not result in equality in a postwar Southern society dominated still by whites.

The 1870 Federal Agricultural Census also provided additional documentary evidence of the Civil War's effects on Bolivar County agriculture, though the war's cumulative impact was already familiar to county residents. Despite the fact that the census was recorded *five years after the war had ended*, Bolivar County (and similar counties across the defeated South) still had not recovered from the devastating and lingering consequences of the war, failing to equal or even approach prewar numbers in key agricultural categories. The 1870 census figures reveal that the cash value of Bolivar County's farms remained more than $7,000,000 less than in 1860. Compared to 1860 only forty-six percent of the county's land was under cultivation (improved acres), which explains why Bolivar's cotton yield of 15,571 bales for 1870 was also just forty-six percent of its prewar yield (reflecting a statewide trend). Furthermore, those supplementary, but vital indicators of a nineteenth century farming community's strength, its horses, mules, and work oxen, also exhibited acute declines from their 1860 totals (Table 4).

Thus, even five years after the war, with economic recovery stalled, many Bolivar County planters continued to remain beleaguered by the same daunting array of problems they had experienced in the days immediately following the war – fluctuating and declining cotton prices, lack of capital and equipment, a shortage of work and feed animals, arable land, and adjustment to a new labor system. Probably, only a nationwide depression could have made things worse.

Just four years after the war's end, Daniel Perkins, thirty-six, and his twenty-two year old younger brother James, the last surviving sons of Jane and William Perkins, died, either at the same time or within weeks of each during April 1869. In his will, recorded on April 15, 1869, Daniel bequeathed his assets to his wife Caroline Campbell Perkins.[54] Since Daniel and Caroline had been unable to have children, his other survivors included his adopted son and an adopted infant daughter, Lelia Perkins, born in

---

[54]Bolivar County, Mississippi, Wills and Inventories 1861-1924, Volume C & D, image 217, Will of Daniel Perkins, accessed September 4, 2012, *Family Search.*

1867.[55] (Lelia was named after Caroline's deceased sister Lelia Campbell who had died in 1852 at age sixteen while away at school.)

Because the Moores were temporarily out of the state, Caroline also accepted responsibility for administering the estate of her young brother-in-law James Perkins.[56] On the same day that she filed for letters of administration for her husband's estate, she also filed the same papers for James' estate. Later, by December 1869, the Moores returned to Mississippi, and Colonel Moore assumed the role as his brother-in-law James' estate administrator on behalf of Jane Moore.

Table 4

Federal Agricultural Census 1860 & 1870, Bolivar County, Mississippi (selected items)[57]

	1860	1870
Improved Acres	85,188	39,020
Unimproved	216,504	unknown
Cash Value of Farms - $	8,759,270	1,449,525
Horses	764	720
Mules	3,180	1,478
Oxen	1,601	261
Cotton - 400 lb. bales	33,452	15,571

[55]Confederate Amnesty Papers, Perkins, Daniel P., Amnesty Petition, July 1865. The names and birthplaces of Lelia's parents went unrecorded in the 1880 census.
[56]Mississippi Probate Records, Bolivar County Minutes 1865-1870, images 146-147, accessed September 4, 2012, https://familysearch.org/pal:/MM9.3.1/TH-1951-30968-2957-96?cc=2036959&wc=MMY2-QHM:1888823323.
[57]Eighth Census, 1860, Mississippi, Agriculture, Bolivar County, 84, 85 and Ninth Census, 1870, Mississippi, Agriculture, Bolivar County, 184-186.

Following Daniel's death and true to his Perkins heritage, his estate held receipts for ninety-nine bales of cotton valued at $10,680. However, not all the proceeds of the sale went to his widow. Among the debts Daniel owed were $2,756 to New Orleans cotton factor J. W. Person (the son of J. J. Person, Stephen Curry's partner from the 1850s) and approximately $5,300 to his sharecroppers, half the value of the bales they had raised during the year. Daniel's estate would also pay a $339 tax bill, his portion of the Southland property taxes that he had shared over the years with his sister Jane.

As a result of the deaths of Daniel and James, the male line of this branch of the Perkins family ceases, as none of William and Jane Perkins' five sons produced any male heir to continue the Perkins name. The childless Jane Moore thus remained the sole surviving heir/child of the Perkins family, having lost in less than twenty years her husband, every male sibling in her family, her brother-in-law Dr. Pugh, nephew J. J. Pugh, and her parents. Presumably, in a double funeral, Caroline and Jane had Daniel and James buried at the Mound Cemetery.

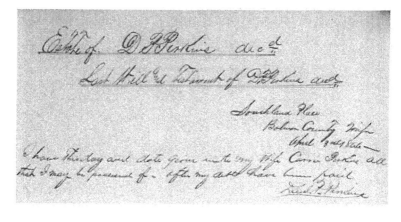

The brief will of Daniel P. Perkins, originally written in April 1866, three years before his death

Shortly after Daniel's death, the widowed Caroline Perkins remarried, perhaps for love, perhaps out of loneliness, or a combination of the two. Later events indicate, though, that she retained her strong attachment to Daniel in the years after his death. She and her new husband, Virginian John H. Hedges, born in 1836, signed papers relating to Daniel's estate in October 1869 as husband and wife, meaning the couple had married within at most six months following Daniel's death.[58] According to a court document, the couple resided on Daniel's one-third portion of the Southland Plantation (the other two thirds were owned by Jane and the deceased James' estate), perhaps because structures on the Mecca plantation were in need of repair.

By July 1870 the Hedges family, with Caroline's two-year old adopted daughter, Lelia Perkins, John 'Barkin' (the adopted son?), and two servants, had relocated west of St. Louis, to a Missouri cotton plantation.[59] Later, while residing in Missouri, they welcomed a son of their own, John S.[60]

In late January 1876, Caroline planned to make a last journey home to her mother in Mississippi. On the way, she stopped in Tennessee: "Stopping in Memphis . . . but in near prospect of death," Caroline, with a Dr. Shannon, the son of her personal physician, visited two acquaintances, lawyers Dabney and J.W. Scales, and instructed them to prepare a will as quickly as possible while she waited.[61]

The will provided that Lelia Perkins would receive one-half of Caroline's estate and her son John Hedges Jr. the other half. She appointed her mother Margaret Campbell and brother

---

[58]Bolivar County Wills and Inventories, images 238 and 244 and Mississippi Probate Records, Minutes 1865-1870, image 162, accessed September 4, 2012, *Family Search*, https://familysearch.org/pal:/MM9.3.1/TH-1951-30968-2871-37?cc=2036959&wc=MMY2-QHM:1888823323.

[59]The 1870 Federal Census of St. Louis County, Missouri, shows a ten-year old John Barkin of Mississippi living with the Hedges and Lelia Perkins. Given the boy's age and birthplace, he is probably the adopted son of Daniel and Caroline. The census taker may have misunder-stood the boy, writing Barkin instead of Perkins on the tabulation sheet. By 1876 John Barkin had disappeared from the family record.

[60]The fact that Caroline and Hedges produced a child together suggests that since she and Daniel had adopted two children, perhaps Daniel's disability had affected his reproductive capability.

[61]Bolivar Wills and Inventories 1861-1924, Volume C-D, images 254-256, accessed September 4, 2012, *Family Search*, https://familysearch.org/pal:/MM9.3.1/TH-1971-30970-21043-71?cc=2036959&wc=MMY2-QH3:743804828.

William as Lelia's guardians while assigning guardianship of John Hedges Jr. to his father. She also expressed her "wish to be buried by the side of my husband Mr. D. P. Perkins and that one thousand dollars of my personal estate be used to defray the expense of erecting a monument over us both & I wish my brother to select this monument and have it erected at once."[62]

Caroline, with death approaching, had chosen to join Daniel for eternity in the Perkins' family cemetery in Bolivar County rather than selecting a plot where she and John Hedges eventually could rest together. With this decision and the reference to Daniel as "my husband," she proclaimed, too, her strong feelings for him even now, seven years after his death. Inasmuch as Hedges did not witness the will, we may assume he was not present for the signing. The following day Caroline Campbell Perkins Hedges passed away in Memphis at 1:30 in the afternoon, and thus was denied the opportunity to see her family and Argyle for one final time.

Whether or not Hedges was present to escort his wife's body on the remainder of its journey is unknown, but eight-year old Lelia may have. Caroline's steamboat voyage down the Mississippi carried her to the Mound Plantation, where in the middle of the cotton fields rose the Perkins' family cemetery. There, at the top of the Indian mound, Caroline joined Daniel.[63]

* * * * *

Between 1867 and 1869 the Moores had moved temporarily to Missouri, possibly leaving the Mound Plantation in Daniel's care until his death in 1869.[64] It is unknown where the Moores resided during their time there, but by late 1869 (or probably before, if they attended the two funerals of Jane's brothers) they had returned to Mississippi. They reoccupied the plantation house at Mound Landing as Colonel Moore tended to legal matters regard-

---

[62]Ibid. Caroline also made provisions in her will that the taxes on her Mississippi property would be paid by February 15, 1876.

[63]Tenth Census, 1880, Washington County, Mississippi, s. v. "Margaret Campbell," *Heritage Quest*, accessed online through author's library account, July 29, 2010. The census shows a thirteen-year old Lelia (line 28) living with her grandmother, Margaret Campbell (line 26).

[64]*Biographical and Historical Memoirs of Mississippi*, 586.

ing James Perkins' estate and also in time to be counted in the Federal Census the following year.

In the 1870s Jane, then in her fifties, and Colonel Moore remained on the Mound Plantation, valued at $50,000. Residing with them was the Colonel's son Thomas Moore, a young Missouri-born merchant and partner with his father in a dry goods store, his wife, and three employees.[65] With Matthew Moore as the proprietor, the store, as early as 1868, recorded sales of $1,000.[66] Located on Moore's land, it probably served as the plantation store for the Moore's sharecroppers while also offering goods to locals. Moore's business would soon become part of a small, but thriving community bearing his name that sprang up in the area.

By 1870, the county had begun to take on a new appearance. Many of the county's 'old guard', who had been among Bolivar's early pioneers, planters like William Cook, William Vick, and others had died. In some cases their plantations had been passed on to their descendants (as had the Mound Plantation). Often, others had been sold, destroyed during the war, or considerably reduced in size. Indeed, large plantations were becoming the exception, not the rule, in Bolivar County. The Burrus family retained 700 acres, just a share of the property they owned before the war, while Frank Montgomery wrote that during this time (approximately 1870), "I had struggled to maintain myself on my plantation, which gradually dwindled down to a small farm, but had wholly failed to adapt myself to the new condition of farming [without slaves and with sharecroppers] and from that time on gave it up."[67]

In the 1870s and into the early 1880s while the Mound Plantation still remained the Moore's hospitable home, a portion

---

[65]Ninth Census, 1870, Bolivar County, Mississippi, s. v. "M. H. Moore, lines 20-21, p. 128," accessed online through author's library account, July 29, 2010, *Heritage Quest*. One of the employees was a South American, the other an Australian.
[66]Mississippi, State Archives, Various Records, 1820-1951, Bolivar County, County tax rolls, 1868-1887, Personal Tax Assessment 1868, Box 3611, image 31, accessed October 23, 2011, *Family Search*, https://www.familysearch.org/search/image/index#uri=https%3A//api.familysearch.org/records/collection/1919687/waypoints. Colonel Moore paid taxes on the store's income indicating he was the owner.
[67]Montgomery, *Reminiscences*, 273.

of their land soon underwent development unseen in that part of the county. Jane and Colonel Moore, who earlier had divided parts of the plantation into smaller plots then rented them to their share-croppers, also began selling a number of lots, eventually leaving them with approximately 1,750 acres valued at about $22,000 in land and improvements by 1883.[68] Approximately 200 of the acres they sold lay directly opposite Arkansas City, Arkansas, on the Mississippi side of the river slightly south of Mound Landing, part of the same historic acreage Jane's father had first purchased in 1842. After the sale the buyer, W. E. Ringo & Company, erected several buildings there. A store owned by Ringo and another oper-ated by Simon & Brown soon competed with each other and Moore's store for local business.[69]

The possibility exists that the reason the Moore's sold off various plots of land was due to the depression then gripping the entire United States. Beginning in 1873 and continuing until ap-proximately 1879, this economic downturn hit Mississippi planters particularly hard. Those planters fortunate enough to have sur-vived the postwar era's economic challenges and declining cotton prices faced mounting debt. One local Bolivar citizen reported that, "The year 1875 dawned upon an impoverished state and an impoverished people. . . ."[70] Near Natchez, Mississippi, in that same year over 150 indebted planters had surrendered parts of their land to satisfy unpaid debts or tax obligations. While it ap-pears that the Perkins clan and the Moores had weathered the

---

[68]Bolivar County, Bolivar County Land Assessment 1883, Box 3611, images 193-195. The assessor noted that part of William Perkins' original purchase back in 1842 in section three had gone into the river. Despite the sales, the 1880 agri-cultural census shows Jane Moore claimed 1,565 acres. She may have added additional acreage between the 1880 Federal Census and the 1883 Bolivar Coun-ty assessment which would account for the difference.

[69]Tenth Census, 1880, Bolivar County, Mississippi, Family 1, 1. According to Sillers, *History of Bolivar County*, 127, the store had a series of owners after the war, Will Robinson (he also operated the landing in 1872), the Ballou Brothers, and finally Ringo. Ringo's land purchase included parts of lots 5-8 in section 3 and lot 1 in section 4. Arron Simon and David Brown held positions as retail grocers in1880. Had William Perkins been alive at that time, he may have sur-prisingly noted the changing character of the county as Simon and his wife were Russians and, despite his name, David Brown was a Prussian, 1880 Census, Fam-ily 500, 46.

[70]Montgomery, Reminiscences, 288.

postwar economic crises better than most, the depression may
have caused the Moores enough concern that selling selected
Mound Plantation land parcels provided them with added financial
security. No evidence exists, however, that the Moores experienced any undue financial problems during the depression's five
and half year run.

Whatever the Moore's rationale for selling, the property
soon evolved into a bustling new settlement, Mound Place or
Moores (1895 Bolivar County map). By 1880, with the depression
nearing its end, W. E. Ringo employed three clerks and a book-
keeper, attesting to the growth of his store and the new community. Later, Moores added its own station/express office for the
railroad spur extending to that part of the county. Moores also
claimed a post office, with Colonel Moore's son Thomas, then
later the Colonel (from 1875-1877), serving as postmasters.[71]

The combined profits from the sales of the Mound Plantation parcels, ongoing cotton production, and sales from their dry
goods store allowed Jane and the Colonel to enjoy life as aging
elders in a changing community. Parties and get-togethers at the
Moore home appear to have been regular events, indicating the
couple must have lived quite comfortably despite the area's postwar difficulties. The Colonel, on the occasion of these social gath-
erings, made it "a habit . . . to greet his guests at the door of the
reception room and to announce with emphasis the name of each
arrival to the assembly."[72]

In 1878 Jane and the Colonel visited Texas, perhaps to
escape the deadly effects of Mississippi's worst yellow fever epi-
demic then ravaging the state. Possibly, too, they made the journey
to celebrate the birth of the first child of Jane's niece, Florence
Pugh Morrison. The daughter of Jane's late sister Ann Pugh, Flor-

---

[71]Beginning in November 1850, locals established a post office situated at Glencoe near the Perkins plantation. Thomas Moore served as postmaster from
August 16, 1875, to September 10, 1875, followed by his father Colonel Moore.
In 1877 Glencoe underwent a name change and became the Mound Landing post
office, or Mound Place, or Moores. With Colonel Moore's resignation, Ringo
assumed the role of postmaster and may have located the post office in his store.
Ringo filled the dual roles of postmaster and merchant for the next twenty-one
years until December 31, 1920, when the Mound Landing post office closed its
doors for the last time.

[72]McCain, *Memoirs of Henry Tillinghast Ireys,* 288.

Bolivar County map showing Mound Landing and Moores on the Mississippi River circa 1895. Moores would continue to appear on Mississippi maps into the 1930s, but by 1940 it seems to have become extinct.[73]

ence had given birth to a son, John Morrison, born prior to July of that year in Robertson County. However, during the Moore's visit, tragedy struck with the unexpected death in Texas of the Colonel. Jane, grieving and now widowed for a second time, tended to burial arrangements for her late husband. Presumably, she conveyed his body to Mississippi and had him buried at the Mound Cemetery, joining so many other Perkins family members already in-

---

[73]"1895 Mississippi" map (Rand McNally?), accessed June 1, 2010, at http://www.livgenmi.com/1895/MS/County/bolivar.htm.

terred there. Moore would be the last male in the long line of Mound Plantation owner/managers. From that time forward, management of the property reverted to Jane Moore as it had done following her mother's death in 1861.

* * * * *

Bolivar County's growth during this period also changed the area's landscape and social climate. Early residents from the 1840s, 50s, and 60s still residing there in the 1880s observed the stark contrast between the new and the old in Bolivar County and in the Mound Landing district. Thirty years earlier roads were absent, scarce, and unreliable, and supplies came upriver on steamboats or had to be purchased in New Orleans or Greenville. Now, stores and new communities like Moores had sprung up. Furthermore, according to an 1895 atlas, tiny Mound Landing counted seventy-four people, ten times more than existed in the William Perkins family at the time they originally occupied the land in the 1840s. As a result of the war and emancipation, locals now noted the novelty of a black lawyer, A. B. Grimes, who practiced law at Mound Landing.

Also, the college-educated former slave, Blanche Bruce, held the post of Bolivar County Sheriff, replacing a former Confederate general. Bruce also became the county tax collector and its superintendent of education. Later, from 1875 to 1881, he served as one of the two United States Senators from Mississippi. Though dramatic changes had occurred in the county over the decades, some local landmarks remained constant.

By 1880 Jane's venerable Mound Plantation, nearly forty years old, still prospered. The buildings and land were valued at $35,000, while farm implements, machinery, and livestock accounted for another $7,500. On the entire plantation, Jane cultivated just 750 of her available 1,565 acres.[74] Cotton, of course, remained her money crop. The generous Delta soil still produced, yielding 400 bales from Jane's 550 acres of cotton, the sale of

---

[74]This figure differs from the 1,750 acres she reported in 1883. Jane also grew six acres of Irish and sweet potatoes (180 bushels) and 100 acres of Indian corn (2,800 bushels). She also produced butter and raised poultry and pigs.

which accounted for the largest part of the $19,000 estimated value of all products produced on the Mound Plantation that year. She did not record a single week in which she used hired labor in 1879-80, evidence that Jane, like so many other plantation owners in the postwar South, still relied on sharecroppers.[75]

As time passed and with the sale of some of her land, Jane saw the number of sharecroppers working in the Mound Plantation's fields decline. By 1883 she counted forty-one black, male sharecroppers on her estate (Appendix H).[76] Though most had worked on Jane's land for at least the past two years, many had not appeared in the most recent Federal Census for Bolivar County; it seems that only ten of the forty-one had resided in the county in 1880, just three years earlier. Such a low number reveals, perhaps, the temporary nature of some sharecroppers' living arrangements at that time.

As late as 1883, Jane still depended on the labor of Sandy Jones II, then forty-nine.[77] (The 1880 census incorrectly showed him as a fifty-two year old.) A slave on the Perkins' plantations in Madison and Bolivar Counties for decades, Sandy also had the distinction of being used by Jane's father, William Perkins, as a gift (to his son Charles) and as collateral for several of William Perkins' loans. A freeman now, Sandy and his twenty-year old son Simon, the great grandson of Sandy I, sharecropped side by side in Jane's fields, tending cotton and other crops to support Sandy's wife and his nine other children.

In 1891 the Chicago-based Goodspeed Publishing Company published its *Biographical and Historical Memoirs of Mississippi,* cited frequently in this work. The *Memoirs* chronicle the

---

[75]Tenth Census, 1880, The Agricultural and Manufacturing Census for Bolivar County, Mississippi, reel 184, 4.

[76]Mississippi, State Archives, Various Records, 1820-1951, Bolivar County, County tax rolls, 1868-1887, (Assessment of Personal Property and Polls, Fiscal year 1883 for Glencoe Precinct), Box 3611, images 363-381, accessed February 12, 2013, *Family Search*, https://familysearch.org/pal:/MM9.3.1/TH-1942-22496-4409-75?cc=1919687&wc=MMYG-VBW:n570224633.

[77]Sandy II appears as a thirty-six year old in the 1870 census, making his birth year 1834. Ninth Census, 1870, Bolivar County, Mississippi, s. v. "Sandy Jones," p.129, line 39, accessed online through author's library account, July 29, 2010, *Heritage Quest.*

stories of many notable Mississippi families and individuals. It appears that from interviews with members of the subject families the unique, irreplaceable, genealogical information found within the book's pages emerged. Possibly in 1889 or 1890, a Goodspeed's representative called at the Mound Plantation and interviewed Jane Perkins Curry Moore. As a result, her recorded recollections became the voice of the William Perkins family for the ages. While some minor errors appear (Jane was at least seventy when the interview was conducted), overall a very accurate, though brief, portrayal of the William Perkins clan eventually became part of the historical record. Given the time frame in which the *Memoirs* were written, these remain Jane Moore's only known reminiscences.

Jane's interviewer related not only historical family biographical information, but he also provided a contemporary description of the Perkins plantation itself. He noted that Jane still resided in the old family home shaded by large trees on the banks of Williams Bayou and that a strong new levee had just been completed along the riverfront "which gives all promise of future protection from the Mississippi river floods."[78] From Jane, whom he described as "a refined, well-educated, and intelligent lady," he learned that the Mound Plantation consisted then of about 1,000 acres of still the most productive cotton land in the Yazoo Delta with "about six hundred acres under a high state of cultivation, and consequently kept in the best of order by the mistress [Jane]."[79] (Bolivar County records for 1889 show that Jane actually owned a total of 1,787 acres, 746 "cleared" and the remainder "uncleared", valued at $11,304.)[80] Subsequently, with its publication, the *Mem-*

---

[78]Ibid., 587. On March 28, 1890, the levee at Mound Landing burst, creating a crevasse 1,500 feet wide. Possibly the construction of the new levee mentioned by the interviewer was a result of this flood.
[79]*Biographical and Historical Memoirs of Mississippi*, 586. No source ever mentioned whether or not Jane had attended college.
[80]Mississippi, State Archives, Various Records, 1820-1951, Bolivar County, County tax rolls, 1889-1897, Box 3612, images 13, 14, accessed October 23, 2012, *Family Search*, https://familysearch.org/pal:/MM9.3.1/TH-1951-22496-5675-50?cc=1919687&wc=MMYG-VBH:n694889328. By 1889 Jane's land holdings thus constituted just about one half the total her father had claimed in the 1840s. She retained acreage in section 3. She claimed land in small portions

oirs contributed to the lore of nineteenth century Mississippi history and provided a first-hand glimpse into the significant, yet nearly forgotten Perkins family of Bolivar County.

In 1896 Mrs. J. P. Moore appeared on a Bolivar County Tax List, the last known Mississippi document bearing her name. Her assessment stood in stark contrast to those of previous years. She paid taxes on two horses, twenty-two mules, three carriages, and a piano. This limited inventory may have been due to the fact that as of 1893 she had moved to Texas, while possibly leaving the plantation house in the hands of a caretaker.

---

of sections 4, 10, 16, 17, 21, and 22, all located in Township 20, Range 9 West. Again, Jane's total acreage claimed differs from that reported in previous years.

XI

Texas, and the End of the Mound Plantation

*The receding floodwaters have unearthed many queer objects and
brought history to light, not the least of which is that of Mound
Landing, the scene of the only crevasse in Mississippi. . . .*

> Youngstown, Vindicator, (Ohio)
> July 22, 1927

*"Turn out of there! The deputy shouted. He was fully dressed –
rubber boots, slicker, and shotgun. "The levee went out at
Mound's Landing an hour ago. Get up out of it!"*

> From William Faulkner's *The
> Wild Palms: (If I Forget Thee,
> Jerusalem)*

From 1883 to 1889 the widowed and childless Jane Moore
had shared her plantation home with her thirty-five year old (in
1883) daughter-in-law Louisa Moore, the wife of Colonel Moore's
son. Together they provided company for each other, with Louisa
undoubtedly looking after the aging Jane. For the six years the two
lived together, Jane generously allotted Louisa fifty acres of farmland to raise crops, most likely cotton. With Louisa either remarried or departed by 1890, Jane apparently lived alone, with nothing
more than memories and treasured family portraits to keep her
company during the next few years.

In approximately 1893 at age seventy-two, Jane Moore
left the Mound Plantation, never to return, and moved to Gainesville, north of Dallas in Cooke County, Texas. There she acquired
property worth $1,500.[1] Whether she rented the Mound Plantation
or eventually sold it remains unknown, but county records show
that as late as 1896 she continued to pay taxes on it. In the decades
following Jane's departure, nothing is known of the plantation's
new residents, but by 1927 or before it apparently had been

---

[1]Texas County Tax Rolls, 1846-1910, Cooke County, Texas, s.v., "Jane P.
Moore," 1893, line 30, accessed June 8, 2012, *Family Search*,
https://familysearch.org/pal:/MM9.3.1/TH-1-13695-822-75?cc=1827575. (Sign
in required-free access).

abandoned.

Jane may well have had mixed emotions in leaving the old home place where she had spent most of the last forty-five years. Proximity to her only remaining relatives appears to have taken precedence, however, over any sentimental attachment she still retained for the Mound Plantation. Her relatives, nieces Sally Pugh, Florence Pugh Morrison, and nephew Nicholas Perkins Pugh, had resided since 1880 in Robertson County nearly 200 miles south of Gainesville. For Jane the decision to move, while it might well have been difficult, would appear to have been the logical one.

Bolivar County remained an agricultural community in the years following Jane's departure. By the turn of the century, the county's larger antebellum plantations for the most part had been divided into smaller farms owned by independent farmers. Additionally, large corporations and railroads began investing in Delta and Bolivar County land. As always, blacks constituted a huge majority, approximately eighty-nine percent of the county's population by 1900. It is probably safe to say that few, if any, of the county's original settlers from six decades earlier still remained alive.

In Gainesville Jane had rented a house at 901 Dixon Street. There, she experienced the novelty of living in a city for the first time since the early 1850s when she and her first husband Stephen Curry had resided in New Orleans. Her unwed niece, forty-nine year-old dressmaker Sally Pugh, the daughter of her late sister Ann and Dr. J. J. Pugh, joined her in Gainesville. Jane evidently had enough money to live comfortably and to employ a housekeeper/servant.[2]

Eventually, Jane owned the Dixon Street home, still sharing it in 1910 with her niece Sally. Jane and Sally, however, were joined by two other relatives, Charlie Pugh, thirty-four, and Jack (John) Morrison, thirty-one. These men were the great grandchildren of William and Jane Perkins. (Charlie was the son of Jane's

---

[2]Twelfth Census, 1900, Cooke County, Texas, s.v., "Jane P. Moore," line 38, accessed online through the author's library account, August 1, 2010, *Heritage Quest*.

nephew Nicholas Pugh, while Jack was the son of Jane's widowed niece Florence Pugh Morrison.) At approximately this time, one or more of these relatives may have been instrumental in initiating a Civil War reimbursement claim for the aging Jane.

In 1871 the United States government created the Southern Claims Commission. This organization provided the means by which Southerners could file claims for reimbursement for personal property losses attributable to Union forces during the Civil War. Claimants had to prove property loss and loyalty to the Union. Residents of the eleven Confederate states and West Virginia were eligible to apply.

While living in Gainesville in 1907, Jane Moore and her lawyer filed a lawsuit in an effort to recover from the United States government by means of the Southern Claims Commission's process the cost of her property Union forces had seized during the Civil War some forty-four years earlier. Quite possibly, because of the eighty-six year old Jane's advanced age, one of her potential heirs may have assisted Jane. She claimed losses in the amount of $23,470 for confiscated animals, grains, cotton, and foodstuffs. (Refer to the chart in Chapter IX for the specific items and their estimated value mentioned in Jane's suit.) Subsequently, Senate Bill 3374 of the Fifty-ninth Congress, *A Bill for the Relief of Jane Moore,* dated March 2, 1907, ordered that the Secretary of Treasury pay to the claimant (Jane) the sum of $10,325, less than half of the value Jane had placed on the items in question.[3]

Because Jane had initiated the paperwork decades after the Civil War had ended, she may have been fortunate to be awarded any compensation at all. In her petition she maintained that she had not presented the claim to the postwar Southern Claims Commission in a timely manner due to her ignorance of the existence of such a commission. Though the Senate had acted in her favor, it appears the United States government appealed the award to the Court of Claims on "loyalty and merit" grounds.

---

[3]"Jane P. Moore v The United States," Senate Document 165, *United States Congressional Series Set*. Jane was suing under the terms of the Tucker Act, enacted on March 3, 1887. In it the United States had agreed to waive its sovereign immunity in regards to certain lawsuits.

Jane's appeal hearing occurred on March 15, 1910. Later, the Court of Claims rendered its "Finding of Fact", declaring "The claimant Jane P. Moore was not loyal to the Government of the United States during the late Civil War."[4] In item two the Court found that the "military forces of the United States by proper authority . . . took from the claimant in Bolivar County, Miss. stores and supplies of the kind and character described in the petition." The Claims Court placed a value of just $3,380 on the appropriated goods, reduced from the $23,470 amount Jane had originally claimed and less than the $10,325 the Senate Bill had allotted her. The Court had disallowed the $12,000 Jane had requested for her sixty bales of cotton stating "the evidence fails to establish to the satisfaction of the court that cotton was taken from the claimant by the military forces of the United States. . . ."[5] Lastly, the panel closed with an admonishment, indicating that no satisfactory proof was adduced as to why Jane's tardy claim was not presented earlier. From the document cited, it is not stated if Jane ever was entitled to receive or did receive any compensation from the government. However, because Jane had failed to meet the loyalty stipulation, it is probable that her claim was denied.

For her remaining years, Jane resided in Gainesville. On December 17, 1913, at 7:15 p. m. Jane Perkins Curry Moore, 93, passed away of "natural decline".[6] She was laid to rest the following day in Fairview Cemetery in Gainesville, possibly the only Perkins family member not buried on the Mound cemetery. She may have willed the house to Sally Pugh, who resided in Gainesville until her death in 1932.[7] Niece Sally may well have retained possession of the Perkins family memorabilia and portraits mentioned by the Goodspeed's interviewer in 1890. Sally Pugh, too, rests in Fairview, near Jane and next to her brother, Nicholas Per-

---

[4] Ibid. Jane had admittedly provided aid to wounded Confederate soldiers.
[5] Ibid.
[6] Her death certificate mistakenly showed her age as "about eighty-eight."
[7] Fourteenth Census, 1920, Cooke County, Texas, s.v. "Sallie Pugh," line 79, *Heritage Quest*, accessed online through author's library account, August 1, 2010. Curiously, Sally Pugh is shown as a widow in this census enumeration. In the 1930 Federal Census for Cooke County, Sally Pugh still lived in Gainesville. Her death record shows that she died on August 17, 1932, but at eighty-three years old, not at ninety as stated on the certificate.

Death Certificate of Jane Perkins Curry Moore (1820-1913)[8]

kins Pugh, presumably the namesake of his distant grandfather, Nicholas Perkins II of seventeenth century Virginia.

With Jane's death the final link to William and Jane Stewart Perkins' family of seven children breaks, ending this line of the Perkins name. Having outlived all her siblings by decades, Jane passed away, far from her plantation home in Bolivar County and farther still from the Virginia and Tennessee of her ancestors the two Nicholases, Constantine, Harden, and Daniel P. Perkins. In her ninety-three years, Jane had experienced remarkable changes and events: the 1835 Livingston slave revolt episode, the settlement and development of Bolivar County, the Mexican War, the

---

[8]Texas Deaths 1890-1976, s.v. "Jane P. Moore," image 957, accessed October 1, 2011, *Family Search,*
https://www.familysearch.org/search/collection/show#uri=http://hr-search-api:8080/searchapi/search/collection/1320964. Access is free after log in.

Civil War, Lincoln's assassination, the end of slavery, and the inventions of the telephone, automobile and airplane. One very personal event that she failed to witness, though, was the destruction of the Mound Plantation.

Years after Jane passed away, life in Bolivar County still depended on the cotton crop and of course the Mississippi River for its livelihood. The river, always the dominant force in the Delta, still obeyed its natural tendency to flood, as it had done for centuries. In the summer of 1926 and continuing throughout

The headstone marking Jane Moore's grave in the Fairview Cemetery in Gainesville, Texas

the spring of 1927, nature unleashed a series of unprecedented rainstorms up and down the length of the Mississippi. Finally, when they could hold no more, levees all along the river broke, but none larger than the greatest single crevasse (break) ever to occur on the river.

On Thursday April 21, 1927, at eight a. m. the levee in southern Bolivar County burst. The raging water's initial surge occurred at Mound Landing and Williams Bayou at the site of the abandoned Moore plantation house. The river's full fury erupted with such force it unleashed into the countryside double the water volume of a "flooding Niagara Falls" in an extraordinary and devastating torrent, eventually flooding an area fifty miles wide and 100 miles long with up to twenty feet of water.[9] Water flowed

---

[9]John Barry, *Rising Tide: The Great Mississippi Flood of 1927 and How It Changed America*, (New York: Simon and Schuster, 1997), 203, 206.

over the tops of homes seventy miles from Mound Landing. At the site of the break, "The water's force had gouged a 100-foot deep channel half a mile wide for a mile inland."[10] Hundreds would eventually die during the flooding, while large swaths of land were inundated for months. Historically, flooding had occurred in or near Mound Landing several times over the decades, most recently in 1882, 1890, and again in March 1897, but with nowhere near the awesome destructive power of the current breech. In reality, no levee, no matter how well constructed, could have withstood the Mississippi's torrent in 1927.

One witness described the scene at the presumably abandoned Perkins-Moore property, set beneath a darkened Delta sky and located at the very center of the break: "[T]he water was leaping, it looked like, in rapids thirty feet high. And right in front of the break was the old Moore [Perkins] plantation house, a mule barn, and two big, enormous trees. And when we came back by there [a few hours later] everything was gone."[11] In a continuous devastating surge, the river's muddy current had swallowed the eight-decades old Mound Plantation, perhaps then neglected, but once the conspicuous icon of the storied William P. Perkins family. The celebrated home, William's palace in his small, self-created kingdom, and the scene of festive dinner parties, sad farewells, joyous reunions, and tragedy, now lay in a watery grave, a victim of the river's rampage. The destructive flood returned much of the Bolivar County countryside and the vast Perkins plantation - in its heyday a symbol and the reality of the nineteenth century slaveholding South - to a primitive state, perhaps an era centuries before the arrival of even the Mound Builders.

Today, a sixty-five-acre lake at the site of the break still covers most of the acreage of William Perkins' original 1840's purchases in sections three, four, and ten. The rampaging Mississippi also sheared off acreage in two of those sections, three and four, leaving only a meager remainder behind. Williams Bayou, a distinctive landmark since the county's inception, is now cut short

---

[10]Ibid., 202. At Mound Landing in 1927, an auto ferry regularly transported cars across the Mississippi River to Arkansas City, 196.
[11]Ibid., 203.

and no longer connects with the Mississippi. (See the 1831 Survey Map and 2006 Highway Map below.)

The beginning of the levee break at Mound Landing, April 1927
Courtesy of the National Oceanic and Atmospheric Administration/Department of Commerce

Florence Sillers, in her *History of Bolivar County*, wrote the Mound Landing's epitaph, "Caving banks [and the 1927 flood] have long since carried into the river the land used for this settlement . . . Mound Landing has passed away and only the memory of its fine citizens remains."[12]

Created in the 1840s, the Perkins family cemetery (on the mound) should have been spared the flooding because of its height and its distance from the river. However, it, too, unexpectedly succumbed to the fury and tremendous pressure exerted by the rampaging water at the site of the levee's breach. And what of the re-

---

[12]Sillers, *History of Bolivar County,* 127. The Perkins plantation was not the only property to succumb to the power of the Mississippi River. Daniel Perkins' in-laws, the Campbells or their descendants, lost the land on which their Argyle Plantation stood sometime prior to 1913 when the riverbank on which it rested caved in and washed it downriver to a sandbar above Greenville. McCain, *Memoirs of Henry Tillinghast Ireys*, 337.

mains of William, Jane, their sons Charles, Daniel, Noland, William, and James, as well Stephen Curry, Caroline Perkins Hedges, and Colonel Moore all interred there?

By late July 1927, the floodwaters of the Mississippi had gradually receded near Mound Landing revealing the residue of its destruction. A survey party in the vicinity reported finding evidence of an Indian civilization dating to before De Soto's expedition (Appendix G).[13] Pottery, clay vases, weapons, peace pipes, and art objects emerged, strewn about the landscape. The surveyors also discovered that the water surge had incredibly swept away the four Perkins mounds and in the process washed off five or six feet of surrounding topsoil, exposing numerous bones and skulls. W. Childs, a member of the surveying party, posited that an old burial ground holding the bones of prehistoric Indians had been unearthed.[14] Based on the remains his team had discovered, Childs' theory has merit, as far as it goes. However, Mr. Childs likely had little or no inkling of the nineteenth century history of the area. Nor was he probably cognizant in 1927 of the eighty-year old Perkins cemetery that had existed on the very land on which he then stood. Had he been so aware, Childs might have considered that among some of those 'Indian' bones strewn across sections seventeen, ten, three, and elsewhere may, in fact, have been the remains of a member or members of the Perkins family. Moreover, also uprooted in the surge, but then reburied by the floodwaters somewhere in the vast expanse of that portion of Bolivar County, were the family's displaced headstones.

In this epic flood of April 1927, the Mississippi had engulfed, in its own act of privilege, much of the Mound Plantation. Not only did it erase the Perkins' house and cotton fields, but it also had taken the cemetery and its family plots. But, wasn't it proper that the River, which had helped bestow such tremendous wealth on the Perkins family, should claim the beneficiaries of its generosity after their deaths? Maybe, then, this was the final design, and a very ironic one – that having been outmoded and abandoned like the Slavery it depended on, it was only appropriate that the plantation and the Mounds too, would be literally washed

---

[13]*Youngstown* [Ohio] *Vindicator*, July 22, 1927, 22.
[14]Ibid.

away by the advance of time and change – disappearing in all but the scattered, disputable, remnant traces and artifacts strewn across those coveted acres William Perkins had purchased in 1842.[15]

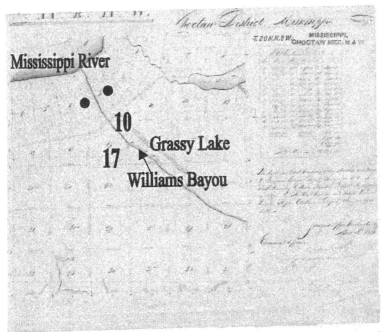

Using this Bolivar County Survey Map of 1831 and the Bolivar County Highway Map of 2006 below, the changes created by the 1927 flood as it swept over the Mound Plantation become apparent. The flood reduced the size and shape of Grassy Lake (1831 and 2006 maps) considerably. Williams Bayou extended to the Mississippi in 1831, but today it reaches only to approximately section 23. Perkins' section 17 and the triangular section 10 are labeled here for comparison with the 2006 map. The black circles show the location of sections 3 and 4.

---

[15]Another culture may have viewed the destruction of the mounds differently. Descendants of the Native-American mound builders might have seen the river's destructive fury as nature's mystical act of revenge for William's blasphemy at the very top of their sacred mound.

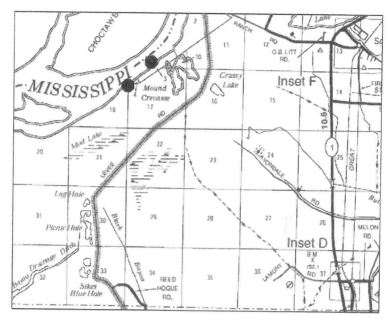

In this 2006 map, notice how the river has reclaimed much of William's original acreage in sections 3 and 4, leaving only small remnants of each section. In the aftermath of the river's surge, the most obvious geographic change is the emergence of the "lake" (Mound Crevasse) covering most of section 10. The Perkins home, swept away by the 1927 flood, stood on the banks of Williams Bayou (not shown), either in section 3 or 17. Section 17, part of which now also lies beneath the waters of Mound Crevasse, almost touches the river here, whereas on the 1831 map it is located considerably farther back. In addition, sections 5, 6, and 19 owned by William's neighbors in 1850 have disappeared entirely.
Map Courtesy of Mississippi Department of Transportation

Mound Landing Crevasse, October 1927.
View of the destruction wrought by the flood at Mound Landing in
April 1927. This photo was taken at or near the location of the
Perkins-Moore home and Williams Bayou, both washed away in
the early minutes of the river's initial surge on April 21. Barely
discernible in the foreground and to the right are logs strewn about
by the force of the flood. In the center two individuals (arrow)
walk along an embankment, the new levee. A levee-constructing
tower machine, state of the art for its day, is just visible in the center at the top of the photo. The depth of the crevasse at Mound
Landing proved to be 130 feet. Courtesy of the Mississippi Department of Archives and History [16]

---

[16]"1927 Flood Photograph Collection." *Mississippi Department of Archives and History*, accessed July 11, 2010,
http://mdah.state.ms.us/arrec/digital_archives/1927flood/index.php?itemno=120.
Mississippi native William Faulkner, in 1939, penned a novel of the flood and the story of two people involved under the title *The Wild Palms*. Faulkner's preferred title was *If I Forget Thee, Jerusalem.*

The *Vicksburg Evening Post* reports the levee breaks at Scott and at Mound Landing on April 21, 1927. The arrow points to the article describing the Mound Landing break.

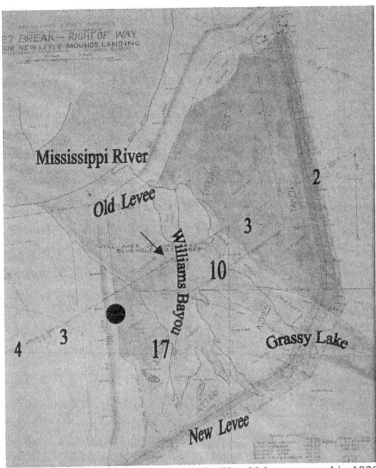

Photograph by Princella Nowell of a Flood Map prepared in 1928
by the Mississippi Levee District showing the levee break at the
Perkins plantation site, referred to as the Mound Landing Crevasse, (arrow) in April 1927. Compare to the original Bolivar
County survey map of 1831 and the Highway map of 2006 above
and with the Google map shown below.
Grassy Lake (formerly Swan Lake) is shown to the right. The
black circle represents the approximate location of the Perkins-
Moore home.[17]

---

[17]Photo courtesy of Ms Nowell. The original map showed incorrect locations for
sections 2, 3, and 4. Those section locations appear above, superimposed with

A 2009 Google aerial photograph of the water-covered Mound Crevasse, the large darkened puzzle-piece like shape left of center. Between the crevasse and Grassy Lake is today's Levee Road shown as a thin line following the path of the 1928 levee and running roughly parallel to the river. A portion of the former Perkins-Moore plantation land lies in and near the Mound Crevasse and extends across today's Levee Road.

their corrected numbers. The distinctive triangular shape of section 10 is shown for ease of comparison with the previous maps. Ms Nowell is the great, great, great granddaughter of Peter Wilkerson, an early Bolivar County resident mentioned earlier.

EPILOGUE

The life of William P. Perkins was not a long one by twenty-first century standards, just fifty-five years. In that short span, however, he emerged as the patriarch of one of the wealthiest, most prominent, and well-connected slaveholding planter families in Mississippi's antebellum era. While we may abhor the use of slave labor by William Perkins and his ancestors, it would be difficult to deny that dedicated and energetic men like William brought a vitality and industriousness to wilderness Mississippi gaining wealth from a plant, with its small white bolls, that somehow magically harmonized with the alluvial soil of the Mississippi Delta. Planters and their slaves transformed this Delta region, particularly the Bolivar County wilderness, into a vital part of the South's Cotton Kingdom. Today, subsequent generations of successful Bolivar County cotton planters and corporations benefit from their now almost forgotten, early to mid-nineteenth century benefactors up and down the river who planted the seed, both figuratively and literally, that brought and continues to bring enduring prosperity to the region.

In the larger picture, whether the crop was Mississippi cotton, Carolina rice, or Virginia tobacco, slave-owning Southern planters like William Perkins, exploiting their slaves over the centuries, emerged as a driving force in the economic, social, and political growth of the South, while changing forever the face of the land in not only Bolivar County but in hundreds of other Southern localities as well. Though the story of the Perkins clan possesses its own unique elements, similar accounts of the lives of other such slaveholding families beg to be told.

In 2010, while standing along the highway that passes near the half-hearted run that is the now-abbreviated Williams Bayou and gazing at the abundance of thriving cotton fields across Bolivar County's still rural landscape, it was not difficult for this writer to visualize scenes of the 1850s. Images of sweating Perkins' plantation field slaves like Joe Ready, Big Louisa, Charlotte, Churchill, Lucky, Little Charlotte, May, and others 'appear', toiling in a sea of white under a scorching Delta sun. It should be they for whom these histories are written, for it was on their backs that men like William Price Perkins achieved their dreams.

It was in 1850 that a teenage slave, Sandy Jones II, might have watched as his grandfather Sandy, with Robert Perkins, departed for the goldfields as slaves of the Kirks and A. G. Perkins. Was it coincidence or a form of tribute that caused Sandy Jones II fifteen years later in 1865 to name one of his sons Carter, after Charles Perkins' 'fugitive' Carter Perkins, the third slave of this gold rush trio?[1] While it seems unlikely, it may be gratifying to believe this unique Gold Rush episode remains safely stored in the lore of the descendants of both the white and black participants and resonates there until this day.

No specific reminders of the Perkins family's presence in Bolivar County remain today. But, those steadfast elements of nature that lured William there in 1842 still survive, the rich soil and the meandering and powerful Mississippi as it moves forever southward past the riverbank at Mound Landing.

---

[1] Ibid., Tenth Census, 1880, Bolivar County, Mississippi, Family 519, 48.

Appendix

Appendix A - Portion of the October 1834 Will of Daniel P. Perkins Sr. of Williamson County, Tennessee.[1]

The will mentions the names of heirs William P. Perkins, and his siblings. Daniel Perkins Sr. specified his property should be sold and the proceeds from the sale divided among his children.

[1]Tennessee Probate Court Files, 1795-1927, Williamson County Court, Wills 1800-1899, s. v. "Peay-Yeargen," Image 10, accessed December 8, 2011, at *Family Search*,
https://www.familysearch.org/search/image/index#uri=https%3A//api.familysearch.org/records/collection/1909193/waypoints.

302

Appendix B - United States Census 1850, Bolivar County - William P. Perkins' family (beginning on line 13).

Appendix C - United States Census 1850, Slave Schedule
Part of a Slave Schedule census page for Bolivar County, Mississippi, showing William Paquinett(e) as "agent for W. P. Perkins."

Numbers and letters on the lines after and below Paquinette's
name represent four of Perkins' 166 *slaves*. The first line opposite
Paquinette's name would 'read' 1 (anonymous) thirty-five year old
male, black. These four may represent a slave family, a male, a
female, and two young children.

304

Appendix D - 1850 Slave Schedule (part 2)

The remainder of W. P. Perkins' slaves listed under Paquinette's name. A separate listing begins on line 40 (arrow) for slaves under William Perkins' name alone. A total of 84 slaves are enumerated on the page.

Appendix E - 1850 Slave Schedule (part 3)

Continued – the remaining 78 slaves listed under William Perkins'
name alone. The entire Slave Schedule for 1850 Bolivar County
shows 2,180 slaves, or 26 such images of approximately 84 slaves
per page.

Appendix F - Bolivar County Censuses 1841-1880[2]

YEAR	BLACKS	Black % of total	WHITES	Total
1841	712	62.7	423	1,135
1845	?	?	387	?
1846 u-60 yrs	1,444	?	*119	?
1850	2,180	84.5	**397	2,577
1853	?	?	418	?
1855 u-60 yrs	3,547	?	*183	?
1858 u-60 yrs	7,322	?	*378	?
1860	9,078	86.6	1,393	10,471
1864	3,624	?	***81	?
1866	6,156	82.1	1,334	7,490
State 1870	7,602	82.7	1,587	9,189
Federal 1870	7,816	80.4	1,900	9,716
1880	15,958	85.5	2,694	18,652

*only free white polls between 20/21 and 65 years

** includes 2 free blacks

*** free whites 21-60 not in Confederate Army

---

[2]Years ending in zero denote Federal Census data except for 1870, which also includes state census numbers. Population data for some years was incomplete in the records consulted. Figures are based on sources previously cited in this work. Note the disparity in the numbers for the 1870 state and Federal censuses. The 1840 Federal Agricultural Census for Bolivar County (not shown) counted 971 blacks and 384 whites, while Bolivar County's own totals as of January 1841 (shown above) inexplicably showed just *712* blacks for the taxable year 1840.

Appendix G – *Youngstown*, [Ohio] *Vindicator* July 22, 1927, p. 22, reporting the aftermath of the Mound Landing flood

Flood Waters Reveal Signs Of Ancient Civilization

Waters Wash Off Top Soil and Mound Landing, Home of Indian Tribe, Discovered

[By The Associated Press]

Vicksburg, Miss.. July 22.—The receding flood waters have unearthed many queer objects and brought history to light, not the least of which is that of Mound Landing, the scene of the only crevasse in Mississippi and the most disastrous in the flood this year.

W. Childs, associate engineer of the Third District. upon his return from the crevasse, reported that the survey party there had found evidence of a civilization before DeSoto discovered the Mississippi, the mound builders that are mentioned in the history of Mexico and the west, who have never before had been mentioned as a phase of Mississippi evolution.

Mound Landing received its name from the Indian mounds in that vicinity. When the waters crashed through the levee and swept away the mounds they washed off five or six feet of top soil. There is no mound in sight now. In its stead are being found bones and skulls, reminders of a past age, scattered over several acres.

Some of the skulls Mr. Childs stated were placed in various positions in accordance with Indian customs. The old burial ground that held the bones of some prehistoric Indians little spoken of in history has been dug up.

Members of the survey party also have found pottery, beautiful clay vases, some implements of warfare, peace pipes and other objects of art. The waters that unearthed the antiques also paved the way for their destruction and if care is not taken in handling, the clay objects crumble.

FOUR VIOLATORS HEAVILY FINED

Appendix H - List of sharecroppers who worked for Jane Moore in 1882 and 1883 in Bolivar County, Mississippi.[3]

1. Willis Allen
2. Mareh Anderson
3. James Bradley
4. George Banks
5. Major Brown
6. Allen Buley (?)
7. Thomas Burn
8. Dave Clark
9. Aaron Cotton (1880)
10. Robert Davis
11. Willis Dickerson (1870)
12. F. P. Givins
13. Derny (?) Gum (?)
14. Wash Green
15. Sam Hunter (1880)
16. Abram Haywood
17. Alex Holiday
18. Nathan Jackson
19. Jake Jones
20. Sandy Johns (Jones) (1880)
21. Simon Jones (1880)
22. Jack Jones
23. R. E. Lee (1880)
24. Edward Lewis (1880)
25. Silas Moore
26. Wilson Morris
27. Perry Porter
28. Robert Porter (1880)
29. Seldon Robinson (1880)
30. James Sanford
31. Steve Sanford
32. Gus Spann
33. Jonas Toliver
34. Joe Toliver
35. Peter Toliver
36. Charles Umbrels
37. Jack Upshaw
38. Jim Vincent
39. Steve Warren (1880)
40. Jack William
41. Buchanan Young

[3]Mississippi, State Archives, Various Records, 1820-1951, Bolivar County, County tax rolls, 1868-1887, (Assessment of Personal Property and Polls, Fiscal year 1883 for Glencoe Precinct), Box 3611, images 363-381, accessed February 12, 2013, *Family Search*, https://familysearch.org/pal:/MM9.3.1/TH-1942-22496-4409-75?cc=1919687&wc=MMYG-VBW:n570224633. The year following some names represents the Federal Census for Bolivar County in which the same name appears.

Bibliography

Works Cited

Books

Anderson, John. *Making the American Thoroughbred, Especially in Tennessee, 1800-1845.* Norwood: The Plimpton Press, 1916.

Annual Report of the Secretary of War for the Year 1883. Vol. II. Washington, DC: Government Printing Office, 1883.

Bancroft, Hubert Howe. *Western American History.* 23, pt.6, New York: Bancroft Company, 1902.

Barker, Eugene (ed.). *Annual Report of American Historical Association.* 2, The Austin Papers. Washington: Government Printing Office, 1924.

Barry, John M. *Rising Tide: The Great Mississippi Flood of 1927 and How it Changed America.* New York: Simon & Schuster, 1997.

Bell, James. *The Evolution of the Mississippi Delta From Exploited Labor and Mules to Mechanization and Agribusiness.* Bloomington, Indiana: iUniverse, 2008.

Biographical and Historical Memoirs of Mississippi Embracing an Authentic and Comprehensive Account of the Chief Events in the History of the State and a Record of the Lives of Many of the Most Worthy and Illustrious Families and Individuals. Chicago: Goodspeed Pub. Co., 1891.

Branton, Catherine, and Alice Wade (compilers). *Early Mississippi Records Washington County, 1827-1880,* IV ed. Carrollton, Ms: Pioneer Publishing, 1986.

310

Brown, Calvin S. *Archeology of Mississippi*. Jackson: University of Mississippi, 1926.

Burnett, Peter Hardeman. *Recollections and Opinions of an Old Pioneer*. New York: D. Appleton and Company, 1880.

Carr, Peter E. *San Francisco Passenger Departure Lists*. 1st ed. San Bernardino, Calif.: Cuban Index, 1991.

Casdorph, Paul D. *Confederate General R.S. Ewell: Robert E. Lee's Hesitant Commander*. Lexington, Ky.: University Press of Kentucky, 2004.

Catalog of the Officers and Students of the College of New Jersey. Princeton: John Robinson, 1845. Accessed July 4, 2010, http://books.google.com/books?id=SS1LAAAAYAAJ&pg=PA82&dq=charles+s+perkins+the+college+of+new+jersey&lr=&cd=2#v=onepage&q=perkins&f=false.

Chambers's Encyclopedia; a Dictionary of Universal Knowledge for the People. Rev. ed. Philadelphia: J. B. Lippincott and Company, 1883.

Cobb, James C. *The Most Southern Place on Earth: The Mississippi Delta and the Roots of Regional Identity*. New York: Oxford University Press, 1992.

Colville, Samuel. *Sacramento Directory For the Year 1855*. Sacramento: James Anthony & Co, 1855.

Comisford, Bill. *History of the Ancestors, Families, and Descendants of Paris Patrick Comisford*. Bowie, Maryland: Heritage Books, 2007.

Crist, Lynda Lasswell (ed). *The Papers of Jefferson Davis Volume 5*. Baton Rouge: Louisiana State University Press, 1985.

Desty, Robert. *The Supreme Court Reporter, 11*. St. Paul: West Publishing Company, 1891.

Dupre, Daniel S. *Transforming the Cotton Frontier: Madison County, Alabama, 1800-1840.* Baton Rouge: Louisiana State University Press, 1997.

Foster, Austin P. *Counties of Tennessee.* Nashville: Dept. of Education, Division of History, State of Tennessee, 1923.

Fouche, Rayvon. *Black Inventors in the Age of Segregation: Granville T. Woods, Lewis H. Latimer & Shelby J. Davidson.* Baltimore: Johns Hopkins University Press, 2003.

Fox, Early Lee. *The American Colonization Society, 1817-1840.* XXXVII, 3 ed. Baltimore: Johns Hopkins Press, 1919.

Frankel, Noralee. *Freedom's Women: Black Women and Families in Civil War Era Mississippi (Blacks in the Diaspora).* Bloomington: Indiana University Press, 1999.

Freeman, John D., and Robert H. Bruckner. *Reports of Cases Decided in the Superior Court of Chancery of the State of Mississippi.* Cincinnati: E. Morgan and Co., 1844. Newman and Beck v Jesse Meek et al.

Garfielde, S., and F. A. Snyder. *Compiled Laws of the State of California: Containing all the Acts of the Legislature of a Public and General Nature, Now in Force, Passed at the Sessions of 1850-51-52-53, to which are Prefixed the Declaration of Independence, the Constitutions of the United States.* Benicia: S. Garfielde, 1853.

Garner, James Wilford. *Reconstruction in Mississippi.* London: MacMillan Co., 1901.

Hall, W. K. *Descendants of Nicholas Perkins of Virginia.* Ann Arbor: Edwards Brothers, 1957.

Harris, G. E., and G. H. Simrall. *Report of Cases in the Supreme Court for the State of Mississippi,* 51. Chicago: Callaghan and Company, 1876.

312

Hendrix, Mary. *Mississippi Court Records from the Files of the High Court of Errors and Appeals, 1799-1859.* Greenville, SC: Southern Historical Press, 1999.

Howard, H. R. *The History of Virgil A. Stewart and his Adventure in Capturing and Exposing the Great "Western Land Pirate" and his Gang, in Connexion with the Evidence; Also of the Trials, Confessions, and Execution of a Number of Murrell's Associates.* New York: Harper, 1836.

Lamar, Curt (ed). *History of Rosedale, Mississippi.* Spartanburg, S. C.: Reprint Company, 1976.

Laws of the State of Mississippi. Natchez, Miss.: E. Barksdale, State Printer, 1854.

Libby, David J. *Slavery and Frontier Mississippi, 1720-1835.* Jackson: University Press of Mississippi, 2004.

Litwack, Leon F. *Been in the Storm So Long: The Aftermath of Slavery.* New York: Alfred A. Knopf, 1980.

Longwith, John. *Since Before the Yellow Fever – A History of Union Planters Bank.* Memphis: Union Planters Corp., 1994.

Lowry, Robert, and William H. McCardle. *A History of Mississippi: from the Discovery of the Great River by Hernando DeSoto, Including the Earliest Settlement Made by the French under Iberville, to the Death of Jefferson Davis.* Jackson, Miss.: R.H. Henry & Co., 1891.

Lloyd, James B. ed. *Lives of Mississippi Authors, 1817-1967.* Jackson: University Press of Mississippi, 2009.

Maclean, John. *History of the College of New Jersey, from its Origin in 1746 to the Commencement of 1854.* Philadelphia: J.B. Lippincott, 1877.

Mann, Joseph Karl. *The Large Slaveholders of Louisiana: 1860.* New Orleans: Pelican Publishing Company, 1998.

McCain, William. *Memoirs of Henry Tillinghast Ireys: Papers of the Washington County Historical Society, 1910-1915.* Jackson: Mississippi Dept. of Archives and History and Mississippi Historical Society, 1954.

McCormick, Thomas. *Carson-McCormick Family Memorials.* Madison, Wisconsin: s.n., 1953.

Miller, Mary Carol. *Lost Landmarks of Mississippi.* Jackson: University Press of Mississippi, 2002.

Monette, John W. *History of the Discovery and Settlement of the Valley of the Mississippi, by the Three Great European Powers, Spain, France, and Great Britain, and the Subsequent Occupation, Settlement, and Extension of Civil Government by the United States, Until the Year 1846.* New York: Harper & Bros., 1848.

Montgomery, Frank A. *Reminiscences of a Mississippian in Peace and War.* Cincinnati: The Robert Clarke Press, 1901.

Moore, John. *The Emergence of the Cotton Kingdom in the Old Southwest: Mississippi, 1770-1860.* Baton Rouge: Louisiana State University Press, 1988.

Morgan, William N. *Prehistoric Architecture in the Eastern United States.* Cambridge, Mass.: MIT Press, 1980.

Niles, Hezekiah. *Niles' Weekly Register Containing Political, Historical, Geographical, Scientifical, Astronomical, Statistical, and Biographical Documents, Essays and Facts: Together with Notices of the Arts and Manufactures, and a Record of the Events of the Times.* Edition 30. Baltimore: Printed and published by the editor, at the Franklin Press, 1826. (Also 1835, edition 49.)

314

O'Brien, Michael. *An Evening When Alone: Four Journals of Single Women in the South, 1827-67.* Charlottesville, Virginia: University Press, 1993.

Official Records of the Union and Confederate Navies in the War of Rebellion. Ser. 1, volumes 1-27; ser. 2, volumes 1-3. Washington: Government Printing Office, 1911.

Olmsted, Frederick Law. *The Cotton Kingdom: A Traveller's Observations on Cotton and Slavery in the American Slave States.* New York: Mason Brothers, 1861.

Otto, John Solomon. *The Final Frontiers, 1880-1930 Settling the Southern Bottomlands.* Westport, Conn.: Greenwood Press, 1999.

Peet, Stephen D. *The Mound Builders: Their Works and Relics.* Chicago: Office of the American Antiquarian, 1892.

Rasmussen, Louis J. *San Francisco Ship Passenger Lists.* Vol. 2. Baltimore: Clearfield, 2002.

Riley, Franklin L. *School History of Mississippi; for Use in Public and Private Schools.* Richmond, Va.: B.F. Johnson Pub. Co.,1905.

Robinson, Charles. *Forsaking All Others: A True Story of Interracial Sex and Revenge in the 1880s South.* Knoxville: University of Tennessee Press, 2010.

Santa Cruz County, California Illustrations Descriptive of its Scenery, Fine Residences, Public Buildings, Manufactories, Hotels, Farm Scenes, Business Houses, Schools, Churches, Mines, Mills, etc.: With Historical Sketch of the County. San Francisco: W.W. Elliott & Co., 1879.

Sandlin, Lee. *Wicked River: The Mississippi When It Last Ran Wild.* New York: Pantheon Books, 2010.

Scott, Robert N. *The War of the Rebellion: A Compilation of the Official Records of the Union and Confederate Armies.* Series I, Volume II, Part II, Confederate Correspondence, Etc. Washington: Government Printing Office, 1898.

Seebold, Herman de Bachelle. *Old Louisiana Plantation Homes and Family Trees.* Second ed. New Orleans: Pelican Press, 1971.

Sillers, Florence Warfield, and Evelyn Hammett. *History of Bolivar County, Mississippi. Compiled by F. W. Sillers* [and others]. *Edited by Wirt A. Williams.* Jackson, Mississippi: Hederman Bros., 1948.

Smedes, W. C., and T.A. Marshall, *Reports of Cases Argued and Determined in the High Court of Errors and Appeals for the State of Mississippi July Term 1843-Nov. Term 1850.* Boston: C.C. Little and J. Brown, 1844. (9 Mississippi 412, 1843).

Smedes, William C. and T. A. Marshall. *Reports of Cases Argued and Determined in the High Court of Errors and Appeals for the State of Mississippi.* Vol. XI. Boston: Charles C. Little and James Brown, 1844.

Smith, Jonathan (ed.). *Death Notices from the Western Weekly Review Franklin, Tennessee 1841-1851.* 2004. Accessed July 28, 2010, http://www.tngenweb.org/records/williamson/obits/wwr/wwr2-15.htm.

Smith, Myron J. *Tinclads in the Civil War: Union Light-Draught Gunboat Operations on Western Waters, 1862-1865.* Jefferson, N.C.: McFarland & Co., 2010.

Smith, William Russell. *Reminiscences of a Long Life: Historical Political, Personal and Literary.* Washington, D. C.: W.R. Smith, Sr., 1889.

Span, Christopher. *From Cotton Field to Schoolhouse: African American Education in Mississippi, 1862-1875.* Chapel Hill: University of North Carolina Press, 2009.

Squier, E. G., and E. H. Davis. *Ancient Monuments of the Mississippi Valley.* Washington: Smithsonian Institution Press, 1998, originally published in 1848.

Stampp, Kenneth M. *The Peculiar Institution: Slavery in the Antebellum South.*[1st ed.] New York: Knopf, 1956.

Steele, R. J., and James P. Bull. *Directory of the County of Placer for the Year 1861; Containing a History of the County, and of the Different Towns in the County; with the Names of Inhabitants and Every Thing Appertaining to a Complete Directory.* San Francisco: Charles F. Robbins, printer, 1861.

Stone, Kate. *Brokenburn, The Journal of Kate Stone, 1861-1868.* Baton Rouge: Louisiana State University Press, 1955.

Sydnor, Charles S. *Slavery in Mississippi.* Gloucester, Mass.: P. Smith, 1965.

The Compendium of American Geneaology. Volume 4. Chicago: Virkus, 1930.

The Medical Examiner and Record of Medical Science. Philadelphia: Lindsay and Blakiston, 1851.

The Revised Code of the Laws of Mississippi: In which are Comprised All Such Acts of the General Assembly, of a Public Nature, as were in Force at the End of the Year 1823. Natchez: F. Baker, printer, 1824.

Thompson, Elizabeth. *The Reconstruction of Southern Debtors: Bankruptcy After the Civil War.* Atlanta: University of Georgia Press, 2004.

Tracy, John (ed.). *Tenth Annual Report of the Saint Louis Agricultural and Mechanical Association.* St. Louis: Missouri Democrat Book and Job Printing House, 1871.

Trimble, David. *Southwest Virginia Families.* San Antonio: s.n., 1974.

Underwood, Nancy Chambers. *Fifty Families: A History.* Dallas: N.C. Underwood, 1977.

United States Congressional Series Set. 64th Congress, 1st Session, 6954. Washington, D.C.: Government Printing Office, 1910.

Wayne, Michael. *The Reshaping of Plantation Society: The Natchez District, 1860-80.* Urbana: University of Illinois Press, 1990.

Whartenby, Franklee Gilbert. *Land and Labor Productivity in United States Cotton Production, 1800-1840.* Reprint. ed. New York: Arno Press, 1977.

Whitley, Edythe Johns Rucker. *Genealogical Records of Buckingham County, Virginia.* Baltimore: Genealogical Pub. Co., 1984.

Wiley, Bell Irvin. *Southern Negroes.* New Haven: Yale University Press, 1938.

Williams, John Rogers. *Academic Honors in Princeton University, 1748-1902.* Princeton, N.J.: Princeton University, 1902.

Williams, Stephen K.. *Cases Argued and Decided in the Supreme Court of the United States and Others.* Lawyers ed. Rochester, N.Y.: Lawyers Co-operative Pub. Co.,1926. See Wm. and D. Hardeman and Wm. P. Perkins (1846).

Wilson, Oleavia. *Woodville Republican, Mississippi's Oldest Existing Newspaper.* Bowie, Maryland: Heritage Books,

318

2009.

Wiltshire (compiler), Betty C. *Marriages and Deaths from Mississippi Newspapers.* Bowie, Maryland: Heritage Books.,
1990.

Wright, E. W. *Lewis & Dryden's Marine History of the Pacific
Northwest: An Illustrated Review of the Growth and Development of the Maritime Industry, from the Advent of
the Earliest Navigators to the Present Time, with
Sketches and Portraits of a Number of Well Known Marine Men.* Portland, Oregon: Lewis & Dryden, 1895.

Journals

Albin, Ray. "The Perkins Case: The Ordeal of Three Slaves in
Gold Rush California." *California History* LXVII, No. 4
(1988): 214-227.

Davis, John. "Indian Murders Around Nashville." *South-Western
Monthly* January, no. 1 (1852): 214.

De Bow, J. D. B. "Opinion of Judge Anderson of the Supreme
Court of California." *De Bow's Review* XXIII (1857):
100-101.

Grace, Karen. "Let the Eagle Screame." *Ozarks Watch,* summer
(1993): 30.

Gross, Mrs. James (ed.). "Wilkinson County Cemetery Records."
The Journal of Wilkinson County History 1 (1990):
239.

Miles, Edwin. "Mississippi Slave Insurrection Scare of 1835."
Journal of Negro History 42, January (1957): 48-49.

Purcell, Aaron. "A Damned Piece of Rascality, The Business of
Slave Trading in Southern Appalachia." *Journal of East
Tennessee History* 78 (2006): 1-20.

Smith, Stacey L. "Remaking Slavery in a Free State: Masters and Slaves in Gold Rush California," *Pacific Historical Review*, 80: No. 1, (2011): 28-63.

Magazines

Montgomery, G. E. "The Lost Journals of a Pioneer." *Overland Monthly and Outwest Magazine*, VII: 1886, 180.

"Monthly Record of Current Events." *Harper's New Monthly Magazine*, XXXI: June-November 1865, 665.

Census

Fourth Census of the United States, 1820, Mississippi. Washington, D.C.: National Archives, 1958. Wilkinson County. Accessed through *Heritage Quest.*

Fifth Census of the United States, 1830. Washington: United States Census Office, 1830. Wilkinson County, Mississippi, accessed through http://www.Ancestry.com.

Sixth Census of the United States, 1840. Washington, D. C.: National Archives and Records Service, 1967. Madison County, Mississippi. Accessed through http://www.Ancestry.com.

Seventh Census of the United States, 1850. Washington, D.C.: National Archives, 1958. El Dorado, Sacramento, and Yuba Counties, California, Bolivar and Madison Counties, Mississippi, and New York County, New York. Accessed through *Family Search,* https://www.familysearch.org/.

Seventh Census of the United States, 1850, Mississippi Agriculture. Washington, D.C.: United States Census Office, 1850.

Seventh Census of the United States, 1850, Louisiana (Slave Schedules). Washington, DC: United States Census Office, 1963. Madison Parish. Accessed through *Family Search*, https://www.familysearch.org/.

Seventh Census of the United States, 1850, Mississippi (Slave Schedules). Washington, D.C.: National Archives and Records Service, 1963. Bolivar and Madison Counties. Accessed through *Family Search*, https://www.familysearch.org/.

Seventh Census, 1850, The Agricultural and Manufacturing Census for Bolivar County, Mississippi. Washington, D.C.: United States Census Office, 1850. Microfilm Reel 175.

Eighth Census of the United States, 1860: Louisiana. Washington: National Archives and Records Service, 1967. Madison Parish. Accessed through Heritage Quest.

Eighth Census, 1860, Mississippi (Slave Schedules). Genealogy, Family Trees & Family History Records. Bolivar County. Accessed at http://www.Ancestry.com.

Ninth Census of the United States, 1870, Louisiana. Washington, D.C.: Census Office, 1870. Madison Parish. Accessed through *Heritage Quest*.

Ninth Census of the United States, 1870, Mississippi. Washington, D.C.: National Archives and Records Service, 1965. Accessed through *Heritage Quest*.

Tenth Census of the United States 1880, Mississippi. Washington, D.C.: Bureau of the Census, 1882. Washington and Bolivar Counties. Accessed through *Heritage Quest*.

Tenth Census of the United States 1880, The Agricultural and Manufacturing Census for Bolivar County, Ms. Chapel Hill: University of North Carolina Library, 1960.

Fourteenth Census of the United States, 1920, Texas. Washington, D.C.: United States Census Bureau, 1920. Cooke County. Accessed through *Heritage Quest.*

California State Census 1852. Genealogy, Family Trees & Family History Records. San Francisco County. Accessed through http://www.Ancestry.com.

Diaries

Westfall, Milton S. *Diary of Milton S. Westfall.* 1861. Unpublished. Mississippi Department of Archives and History.

Newspapers

"Advertisement." *New Orleans Picayune,* June 23, 1849: 1.

"Pearl River Female Academy." *Canton Herald* [Mississippi], April 21, 1837: 3.

"Cotton Prospects." *The Charleston Daily News* [South Carolina], July 29, 1867: 1.

"Died at Memphis," *New Orleans Daily Crescent,* April 20, 1860: Column 4. Copy of article in author's possession.

"Fugitive Slaves." *The Pacific* [San Francisco], 18 June 1852: 2. Transcribed copy of article in author's possession.

"Fugitive Slave Case." *Weekly Christian Advocate* [San Francisco], August 15, 1852: 150-151.

Memphis Daily Appeal, April 28, 1857: 2.

National Era [Washington], Oct. 14, 1852: 4.

New York Tribune (New York), June 16, 1852.

"Speculation in Tickets." *Panama Star and Herald*, August 11, 1849: 2. Transcribed copy of article in author's possession.

The Daily Phoenix, [Columbia, South Carolina], January 31, 1866: 1.

The Placer Herald [Auburn, Ca], September 18, 1852: 4. Transcribed copy of article in author's possession.

"The Slave Case." *The Placer Times*, May 27, 1850.

"Slave Case." *San Francisco Herald*, June 12, June 19, July 29, 1852: 2. Transcribed copies of articles in author's possession.

Weekly Alta California [San Francisco], April 10, 1852: 2, column 3.

Online Newspapers

Brooklyn Daily Eagle, July 22, 1927, 2. The postcard. http://fultonhistory.com/Fulton.html, "Skulls at Mound Landing," (accessed July 11, 2010).

The Liberator (Boston), "Slavery in California," June 22, 1849. http://www.theliberatorfiles.com/slavery-in-california/ (accessed July 7, 2011).

New Orleans Commercial Bulletin, "Advertisement," June 21, 1849.http://news.google.com/newspapers?nid=9u2w3wkY HSMC&dat=18490621&printsec=frontpage&hl=en (accessed June 15, 2011).

Sacramento Daily Union, "Fugitive Slaves," June 3, 1852. http://cdnc.ucr.edu/cdnc/cgi-bin/cdnc?a=d&d=SDU18520603&cl=CL1%2eSDU&e (accessed August 24, 2011).

Virginia Gazette (Williamsburg), "Runaway," August 1, 1766.
http://research.history.org/DigitalLibrary/VirginiaGazette/
VGImagePopup.cfm?ID=1569&Res=HI (accessed April
11, 2010).

Websites

"Passenger Manifest," Louisiana Secretary of State.
http://www.sos.louisiana.gov/tabid/248/Default.aspx
(accessed May 27, 2011).

"Digital Library on American Slavery." University Libraries, The
University of North Carolina at Greensboro (UNCG).
http://library.uncg.edu/slavery/about.aspx (accessed
December 11, 2010).

"Mississippi State Archives, Various Records, 1820-1951."
Family Search.
https://www.familysearch.org/search/image/index#uri=htt
ps%3A//api.familysearch.org/records/collection/1919687/
waypoints (accessed October 22, 2011).

Bolivar, Madison, and Wilkinson Counties, "1927 Flood Photo
graph Collection." Mississippi Department of Archives
and History. mdah.state.ms.us/arrec/digital_archives/
vault/projects/1927flood/large/97238.jpg. (accessed July
11, 2010).

"Bolivar County, Mississippi 1895 [map]." Livingston County, MI
- Historical & Genealogical Project.
http://www.livgenmi.com/1895/MS/County/bolivar.htm
(accessed June 25, 2010).

Bateman, Mary. "Mary E. Bateman Diary, 1856-1856." University
of North Carolina, Southern Historical Collection.
www.lib.unc.edu/mss/inv/b/Bateman,Mary_E.html
(accessed February 25, 2011).

324

"Binns Genealogy." 1790 & 1800 Virginia Tax List Censuses. www.binnsgenealogy.com/VirginiaTaxListCensuses/Buck ingham/1788PersonalA/11.jpg (accessed December 31, 2010).

Brophy, Alfred. "Considering Reparations for the Dred Scott Case." Social Science Research Network. http://papers.ssrn.com/sol3/papers.cfm?abstract_id=99790 0 (accessed June 25, 2011).

"California State Census 1852." Genealogy, Family Trees & Family History Records at Ancestry.com. http://www.Ancestry.com (accessed January 15, 2011). San Francisco County.

"Case Files of Applications from Former Confederates for Presidential Pardons 1865-1867." Fold3. http://www.fold3.com/s.php#query=daniel+p.+perkins&o cr=1&w=hCLUo81Ws%09 (accessed September 20, 2011). Confederate Amnesty Papers.

"County Formation in Acts of Tennessee 1799." Tennessee State Library. http://tennessee.gov/tsla/history/county/actwilliamson.htm (accessed September 10, 2011).

"Historic American Newspapers." Library of Congress. http://chroniclingamerica.loc.gov/search/pages/results/?sta te=&date1=1836&date2=1845 &proxtext=canton%2C+mississippi&x=14&y=9&dateFilt erType=yearRange&rows=20&searchType=basic (accessed January 21, 2012).

"Land Patents." Bureau of Land Management. www.glorecords.blm.gov/ (accessed March 17, 2010).

McKibben, Davidson Burns. "Negro Slave Insurrections in Mississippi, 1800-1865." *The Journal of Negro History* Vol. 34, No. 1 (Jan. 1949): 73-90, s.v. Google, "Negro

Slave Insurrections in Mississippi, 1800-1865", - JStor (accessed May 2, 2012).

"Mississippi Atlas Map 1856." Mississippi County Maps and Atlases.
http://www.familyhistory101.com/maps/ms-maps.html (accessed September 8, 2010).

"Mississippi Digital Map Library," U. S. GenWeb Archives Mississippi.
http://usgwarchives.org/maps/mississippi/ (accessed March 26, 2010).

"Mississippi Enumeration of Educable Children, 1850-1892, Bolivar." *Family Search.*
https://familysearch.org/pal:/MM9.3.1/TH-1-14208-37344-78?cc=1856425&wc=10917670 (accessed January 28, 2013).

"Mississippi Marriages, Hinds County, 1776-1935." Genealogy, Family Trees & Family History Records at Ancestry.com.
http://www.Ancestry.com (accessed June 15, 2011).

"Photo Gallery." Bolivar County GenWeb.
msgw.org/bolivar/photogallery.htm (accessed July 11, 2011).

"Pioneers of Placer County." California GenWeb Placer County, CA. http://www.cagenweb.com/placer/pioneers.htm (accessed September 22, 2011).

Robertson, Rhonda. "Washington County, VA Survey records abstracts 1781-1790." USGenWeb archives.
http://files.usgwarchives.net/va/washington/deeds/surv100 4.txt (accessed January 11, 2011).

"RootsWeb: MSWILKIN-L William P. Perkins/Jane Perkins." RootsWeb Mailing List Archives.
http://archiver.rootsweb.ancestry.com/th/read/MSWILKI

N/2006-11/1164386438 (accessed May 27, 2010). Or, Google s.v. 'william p. perkins, jane perkins, wilkinson county'.

"Texas Deaths 1890-1976." Family Search. https://www.familysearch.org/search/collection/show#uri= http://hr-search-api:8080/searchapi/search/collection/1320964 (accessed October 1, 2011).

"The Thirteenth Annual Report of the American and Foreign Anti-Slavery Society." http://archive.org/details/thirteenthannual00amer (accessed December 11, 2011), 40-41.

"United States IRS Tax Assessments List. Mississippi, District 3 Annual Monthly and Special Lists, December 1865-December 1866 (Bolivar County)." Genealogy, Family Trees & Family History Records at Ancestry.com. http://www.Ancestry.com (accessed March 10, 2011).

"University of Notre Dame Rare Books and Special Collections, John Munn Letters, 1836-1837." Manuscripts of Early National and Antebellum America. http://www.rarebooks.nd.edu/digital/early_american/letters/ (accessed July 8, 2010). See John Munn Letters.

"Northern Neck Grants and Surveys/ Virginia Land Office Patents and Grants." Online Catalog, The Library of Virginia. www.lva.virginia.gov/siteIndex.asp (accessed March 17, 2010).

"War of 1812 Service Records." Genealogy, Family Trees & Family History Records at Ancestry.com. http://ancestry.com (accessed May 27, 2011).

"Wilkinson County Newspaper Slaves Ads, Mississippi, 1823-1849." Genealogy, Family Trees & Family History

Records at Ancestry.com. http://www.ancestry.com (accessed February 15, 2011).

"1927 Flood Photograph Collection." Mississippi Department of Archives and History. http://mdah.state.ms.us/arrec/digital_archives/1927flood/index.php?itemno=120 (accessed July 11, 2010).

Unpublished Sources: Microfilm

Agricultural and Manufacturing Census Records of Fifteen Southern States for the Years 1850, 1860, 1870 and 1880. Chapel Hill: University of North Carolina Library, 1960. 1860 Bolivar County. Microfilm roll 178.

Bolivar County, Mississippi Deed Books 1841-1857. Salt Lake City: Mormon Family History Library. Book B, microfilm reel 886085, Books C, D, microfilm reel 886086, Book F microfilm roll 886087.

Bolivar County, Mississippi, Wills and Inventories 1861-1924. Salt Lake City: Mormon Family History Library. Microfilm roll 886101.

Madison County, Mississippi, Deeds. Salt Lake City: Mormon Family History Library. Book B, microfilm roll 886074, Book D, microfilm roll 886075, Book F, microfilm roll 886077, Book G, microfilm roll 886078, Book K, microfilm roll 886082.

Mississippi Will Book 2, Wilkinson Co. Salt Lake City: Mormon Family History Library. Microfilm roll 877079.

United States Customs Service Records, Port of New Orleans, Louisiana, (Outbound) Slave Manifests 1847-1850, Outward Slave Manifests 1812-1860, microfilm M1895, Roll 25, November 1847-June 1850.

Seventh Census, 1850, The Agricultural and Manufacturing Cen-

sus for Bolivar County, Mississippi. Washington, D.C.:
United States Census Office, 1850. Microfilm roll 175.

*Tenth census of the United States 1880, The Agricultural and
Manufacturing Census for Bolivar County, Ms.* Chapel
Hill: University of North Carolina Library, 1960.
Microfilm roll 184.

*Wilkinson County, Mississippi Court Minutes, July & August,
1823.* Salt Lake City: Mormon Family History Library.
Microfilm roll 877088.

*Wilkinson County, Mississippi Chancery Court Records, Suits
1822-1871.* Salt Lake City: Mormon Family History
Library, 1823. Microfilm roll 877088.

Wilkinson County, Mississippi Courthouse Land Record. Salt Lake
City: Mormon Family History Library, 1824. Book D,
Book E, microfilm roll 876533, Book G, microfilm roll
876534.

Documents

Cornelius Cole Papers, Cornelius Cole, "Essays," Department of
Special Collections, University of California, Los Angeles.

In re Perkins, Case File. California State Archives, Sacramento.
Copies in author's possession.

Naglee Family Collection, BANC MSS C-B 796, Box VII,
(folder) MR552. University of California, Bancroft
Library, Berkeley, California.

William Henry Seward Papers, (Letters from Cornelius Cole).
University of Rochester, New York.

Index

Ray Albin's background includes a BA and a Masters degree in history from San Jose State University. He taught in the San Jose public schools and occasionally at junior college for more than thirty years. In the Vietnam War, he served in the First Infantry Division earning the Bronze Star, Army Commendation Medal, Air Medal, and the Combat Infantry Badge. Born in Detroit, Michigan, he grew up in California and currently resides in San Jose. He has published two historical articles, "Colonel Edward D. Baker and California's First Republican Campaign" and "The Perkins Case: The Ordeal of Three Slaves in Gold Rush California," which was listed as recommended reading in the *Harvard Guide to African American History*, 2001 edition. This is his first book.

Printed in Great Britain
by Amazon